THE WORLD
THROUGH
ARAB EYES

ALSO BY Shibley Telhami:

The Stakes

THE
WORLD
THROUGH
ARAB
EYES

ARAB PUBLIC OPINION AND THE RESHAPING OF THE MIDDLE EAST

Shibley Telhami

BASIC BOOKS

New York

Books published by Basic Books are available at special discounts for
bulk purchases in the United States by corporations, institutions, and other
organizations. For more information, please contact the Special Markets
Department at the Perseus Books Group, 2300 Chestnut Street, Suite 200,
Philadelphia, PA 19103, or call (800) 810-4145, ext. 5000, or e-mail
special.markets@perseusbooks.com.

A CIP catalog record for this book is available from the Library of
Congress.
ISBN: 978-0-465-02983-9 (hardcover)
ISBN: 978-0-465-03340-9 (e-book)

10 9 8 7 6 5 4 3 2 1

In memory of my parents, Terese Khalil Kabour Telhami and Zeki Shibley Telhami, who had been prevented by war from achieving their dreams, but who had the courage to send their firstborn teenaged son across a continent and an ocean to live his.

CONTENTS

CONTENTS

INTRODUCTION
TWO DECADES OF STUDYING
ARAB PUBLIC OPINION

FOR THE PAST TWO DECADES I have sought to understand the attitudes of ordinary Arabs and to make a case that these attitudes fueled politics in the region in both the short and the long term. When I started this work, in 1990, most political scientists and foreign policy analysts discounted the importance of public opinion because the countries of the region were dominated by authoritarian rulers. Then the 2010 Arab uprisings arrived, seemingly from nowhere, and suddenly the attitudes of ordinary Arabs were inarguably the driving force across a large swath of the Middle East, not only shaping events as they happened but also laying the foundation for politics in the years ahead.

In a way I felt vindicated. Mostly, though, I wondered—and still do—whether and when this awakened giant will find its bearings. In my view, the key to understanding the region still lies in looking closely at the strongly held values and beliefs of people in the region and how they define themselves. Of course, these beliefs and notions of identity did not emerge from whole cloth in 2010; they evolved over time. And we now are better able to study their evolution, using the accumulated public opinion research of the past decade. That is the purpose of this book.

* * *

MY JOURNEY INTO understanding Arab hearts and minds began as the cold war ended and just as Iraq's Saddam Hussein was emerging as the perceived winner of the devastating Iraq-Iran war that dominated the 1980s. To be exact, it started with a trip to the region that took me to Baghdad in early June 1990, just two months before Iraq's army invaded Kuwait. I had taken a leave from teaching political science at Ohio State University to serve, through a Council on Foreign Relations International Affairs Fellowship, as advisor to Congressman Lee Hamilton, then chair of the House Subcommittee on Europe and the Middle East. I would tour the region that spring and summer to research a report for Hamilton on the implications of developments in the region for the global balance of power.

The Arab governments and people I met and interviewed on that trip were clearly apprehensive about an impending era of American dominance, without the counterweight of the Soviet Union. To their minds, America now would be free to intensify its support for Israel, leaving Arabs still more vulnerable. Ever since the 1967 Arab-Israeli war, the United States had been the principal supplier of cutting-edge weapons to Israel, a substantial provider of economic aid, and Israel's protector at the United Nations. Indeed, the majority of cases in which the United States employed its veto power at the UN Security Council during the cold war had related to Israel. The prevailing sentiment was that American support for Israel stood in the way of compelling Israel to withdraw from the Arab territories it occupied in 1967—and that in the post-cold-war era, this would be even more the case.

No Arab leader, however, had expressed these concerns publicly more often and more forcefully, and in some ways more surprisingly, than Iraq's ruler, Saddam Hussein. Although it seems almost impossible to believe now, Saddam had been on America's good side throughout his eight-year war with Iran, which he fought with significant U.S. military and intelligence support. By the start of the new decade, though, the bloom was off that rose. In a speech in Amman in February 1990, Saddam expressed what I discovered to be a common feeling among Arabs: "Given the relative erosion of the role of the Soviet Union as the key champion of the Arabs in the context of the Arab-Zionist conflict and globally, and given that the influence of the Zionist lobby on U.S. policies is as powerful as ever, the Arabs must take into account that there is a real possibility that Israel might embark on new stupidities within the five-year span I have mentioned. This might take place as a result of direct or tacit U.S. encouragement."[1]

By that summer, anger with American policy was more widespread. Driving immediate Arab sentiment were five factors: the perception that the

---

1. S. Husayn, "Iraq's Suddam Husayn." Speech presented at Arab Cooperation Council, Amman, Jordan, February 27, 1990 (FBIS-NES-90-039).

Arab-Israeli peace process was dead, the tilt to the right in Israeli politics, a U.S. veto of a UN Security Council resolution on protecting Palestinians, a resolution by the U.S. Congress declaring Jerusalem to be the united capital of Israel, and the immigration of Soviet Jews to Israel. The prevailing view was concisely summarized by a former Egyptian ambassador to the United States who had widely been considered "pro American": "Arabs are sick of their governments pathetically begging the U.S. to plead with Israel to please let them have peace."[2] The official spokesman of the Islamic deputies in the Jordanian House of Representatives echoed the feeling: "The U.S. hostility and arrogance must motivate our Arab and Islamic nation to put an end to the course of begging and capitulation that it is immersed in."[3] Saddam Hussein sought to exploit this sentiment by hosting an Arab summit in Baghdad at the end of May, ostensibly to address the Palestinian question but also to celebrate his own emergence as the Arab leader most to be reckoned with by the West.

* * *

MY TRIP THAT SPRING and summer would take me to Syria, Jordan, Egypt, Iraq, the Palestinian territories, and Israel. I met with many government officials. I also met with and interviewed journalists, academics, and businesspeople—talking to students and faculty at academic institutions, chatting in cafes, and visiting people in their homes—and I made a particular effort to engage people informally, always in Arabic, and to find out whether Saddam's concerns were widely shared. Even a flight from Baghdad to Cairo was helpful. Flying in economy on Egypt Air, I found myself in the middle of a plane full of Egyptian workers returning home from Iraq. During the Iraq-Iran war, Baghdad had relied heavily on Egyptian labor to replace Iraqis who were doing the fighting. The stories these workers told went beyond foreign policy. Although they expressed admiration for Saddam Hussein for standing up to Israel and the United States, they told stories of mixed treatment in Iraq and distinct cultural differences, even though they were Arabs like Iraqis.

---

2. Ashraf Ghurbal interview with author, Cairo, Egypt, June 1990.
3. Statement by official spokesman of the Islamic deputies in the Jordanian House of Representatives, *FBIS Daily Report*, May 10, 1990 (FBIS-NES-90).

My trip, starting in Syria, had been timed to coincide with a summit of most of the Arab heads of state, who came to Baghdad at the end of May to address the Palestinian question, which for most of the previous decade had been overshadowed by the bloody Iran-Iraq war. But in recent years it had again come to the fore, first due to the Palestinian uprising (what would come to be called the first intifada) in 1987 and then following the end of the Iran-Iraq war, which most around the world interpreted as an Iraqi victory. Saddam Hussein reigned supreme.

In Baghdad my views on Arab public opinion were both enriched and challenged. I arrived there shortly after the summit ended. U.S. ambassador April Glaspie, my host in Baghdad, invited me to accompany her to a dinner at the house of the Italian ambassador. She told me on the way that Palestine Liberation Organization chairman Yasser Arafat was still in Baghdad as the guest of Saddam Hussein. At the time, the United States had frozen its dialogue with the PLO, and neither she nor lower-level American officials could meet with him or his subordinates. Glaspie asked if I would be prepared to meet with him if the opportunity arose during my brief visit. Her reasoning was that I was not subject to the same restrictions that American officials faced and that Arafat might be happy to get a sense of how the American Congress viewed the Palestinian-Israeli conflict and that he, in turn, might want to share his views with Washington. She also reasoned that Arafat might feel more comfortable communicating in Arabic. On my side, I saw this as an extraordinary opportunity to meet and evaluate a central Palestinian figure I had only read and written about but never before met.

At dinner that evening Ambassador Glaspie asked the Egyptian ambassador to arrange a meeting. Knowing that I was scheduled to leave to Cairo the next day, the Egyptian envoy somehow managed to arrange it for early morning. I was met at the Sheraton hotel by Arafat's driver, who whisked me to Arafat's guesthouse—a low-key, modest villa, one of many the Iraqis had built to host visiting dignitaries.

Arafat moved from behind his desk to greet me but otherwise said little, at least initially. Instead, he quietly took my measure as I spoke at length, summarizing the attitudes that Hamilton and other members of Congress held toward the PLO and the Palestinian issue. Soon, though, he was keen to express his own take on events, and our initial conversation, though arranged at the last moment, lasted more than an hour and a half, brought to a close by Arafat's appointment with a Soviet diplomat. As I prepared to leave, Arafat seemed anxious to extend our conversation. His meeting with the visitor would be quick, he said, and he suggested I stay for more conversation and also for lunch. Thus, I got to experience Arafat's charm at the lunch table, when he took my plate and deboned the fish before serving me as some of his aides and a visitor from Mauritania looked on.

As Arafat and I worked our way into the conversation, we moved beyond the specific issues of the American-Arab relationship. Reading what he felt was a highly anti-American Arab public sentiment, Arafat voiced his strong belief that pro-American Arab leaders would soon face a moment of reckoning. Saddam Hussein and the Iraqi people were true Arab nationalists who genuinely cared about the Palestinian people, he said, and both were gaining widespread Arab public admiration.[4] The pro-American Arab leaders, especially King Fahd of Saudi Arabia, looked weak and vulnerable in comparison. There had already been an incident, Arafat noted, in which a public demonstration had prevented the motorcade of the king of Saudi Arabia, "with all his majesty," from entering the city of Medina.

As I was leaving, Arafat implied that Saddam Hussein would be able to use his popularity to influence foreign policies throughout the Arab world, and indeed in the wake of the summit, rulers in the region did increase their financial commitments to the Palestinians. That same time frame also brought public airings of criticism of U.S. foreign policy by some of America's closest allies in the region. By the end of June 1990, even Kuwaiti newspapers were calling on Arabs "to adopt serious and objective stands against the U.S., which persists in a position hostile to Arab causes."[5] Egyptian president Hosni Mubarak also warned that "the biased U.S. positions will certainly return the region to dependence on the military option."[6]

---

4. Saddam Hussein actually projected these beliefs in private conversations with his closest aides. In tapes and documents that fell into American hands after the 2003 Iraq war, hours of conversations dating from the early 1980s into the time of the 2003 war, it appears that most of Hussein's publicly expressed attitudes about the United States, Israel, Arab nationalism, and Palestine were consistent with his private views. For some documentation, see Kevin M. Woods et al., eds., *The Saddam Tapes: The Inner Workings of a Tyrant's Regime, 1978–2001* (Cambridge: Cambridge University Press, 2010).
5. Reports in Kuwaiti newspapers, *FBIS Daily Reports*, June 25, 1990 (FBIS-NES-90–122).
6. Statement by Hosni Mubarak, *FBIS Daily Report*, June 5, 1990 (FBIS-NES-90–108). For further background, please see Shibley Telhami, "Arab Public Opinion and the Gulf War," *Political Science Quarterly* 8, no. 3 (Fall 1993).

For Saddam Hussein, the Arab summit was also the public relations coup he had longed for. Widely televised across the region—in what was a rare moment for mostly government-controlled media—the meetings helped portray him as the emerging leader of the Arab world, one able to deal with the consequences of this new, single-superpower globe.[7] His personal popularity soared as well, particularly after he was seen to have "won" the war with Iran and boasted of weapons that could reach Israel.

* * *

I WAS BACK IN THE STATES as Saddam basked in the afterglow of his summit. The report I submitted to Congressman Hamilton concluded that resentment of American foreign policy over the Arab-Israeli issue was perhaps at the highest level since the late 1950s, following the Suez crisis. Simultaneously I was preparing to move to the U.S. Mission at the United Nations as advisor—unaware that the UN Security Council would almost immediately be dealing with the biggest crisis of the post-cold-war era: the Iraqi invasion of Kuwait on August 2.

In retrospect, Saddam's decision to send forces in Kuwait seems like a huge miscalculation, but by midsummer he had seen close-up the potential power of inciting Arab opinion against the West to neutralize the region's autocrats. He believed that regional rulers, especially the Saudis, would not risk the anger of their people by inviting American troops on to Arab soil, and without the deployment of ground forces America's efforts to reverse his occupation of Kuwait would fail. What he failed to realize but quickly learned was that, faced with a crisis, Arab rulers would choose what they perceived to be the lesser of two evils. For an analyst with a realist's understanding of the calculations of states and rulers, it was not particularly surprising that the king of Saudi Arabia and the president of Egypt would

---

7. On June 2, 1990, while I was in Baghdad, the *Economist* quoted an Iraqi passerby as saying, "Nasser made promises, but could not deliver. But when Saddam speaks, he acts." Many Arabs, including millions beyond Iraq, seemed inclined to agree. On May 19, 1990, the *Economist* ventured, "By meeting in Baghdad, Iraq's capital, the Arabs hope to show the world that they stand fully behind their newest hero, with his mysterious new monster gun and his promise to destroy 'half of Israel' if Israel dares to attack him." This picture corresponded well to my own conclusions during my visit to the region in May and June of 1990. (Originally cited in my "Arab Public Opinion and the Gulf War.")

see in Saddam Hussein's ambitions a greater threat to them than the threat of an angry public—even as public opinion visibly influenced their decisions.

Nonetheless, two immediate questions arose: In the absence of Arab public opinion polls, was I misreading the general public sentiments, based merely on meetings with a limited number of people and the media? And in what way is public opinion a factor in the decisions and behavior of rulers, if it is a factor at all? I thus began a journey of what is now more than twenty years of research.

Three issues, all arising from the Gulf War, were at the root of my original inquiries. First were the assumptions that Arab rulers have been making for decades about the consequences of public anger. It is true for the most part that as authoritarian leaders, Arab rulers had the capacity to repress and control public opinion in their countries, but they have also displayed moments of fear of the consequences of too much public anger and always behaved as though public opinion mattered to them. Thus, for example, in the story Arafat had related to me, the Saudi royal motorcade allowed itself to be stopped by the demonstrators in Medina when the king might have just as easily called on troops to disperse the crowd, or worse.

In some cases, this sensitivity to public opinion appeared to matter to the point of complete foreign policy reversals. One such episode pertained to the Gulf War itself: the behavior of one of America's closest allies in the Middle East, King Hussein of Jordan. Not only had the Jordanian monarch been dependent on American support; he also had the most conciliatory behind-the-scenes relationship with Israel. Yet now he found himself going against the American-led coalition and risking support both from the United States and from the oil-producing states. His behavior simply could not be understood without reference to his concerns about Jordanian public opinion. The king's behavior was also similar in 1967 when he joined forces with his otherwise political opponent Egyptian president Gamal Abd Al-Nasser in the latter's confrontation with Israel—an alliance that resulted in Hussein's losing the West Bank of the Jordan River to Israel. And so I began to wonder how Arab rulers factored in public opinion, and under what circumstances they felt compelled (or the opposite) to respond to it.

Second, it was obvious that the Arab governments' near monopoly of the media was crucial to limiting public discontent. There were always limits to such control—radio stations such as the BBC had long been broadcasting into the region—but the sense prevailed that the control of narrative was almost limitless. In one telling episode during the 1978 Camp David negotiations between Israel and Egypt, Egyptian president Anwar Sadat argued that he was unable to make the concession the Israelis were demanding because public opinion in his country would reject it. Israeli prime minister Menachem Begin's sharply worded response—"the people of Egypt could be easily manipulated by Sadat, and their beliefs and attitudes could be shaped by their leader"[8]—so angered Sadat that the two leaders had to be separated for the rest of the Camp David negotiations. In the end, both sides made concessions and an agreement was reached for which Sadat paid with his life.

The United States was not above trying to control the Arab narrative either. During the Gulf War, the United States disseminated reports, through the principally government-controlled Arab media, portraying a broad and united Arab international front against Iraq.[9] This certainly helped limit the damage of Saddam's attempt to portray the war as an act of American imperialism and as one designed to help Israel. King Hussein's unwillingness to present the American line and the fact that the Jordanian media aired the Iraqi narrative of events was one of the few significant holes in the unified media strategy that the United States and its coalition partners tried to implement—which was a key reason for American anger with the king of Jordan.

Third, although many Arab governments prevailed in going against pervasive regional public sentiments, it was also clear that important differences existed among Arabs from region to region and, not surprisingly, country to country. There were also dramatic differences in how the Arab public responded to the war. What explains these variations, and under what circumstances are the Arab people prepared to act?

These questions made me want to conduct a more systematic study of the differing reactions of Arab publics to their governments' responses to the

---

8. See Jimmy Carter, *Keeping Faith: Memoirs of a President* (Fayetteville: University of Arkansas Press, 1995), 358.
9. Following Iraq's invasion of Kuwait in August 1990, I moved to the U.S. Mission to the United Nations, where I served as advisor to Ambassador Thomas Pickering on the Middle East and focused primarily on the Iraq-Kuwait crisis.

war.[10] Using chronologies from the media and academic journals, I tracked the variation in popular responses to the war in different countries and began to draw hypotheses about the circumstances under which public opinion produces measurable public action, especially regarding reported demonstrations during the Iraq-Kuwait crisis. I had several hypotheses—but the ability to test them and reach strong conclusions had always been hampered by the absence of polling data on Arab public opinion.

As I traveled across the region during the 1990s, from Tunis to Cairo and Damascus, something else was already noticeable about public opinion in the region, especially elite opinion: a more uniform worldview. Arab businessmen and academics had ready access to transnational newspapers such as *Al-Sharq Al-Awsat* and *Al-Hayat* in almost every major hotel—in the same way that a traveling American would get the *New York Times* or the *Wall Street Journal* across the United States. They could also watch new satellite TV stations, such as the Saudi-funded MBC. I began thinking about the consequences of this spreading phenomenon. Then in 1996 came the launch of Al Jazeera TV just as the price of satellite TV equipment was becoming more affordable for the average Arab consumer—a confluence of forces that had a profound impact both on the availability of information across the Arab world and on the political narrative. Governments rapidly lost the dominance of information within their own boundaries.

These changes made me realize that this information revolution would affect not only Arab public opinion and the government's ability to control it, but potentially how Arabs identified themselves as Arabs and Muslims (and Christians), as citizens of their countries, and citizens of the world. And identity is a key factor in forming opinion.

Simultaneously, research I was doing with Jon Krosnick on how American public opinion affected U.S. policy toward Israel introduced me to the importance of the "issue public," or that segment of the public that ranks a particular issue high in its priorities. To test our hypotheses, we designed a public-opinion survey aimed at identifying the segment of the American public that ranked Israel high in its priorities and compared the opinion of that segment with the opinions of the rest of the public and also with governmental policy. Our findings confirmed what recent American political life

---

10. Telhami, "Arab Public Opinion and the Gulf War."

has borne witness to: that the intensity of an opinion matters more than raw numbers about opinions themselves.

But this research involved Americans—a much-polled group. What was clear (once again) was that we lacked comparable scientific information about Arabs, both about public opinion and about media viewership in the region. Scholars and analysts inevitably relied on limited information when describing "Arab public opinion" (based on encounters and interviews with a relatively small set of people) and lacked confidence when generalizing about broader public opinion. In the absence of data, it was also hard to measure the impact of the media on public opinion. So I began exploring whether it was possible to carry out credible public-opinion polls in the Arab world on political issues.

* * *

THERE HAD BEEN LIMITED STUDIES, both by scholars and also, behind the scenes, by the U.S. government, to measure Arab public attitudes on a number of issues. But there were no major regional political studies that would be repeated, year after year, to measure change over time and certainly not on the big foreign policy issues facing Arabs. In exploring the possibilities, I found that commercial polls were being conducted largely on issues related to consumer behavior in the marketplace, including one carried out by Zogby International. I approached Zogby with the possibility of inserting several political questions in the consumer polls that were being conducted. Facing no major political obstacle in carrying out the experiments over a period of two years, I eventually designed major public-opinion polls on political issues.

Of course, there were significant challenges to be faced in countries in which the leaders controlled politics and sometimes even aspects of society, not least that they were unlikely to look favorably on any poll that made them look bad. From the beginning I knew I had to avoid sensitive questions about local governments and rulers' popularity, but there were ways around the issue. For example, whenever I asked respondents to compare and rank leaders they admired, I always added the qualifier "outside your own country."

Significant logistical challenges existed as well. Unlike in the United States, many people I sought to reach, particularly at the beginning of the study, did not have telephones. Even when they did, the understandable fear of, say, local security forces listening in severely limited responses. The lesson: To be meaningful, interviews would have to be conducted in person whenever possible. This required a significant force on the ground and far more expense than originally anticipated.

Given my budget, I had the capacity to carry out an annual poll in only six Arab countries, and I sought to get the most meaningful combination. To my mind, the survey had to include both Egypt, the most populous Arab state, and Saudi Arabia, the most prosperous, given their centralities. I sought another North African country and eventually chose Morocco, also because of the feasibility of public-opinion polling there. I added Lebanon, too, partly because of its accessibility but also because its ethnic and religious diversity provided an excellent laboratory for exploring sectarian divisions and correlations. Jordan was a crucial part of the mix, as well—for its pivotal role in the Palestinian question, its complex demographic makeup, and its proximity to Israel. I would have liked to have included Syria, given its geographic centrality and complex ethnicity, but the iron hand of the Assads made credible political polling there impossible. I then added the United Arab Emirates—an additional Gulf-region state where polling was being conducted already. Together, these six cases provided the backbone of what would become a decade-long study of public-opinion in the Arab world.

My initial research (and therefore my future repetition) was limited to polling in urban areas, due to practical concerns about the reliability of data in the rural areas, the safety of the pollsters, and intra- and intercountry consistency.

But the greater challenges were twofold: putting this data into a larger context and getting correct Arabic wordings of the questions. This book is the largest context toward which all this data has been pointing since I first began polling. As for the wording of the questions themselves, that has been a never-ending (and never-ignored) concern.

As is the case with most polling designed by American experts, the questions are typically prepared in English, then are translated by professional translators working for the polling firms. Most of the translations were highly professional, prepared by skilled experts who are in command of both English and Arabic, and who are also knowledgeable about public opinion surveys, but I always had a final shot at reviewing the translations, and sometimes my intervention was needed.

In one recent such case of otherwise excellent translations, an option in a question about identity listed in English as "a citizen of my country" was translated as "a citizen loyal to my country"; a question about which leader was most admired in the world "outside your own country" was translated as "outside the president of your own country"; and a query about whether public attitudes about the United States were "favorable" or "unfavorable" was translated as "supportive" or "unsupportive." Had these mistranslations not been identified and corrected, the polling results would have been significantly distorted.

From the outset, in seeking funding for the project from the Carnegie Corporation of New York, my aim was to study the relationship between the media that people rely on for information, on the one hand, and their sense of identity and opinion on political and social issues, on the other. This entailed a series of questions measuring people's primary sources of news, their frequency of use, and their preferred outlets. I also asked about first and second media choice to further zero in on the relationship between media, opinion, and identity. (Think of your own first and second choices, and how telling that is about what you learn and what you want the world to look like.) I thus have accumulated considerable information about media trends over the decade and an ability to analyze their relationship to changing opinions and notions of identity.

As noted earlier, self-identity is critical to understanding where opinions originate and how deeply forged they are. Many of my questions would get at this issue indirectly, but two confronted it head-on. One asked which identity was most important or second most important to them, typically giving four choices: Arab, Muslim or Christian, citizen of their country, or citizen of the world (while acknowledging that they could be a combination of these at the same time). Another set addressed people's expectations: whether or not they expected their governments to serve the interests of Arabs, Muslims, their citizens, or citizens of the world.

Throughout, my approach has been to design questions that delineate the prism through which Arabs view the world and their aspirations and fears. This often has entailed indirect questions: "Name the world leader you admire most, outside your own country." The aim of such questions was not really to identify specifically who was most popular or to assume that Arabs had full information about multiple world leaders. Instead, this type of question was employed to analyze the logic of the choices. What framework did people employ when they identified a leader like Jacques Chirac or Saddam Hussein?

The surveys also included questions on social and political issues such as the role of religion and women and views of democracy, as well as views of the outside world, particularly the United States, and perceptions of regional issues, from Iran to the Iraq war and the Palestinian-Israeli conflict. There was a particular focus on two issues identified in the early polling as priority issues: the Iraq war and subsequent American presence, and the Arab-Israeli conflict. Every year I repeated a set of core questions so that I could credibly assess change over time and broad trends in public opinion, while also adding some new questions that were either timely or helped refine old questions.

* * *

ALL OF THIS WORK would have been valuable in its own right, but two events gave added urgency to our work and lent immeasurable importance to our findings. The first, of course, was 9/11. As one of the few researchers annually gathering hard data in the Arab world, I suddenly found myself advising Congress, testifying before committees, and invited to White House gatherings. Always the subtext was how little we in the West really knew about the opinions of Arabs, their wants and needs, their self-identity, their heroes and villains.

I had been in the field long enough by then that I was able to provide guidance, but I also realized the need to dramatically expand our inquiries in the Arab world to understanding attitudes toward the United States and toward specific American policies. Did the Arab media drive public perceptions there, as some were arguing? Were viewers of Qatar-based Al Jazeera more likely to express anger with American foreign policy? How great were the variations of attitudes across demographic categories and country to country?

All of these questions and many more became part of the standard repertoire of my six-country poll and of many other surveys. And the data were all waiting there in late 2010 when the Arab uprisings again showed the West how little we know about this critical area of the world and how much we have to learn.

I have been back in the field multiple times since then, asking (among many other questions) how Arab views of America, American leaders, and the American role in the world have been changed by the uprising. My ongoing six-country Arab public opinion poll was most recently undertaken in October 2011 just before Egypt's parliamentary elections. Was the United States the model of democracy that these young Egyptians were looking to, or was their paradigm to be found elsewhere? I also undertook a study in Egypt in May 2012, on the eve of presidential elections. This time I was able to ask far more intrusive questions than I dared to attempt in prior years, as everyone was more eager to give their views. I also included rural as well as urban areas in an attempt to assess the possibility of anticipating electoral behavior in the presidential election.

Supplementing these public opinion polls in the Arab world, I designed a new poll beginning in 2009 to study Arab/Palestinian citizens of Israel as a control group. This group had the distinction of living in a democratic media environment where both satellite Arab TV and Israeli TV are readily available. That, coupled with fluency in both Arabic and Hebrew, provided an opportunity for testing hypotheses that emerged out of the research in the Arab world. Would they see the world differently? Would they be more inclined to feel empathy for Jews whose families had suffered in the Holocaust? I probed the same issues with Israeli Jews. How did proximity to Arab-Israelis affect their sympathy for suffering among Palestinians?

While most of the research in the past two decades, and certainly the survey research, has focused on Arab public opinion, I also pursued a track of assessing American public opinion toward Arabs, Muslims, and Middle Eastern issues broadly. Some of those polls were conducted before the Arab uprisings and some took place since, giving us a picture of change that allows an assessment of whether the 9/11 paradigm of American public perceptions is being replaced by a Tahrir Square paradigm.

As this book goes to press, it is tempting to conclude that the Arab uprisings have rendered the region a clean slate. But although the circumstances in the region have certainly changed drastically, not all opinions have migrated with them.

An example: One of the assumptions about the Arab uprisings has been that they are driven principally by internal issues, not foreign policy issues. Economic deprivation does count, as does freedom from authoritarianism.

But the Arab public notion of "dignity" cannot be separated from personal and collective aspirations, which in turn cannot be extricated from the way Arabs see the outside world and their place in it. In the end this drive to dignity is tied to broader national and international aspirations that were not born during the uprisings and cannot be fully understood until we know what Arabs want and how they define themselves.

To drive this point home, here is a seeming puzzle. In 2011, a year after the uprisings started, my poll in Saudi Arabia showed that the "most admired world leader" there was the late Iraqi ruler Saddam Hussein, one of the most authoritarian rulers in the Arab world. Here was the moment of Arab aspiration for freedom and dignity, and yet Saddam Hussein outshone perceived Muslim democrats such as Turkey's prime minister, Recep Tayyip Erdogan, and others. Why? The answer lies not only in the relationship between citizen and ruler, but also in the relationship between Arabs and the outside world.

What follows is an attempt to use the information I have gathered from public opinion polls and analysis of Internet and media content to provide a portrait of how Arabs view the world, and the complexity of the prisms through which most perceive central issues of the day. In the process, I hope to offer a perspective, informed by extensive data, on how Arab public aspirations and fears are likely to influence the reshaping of the Middle East—a process that began in Tunisia in 2010 and has since spread like wildfire through much of the Arab world. Even as many Tunisians, Egyptians, Yemenis, Syrians, and other Arabs strive for a better life and more freedom for themselves at home, their aspirations remain connected to the aspirations of other Arabs and Muslims, and to a vision of their collective place in the world. Above all, they want to hold their heads high.

CHAPTER 1

ARAB IDENTITIES

IN FEBRUARY 2011, shortly after the fall of Egyptian president Hosni Mubarak, I joined one of the large gatherings in Cairo's Tahrir Square. I had been to the Square many times before, but this was not the same place I had visited previously. It had been transformed from an impersonal, well-groomed but traffic-congested space into a massive public gathering place. The solidarity, the pride, the optimism were infectious. Only a few days earlier, hundreds of thousands of Egyptians had gathered here to celebrate their revolution. Their chant then was as mesmerizing as it was memorable: "Raise your head high, you are an Egyptian." Similar forceful expressions of restored dignity were to be heard all across the Arab world, in Libya, Yemen, and elsewhere.

But as much as these chants were a celebration of newfound power and hope for a new era of freedom from autocratic rule, they also say much about the causes of the Arab uprisings and still more about how Arabs define themselves. As Arab demonstrators everywhere made abundantly clear, the uprisings were in the first place about *karamah*, or dignity, and about ending a pervasive sense of humiliation. The dignity they hoped to restore was not simply in the relationship between rulers and ruled, but also in the relationship between their nations and the outside world. Those two relationships cannot be easily separated, because many Arabs saw their repressive rulers as subcontractors of Western masters.

Most people of the Arab world are at once citizens of their states, Arab and Muslim. But the degree to which they favor one identity over the other changes over time, and an understanding of these changes can provide clues to core Arab aspirations—including those fueling the great Arab awakening that started in 2010.

First, some context for the Arab uprisings: Fundamentally, most Arab citizens across the region were hungry for freedom, economic opportunity, dignity, and individual rights and liberty. At the same time, as many Egyptian demonstrators made clear, they also sought *eish*, or bread (shorthand for basic economic needs). But if the decade that preceded the Arab uprisings had been particularly disruptive, beyond the extraordinary—and important—information revolution, it was not because of a historically new type of economic deprivation or new modes of repression unknown by Arabs in decades past. The most striking events of that decade were the collapse of the Palestinian-Israeli peace negotiations and the violent consequences beginning in 2000, the confrontation between the United States and Muslim countries following the tragedy of 9/11, the wars in Afghanistan and especially Iraq, the bloody battles between Israel and Hezbollah in Lebanon, and, closer to home for Egyptians, the Israel-Gaza war in 2008–2009.

For most Egyptians it was particularly painful that on all these difficult and consequential issues—issues that went directly to their collective essence—their government had taken positions at odds with public opinion and contrary to how Egyptians envisioned their role in the region. For instance, most Egyptians strongly opposed the Iraq war and saw it as an American attempt to weaken Arabs and Muslims, but the Egyptian government appeared to cooperate with the United States. Similarly, they believed it was important for their government to act to stop Israel's war with Hamas in 2008, but their government seemed at best impotent and perhaps even hopeful that Hamas would be weakened by the war. As a result of such inconsistencies, Egyptians experienced a crisis of identity—brought about, not by confusion about who they are, but by a role in the world undertaken by *their* rulers in *their* name that looked nothing like who *they* are.

It was the sense of liberation from this painful dilemma and the assertion of a proud identity as Egyptians that they celebrated collectively in Tahrir Square. Above all, the revolts were about restoring dignity, but the causes went deeper than a single decade of Arab history and spread far wider than the Arab world itself.

In their own minds, Arabs have never fully divorced the authoritarianism of their rulers from the Western-dominated international order that they see as having cultivated and entrenched these rulers in power from the very inception of the modern political system in the Arab world at the end of World War I. Arabs despised their rulers for their authoritarianism but also for their subservience to Western powers whose aims they suspected and opposed— and whose policies were offensive to Arabs' core identities. In that sense the revolts were not simply rejections of particular regimes as such—they also rejected what most Arabs saw as a rotten political order of autocratic rulers anchored around and enabled by Western powers—principally the United States, in recent years.

One more preliminary note on identity: Yes, Egyptians (like Libyans and Yemenis) identified with their country at their moment of victory, declaring themselves "Egyptian," not "Arab" or "Muslim," as they chanted in Tahrir Square. But to conclude that this was only a national, not also a Pan-Arab, moment is dangerously mistaken.

Arabs—including Egyptians, Yemenis, Libyans, and others—continue to refer to the uprisings (or "spring" or "awakening" or "revolutions") sweeping the region as "Arab." In Tahrir Square immediately after Mubarak's fall, placards displayed images of Arab rulers, monarchs, and presidents, with images of Mubarak and Tunisia's Bin Ali—both of whom had already been toppled—crossed out, and asked when the others will follow. It was hard to miss that this was at once an Egyptian and an Arab moment. What is more, there was an obvious spillover from country to country. The movement has also remained entirely within the Arab world, not spreading even to Muslim-majority countries.

That is why it is essential to explore the issue of identity in the *Arab* world and what *Arabs* mean when they identify themselves as "Arab," or "Muslim," or in terms of their country. How these notions of identity have evolved in an era when media transcend political boundaries also requires examination. Will the empowerment exhibited in the uprisings sweeping the Arab world, and the emergence of governments that are more responsive to the public will, change the way Arabs define themselves?

Changing Notions of Identity in the Arab World

As discussed in the Introduction, my polling on Arabs' self-identity has focused on four distinct identities commonly asserted in the region: as citizen of a country, as Arab, as Muslim (or Christian), and citizen of the world. From 2003, the year I started polling directly on the issue of identity, I sought to probe not necessarily separate communities that identify themselves differently, but the ongoing struggle within each individual. Every Arab, like everyone else around the world, typically holds multiple identities that are often equally cherished. Most Egyptians, for example, also see themselves simultaneously as Arabs, Muslims or Christians, and for some, citizens of the world. Their assertion of each aspect of their identity may also vary, depending on the context.

Similarly, although most Arabs are active Muslims—people for whom religion plays a vital role in daily life—they do not always identify themselves by their religion. Besides, being a "Muslim" is not necessarily about being religious. As we will see, most people in the Middle East identify with a particular community, regardless of their beliefs or absence of belief. In a Lebanese joke popular during the civil war years, a man declares himself an atheist. "What kind of atheist," the reply comes, "a Christian atheist or a Muslim atheist?"

Emphasizing one aspect of identity at any given time also does not imply that other aspects are unimportant. Often the emphasis is contextual: Arabs may identify themselves differently to other Arabs, to their own countrymen, or to foreigners. In a 2002 Zogby poll of eight Arab countries, this issue was specifically explored by asking respondents to rank their identities when they are representing themselves to other Arabs and, as a follow-up question, to Americans.[1] There were noticeable differences. For example, 55 percent of Moroccans said they identify themselves to Americans as Muslim, while only 33 percent say the same to other Arabs; 40 percent of Egyptians said

1. James J. Zogby, "What Arabs Think: Values, Beliefs and Concerns," Washington, DC, Zogby International/The Arab Thought Foundation, September 2002. Available online at: www.google.com/url?sa=t&rct=j&q=&esrc=s&source=web&cd=1&ved=0CDAQFjAA&url=http%3A%2F%2Fwww.al-sahafa.us%2FDocuments%2FWhatArabsBelieve.doc&ei=FXy3UJGCHcTjqAHWyYC4Dg&usg=AFQjCNFxsusuF_hIxjyO9Xgt98XHqtVFpA&cad=rja.

they would identify themselves as Arab to Americans, versus 33 percent to other Arabs; and so on. The moral: Context matters.

The meanings of the terms "Arab" and "Muslim" also vary, sometimes contextually. Identifying as an Arab could imply an Arab nationalist or a secularist outlook, or simply be a statement about cultural and ethnic identification. Doing so also may or may not have significant political implications. It could indicate seeking to avoid being identified as an Islamist or a religious Muslim. Again depending on the context, it could be a way of highlighting commonalities with other Arabs or an expression of defiance toward those who challenge them.

And to say that one is an "Arab" or "Muslim" is sometimes simply an expression of pride, as when a Jordanian felt pride when the Egyptian-American chemist Ahmed Zewail won the Nobel Prize in Chemistry or the Algerian-French soccer star Zinedine Zidane led France to the World Cup.

In some cases, "Arab" and "Muslim" are simply so intertwined that separating them is almost impossible. In Morocco, where "Christian" could mean "Western" and where, unlike in Egypt or the Levant, the concept of a "Christian Arab" appears foreign, the terms "Muslim" and "Arab" may be interchangeable. Sometimes "Arab" is not a real option for citizens of the Arab world, like the Kurds in Iraq, who are Muslim but not Arab (even though most speak Arabic), or the Berbers in North Africa, who are also Muslim but many of whom do not see themselves as Arab.

Even politically, dramatic shifts and swings often occur at the level of the individual. Witness how so many Arabs readily shifted from embracing the secular nationalist movement to jumping on the bandwagon of Islamist groups. One example of this is Ahmed Al-Jaabari, the leader of the Palestinian Islamist Hamas movement who was assassinated by Israel on November 14, 2012. Al-Jaabari started his political activism as a member of Hamas's arch-opponent, the secular nationalist movement Fatah, but later joined Hamas and became one of its leading military commanders. Khairat El-Shater, a leader of Egypt's Muslim Brotherhood who was initially proposed as their presidential candidate in the 2012 elections, started his political activism as a follower of Egypt's Arab nationalist leader, Gamal Abd Al-Nasser, who repressed the Brotherhood. Sometimes these are profound transformations of beliefs. Sometimes they are choices about the most effective instrument to attain individual and collective aims. Either way, the point is twofold:

Identity is no more set in stone in the Arab world than in any other, and identity can rarely be separated entirely from aspiration.

Between Aspirations and Identity

For the overwhelming majority of Arabs, as for any other broadly defined group, collective aspirations help determine the relative power of identities at any given time. When Arabism seems more effective as a vehicle for the attainment of these aspirations, a shift occurs in how people identify themselves; when Islam appears as a more effective vehicle, another shift occurs.

The shift in the 1950s in favor of Arab identity in the Arab world was illustrative. Arabs quickly rallied behind the Arab nationalist president of Egypt after the 1956 Suez crisis. Huge public demonstrations and revolts swept much of the Arab world, toppling pro-Western governments in Iraq and Syria, and threatening others. As always, Arabs had multiple identities, even as states were young and affiliation with country was stronger in some states than in others. In Egypt, the Muslim Brotherhood, advocating a mix of Islamic values and Egyptian nationalism while also providing essential services to its constituents, was already established and had developed a strong grassroots organization that highlighted Muslim identity. At the same time, Egyptians had a robust sense of national identity—one that was missing in many other countries in the region that were still adjusting to artificial boundaries imposed by the European colonial powers after World War I. An Arab identity was present as well—in the sense that Egypt had always aspired to lead the region and played a key role in the inception of the Arab League, which joined Arab states in 1945—but not as a dominant political and ideological movement advancing collective Arab action.

Arabs' aspirations in those days were tied to finally achieving political and economic independence from Western domination as World War II came to an end. Those aspirations were dashed, first in the devastating loss in the 1948 war that resulted from Israel declaring its independence as a Jewish state, next in the resulting displacement of the Palestinian population, and then eight years later as Western colonial powers Britain and France joined Israel to invade Egypt in response to Nasser's nationalization of the crucial Suez Canal. The pervasive Egyptian and broader Arab mood was one of humiliation and dashed aspirations.

Yet for the man who provoked the Suez crisis, it was hardly a disaster. In Arab eyes, Egyptian president Gamal Abd al-Nasser stood up to France, Britain, and Israel and managed to survive and get away with nationalizing the Suez Canal. In the aftermath, Nasser's popularity soared, less because of the secular Arab ideology and more because he championed anticolonialism and the Palestinian cause, and was seen to have succeeded. Nasser appealed to the core aspirations of Egyptians and Arabs and thus was seen as having restored Egyptian and Arab dignity, especially after the humiliating defeat of 1948. One can wonder whether, had Nasser been a member of the Muslim Brotherhood, Islamism, rather than secular Arab nationalism, would have become the dominant identity embraced by Arabs, assuming that Nasser had still charted his anticolonial, anti-Israel, pro-Palestinian, redistribution-of-wealth path. In any event, even before Nasser died in 1970 the popularity of the Pan-Arab movement in the Arab world declined dramatically after the disastrous performance of Egyptian and Arab forces in the 1967 war—one that left Israel even stronger with newly occupied Arab territories and made Arabs even more dependent on foreign powers. In short, a movement, a party, or a leader is favored by the public when it or he (or she) is seen to provide the best promise for delivering on core aspirations—and it is those aspirations that have to be identified and understood.

Fast-forward a half century. Just before the Iraq war in 2003, I conducted my annual poll in six Arab countries: Egypt, Saudi Arabia, Morocco, Jordan, Lebanon, and the United Arab Emirates. Respondents were presented with a list of world leaders, past and present, including leaders from the West and other parts of the world and two prominent Islamists—one current, Yousef al-Qaradawi, and one an important past thinker of the Muslim Brotherhood, Sayyid Qutb—and were asked to identify the two they admired most. This was at the height of the post-9/11 discourse about a possible clash of values between Islam and the West. Nasser was the preferred leader, followed by two non-Arab leaders known for their anticolonialism, Nelson Mandela of South Africa and Mahatma Gandhi of India. Jump ahead another eight years, to 2011, and the most admired world leader for Saudis (not including Saudi leaders themselves) was the secular Arab nationalist (and dead) Saddam Hussein of Iraq, probably because he was seen to have stood up to the United States and Iran, and because Saudis identified with the Iraqi Sunnis who were weakened as a result of the war. So, at the time when all the talk was about

Islamic values and a possible clash of civilization driving public preferences in the Arab world, neither of the top-ranked leaders was specifically Islamist.

The new democratic politics in Egypt the following year were even more telling about who Egyptians looked up to. Islamist groups had swept the parliamentary elections in 2012, and the future seemed on their side. But the symbols to which they appealed for public support, especially in the May 2012 presidential elections, focused on aspirational issues, even as religion and religious law also played a central role. One of the candidates who led in early polls, Abdel Moneim Aboul Fotouh, had been a leader of the Muslim Brotherhood but ran as an independent moderate Islamist. The first Egyptian leader he invoked in his campaign video was Nasser, even though Nasser had repressed, even devastated and outlawed, the Muslim Brotherhood in Egypt—and indeed, even though a Brotherhood member had made an attempt on Nasser's life more than a half century earlier.[2]

In the first round of the presidential elections, when the candidate of the ultra-religious Salafi Islamist party was disqualified, many of the party's stronghold districts voted not for other Islamist candidates but for the Nasserist secular Arab nationalist candidate, Abdin Sabahi. After the Muslim Brotherhood's candidate, Mohammad Morsi, won the election, he attended the conference of the Nonalignment Movement in Tehran, Iran, in August 2012. Despite Nasser's dark history with the Brotherhood, Morsi saluted him for his anticolonial stance and for leading the movement for nonalignment. Morsi was, of course, not paying homage to the man but to the popular aspiration for which he stood and for the dignity he sought to restore—still the driving forces beyond and above how people of the region identify themselves.

When Islam itself is seen to be under assault from external forces, as Muslims overwhelmingly saw it to be in the decade following 9/11, it becomes especially difficult to separate the profoundly religious and ideological aspect of an Islamic identity from its aspect of defiance against imperialism. For some Egyptians an assertion of an Islamic identity is about faith, but for many others it is merely asserting the right to be Muslim, the right to accept Sharia law, plus a measure of defiance in the face of perceived

---

2. A member of the Muslim Brotherhood attempted to shoot Nasser as he gave a speech in Cairo's Tahrir Square on October 26, 1954, but the attempt failed.

Western assault. Muslims simply do not want to have to apologize for who they are, for their faith and for all that it entails.

In the coming years, whether the Islamic thrust in Egypt will be considered legitimate by Egyptians will be in good part a function of the government's ability to deliver security, food, and jobs. But in the Arab world broadly, and partly in Egypt, the strength of Islamic identity will depend on how the Islamist president performs, not on religious issues but in meeting the broader aspirations held by Arabs.   *wrong*

Measuring Identity

Regardless of the meaning of "Arab" or "Muslim," one thing is clear and consequential: When they assert either of these as a core identity, citizens of the Arab world are identifying themselves mostly in connection with people outside the boundaries of their own states. For example, when an Egyptian identifies herself as an "Arab," she is indicating commonality with Lebanese, Saudis, Jordanians, and every Arab in the world. This feature has important implications for these individuals' relationships with their governments, for transnational relations, and also for media viewership.

What is good for Egypt is a matter for its people and government to decide, within Egyptian boundaries, but what is good for Arabs and Muslims cannot be decided by Egyptians, Moroccans, or Saudis alone. In this broader context, what other Arabs and Muslims think matters for legitimizing an action—or, more important, a government. Whenever identification with the state is superseded by a combination of Arab/Muslim identities, this creates what I call "legitimacy interdependence." Such interdependence is the reason the media battle for narrative becomes central, and the reason the information revolution has been so threatening to the legitimacy of governments in the region. As I will show in the next two chapters, one of the most important consequences of the information revolution has been the degree to which it can effect identity change. As Arabs have had more access to media from outside their borders, their identification with their own states has declined. This in turn has further undermined the legitimacy of national governments.

So the question of how Arabs rank their multiple identities is critical. And the transnational media help provide "clues" on what Arabs and Muslims consider good. When a government projects a particular decision as being "good" for Arabs and Muslims and its public hears other Arabs and Muslims

25

say it is not, the legitimacy of the government's decision—and thus the government itself—is undermined.

It is too early to tell how Arabs may come to define themselves if they develop well-established democracies, with the legitimacy of a government being defined through the results of legitimate elections. What is certain is that the absence of electoral legitimacy in the Arab world has for a long time undermined the legitimacy of Arab rulers. While governments have over the years used the instruments of government—from military services to national sports and media—to bolster identification with the state, the longevity of Arab rulers and the absence of the public's right to choose their leaders have blurred the difference between country and rulers. The term *Addawlah*, or *al-Dawlah*, "the state" in Arabic, is sometimes used by Arabs simply to refer to those in power. Tellingly, it equally can be used to refer to inefficiency, ineffectiveness, and corruption.

Arab rulers have been adept at deflecting questions about their legitimacy by concocting issues to rally public support against a perceived common exterior threat. One of the most striking examples of this came in 2009, less than two years before the Egyptian revolution, when the government's media and officials exploited a confrontational soccer match between Egypt and Algeria, played in Sudan, to whip up national sentiment against an otherwise harmless "enemy," with insignificant stakes. Explosive headlines like "Barbaric Attacks on Egyptian Fans in Khartoum" and "Algeria: A Legacy of Blood, Hatred and a History of Violence" became commonplace in Egyptian newspapers. "One Egyptian TV program even invited viewers to express an opinion on whether Algeria might be in league with Israel."[3] The saga was a leading story for weeks, and it offended many Egyptians who understood the episode for what it was: a naked attempt to rally the public behind the flag and create a false enemy—in the hope of bolstering the standing of a government that was increasingly illegitimate in their eyes. The Egypt that their rulers pushed—and the false pride they advanced to bolster it—was not the Egypt with which most Egyptians proudly identified.

Arabs have been sorting through their own identity (or identities) in a post-Arab awakening world. For some, ideology or dogmatic religious be-

---

3. Associated Press, "Egypt's Media Stoked Soccer Fan Anger," November 22, 2009. Available online at: www.guardian.co.uk/world/feedarticle/8822006.

[handwritten margin notes at top: "again: See the paucity (still) of educ in the demand for sharia law" / "The Hijab (still)..."]

liefs trump all else, but for most people the awakening has been about which vehicle is most able to deliver their key aspirations. They are at once Arab, the citizen of a nation (an Egyptian, a Moroccan, and so forth), and Muslim (or Christian), and they will rally behind any of these identities when it is assaulted. But they will rally even more behind the particular identity that shows the most promise of delivering what they aspire to. Broad individual and collective aspirations are at the core of all these identities and are the driving forces for most—even more than the ideological core that each identity represents separately.

[handwritten margin note: "No. This is a v simplistic & superficial U.! of ID."]

In my public opinion research, therefore, I sought to understand how most Arabs prioritize these multiple identities and whether any shifts have been engendered by the issues Arabs have faced over the decade or by the very transnational nature of the new media in the Arab world.

The Findings

Since 2004, one year after the start of the Iraq war, I have been asking respondents this question: "There are various aspects to one's sense of self or identity. Some are more important than others. When you think about yourself, which of the following is your most important identity?" The respondents are presented with four identities: Arab, their religion, their country, and citizen of the world. (In Lebanon, and among Arab/Palestinian citizens of Israel, other applicable options are also presented.[4]) Acknowledging at the outset that there are multiple aspects to one's identity is important, as sometimes people are reluctant *[handwritten: "So?"]* to choose one identity lest they be misunderstood as saying that other identities are irrelevant to them. I follow up with another question about the "second most important" identity, as the choice is often difficult for most people.

In the decade following the Iraq war, identification with country was superseded by transnational identity (a combination of Arab/Muslim) in every year *[handwritten: "19 50%..."]* and almost every country; the exception was Lebanon. Over the decade, identification with country also grew weaker, dipping after the 2006 Lebanon war and declining after the 2008 Gaza war. These trends reflect the weighted average[5]

---

4. In Lebanon, I presented sectarian options: Sunni Muslim, Shiite Muslim, Christian, and Druze. Among Arab citizens of Israel, I presented sectarian options (Christian, Muslim, Druze) as well as "Palestinian."

5. Note that the six-country totals are weighted by population based on the data from the *CIA World Fact Book* from the previous year.

too broad

of the six countries studied for those who ranked a particular identity as either their first or their second most important. The decline of affinity with country is particularly pronounced when one combines the top two choices together (Figure 1.1). In this case, not only has identification with country declined, but it also is lower than each of the other two dominant identities, Muslim and Arab.

What does this say.

FIGURE 1.1 Identity Change, 2004–2011

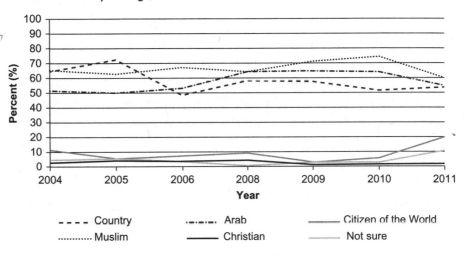

FIGURE 1.2 Identity, 2008–2010

When your government makes decisions, do you think it should base its decisions mostly on what is best for:

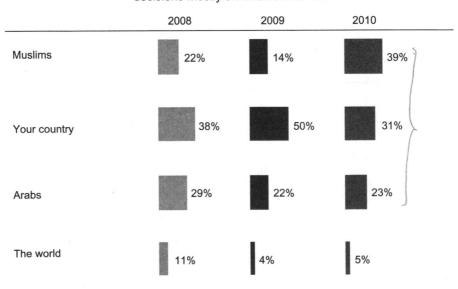

	2008	2009	2010
Muslims	22%	14%	39%
Your country	38%	50%	31%
Arabs	29%	22%	23%
The world	11%	4%	5%

These identifications are consequential for people's expectations about their own governments, as indicated by poll findings. Asked whether their governments should do what is good for their citizens, for Arabs, for Muslims, or for citizens of the world, in 2008, 2009, and 2010 half or fewer than half of all respondents said that governments should do what is good for their citizens. What is particularly striking is that nearly half or more said they *Wuelev. finding* expected their governments to do what is good for either Muslims or Arabs—which obviously places foreign policy on center stage.

There are variations across the six countries, less so in the trends than in the broad ranking of each identity. To illustrate, focus on three countries that showed contrasting results: Saudi Arabia, Lebanon, and Egypt. In Saudi Arabia, Muslim was consistently chosen as the most important identity, although there was a noticeable decline after 2009 (Figure 1.3). In Lebanon, respondents consistently ranked "Lebanese" as their most important identity, which held for every one of Lebanon's sects. In Egypt, there were shifts over time.

These variations are a reminder of the diversity of the Arab world and of the local circumstances that influence identity and opinion, even with *S.f.* the presence of much commonality and shared aspirations. The consistently high ranking of Muslim as a most important identity for Saudis, for example, is not particularly surprising. Saudi Arabia is the birthplace of Islam, and

FIGURE 1.3 Identity Change in Saudi Arabia, 2004–2011, First Choice

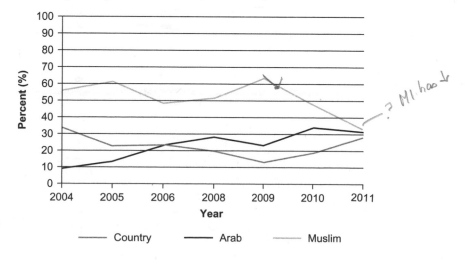

every year millions of Muslims from all over the globe, Arab and non-Arab, converge on the country for the annual Haj. Although the country is ruled by a monarchy, the king's chosen title is "The Custodian of the Two Holy Mosques," a reference to the mosques in Mecca and Medina. And Sharia law is applied more strictly in Saudi Arabia than anywhere else in the Arab world.

What is a little more puzzling, however, is the low ranking among Saudis of identification with country, both in comparison with other Arab states—Saudis give it the lowest ranking—and in comparison with Arab identity, especially after the 2006 Lebanon war (Figure 1.4). Most likely this is the consequence of the government's failure to cultivate a deep sense of national identity, something that the royal family itself appears to have recognized. In 2010, for the first time, the kingdom's rulers began to emphasize and celebrate Saudi National Day, and in 2012 they decided to give public employees an extra day off to mark the occasion.

In contrast, Egyptians tend to merge the three identities into one (Figures 1.5 and 1.6). That all three are strong in Egypt is again not particularly surprising. Egypt has one of the longest-standing country identifications of all Arab states, it led the Pan-Arab movement for two decades, and it is the birthplace of the Muslim Brotherhood, the most influential Islamic

FIGURE 1.4 Identity Change in Saudi Arabia, 2004–2011, First and Second Choices Combined

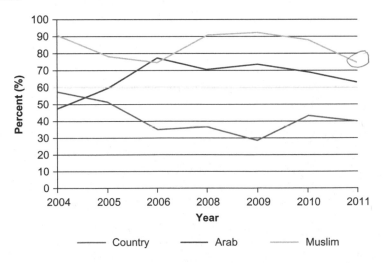

FIGURE 1.5 Identity Change in Egypt, 2004–2011, First Choice

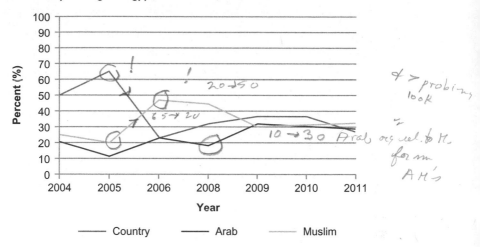

FIGURE 1.6 Identity Change in Egypt, 2004–2011, First and Second Choices Combined

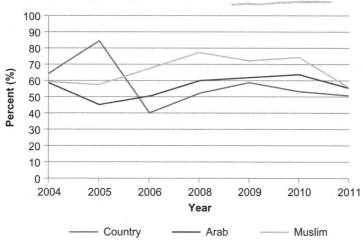

movement in the Arab world. Still, despite the relative closeness of these identities, we can see identification with country declining over time, especially vis-à-vis Arab and Muslim identifications.

Lebanon: Rallying Behind a State Under Assault

For Arabs generally, the two years after the start of the Iraq war witnessed the highest ranking of identification with country for the rest of that decade.

Although I did not ask the same question about identity before the Iraq war, other questions in the 2002 Zogby poll indicate that state identity was weaker than either Muslim or Arab identities, so probably there was a bump in 2004 and 2005.[6] This is likely due to the fear of the anarchy and devastation that swept Iraq after the demise of Saddam Hussein's regime, as well as concern that the Bush administration would move on from Iraq to other countries in the region. This fear factor helped authoritarian rulers rally their publics behind them.

This dynamic of rallying behind the state may also be at work in the Lebanese people's continued strong identification with their country despite—maybe even because of—Lebanon's deep sectarianism (Figures 1.7 and 1.8). None of its many sects constitute a majority, and its system allocates government positions based on sect; the president must be a Maronite Christian, the prime minister a Sunni Muslim, the speaker of the Parliament a Shiite Muslim. After the start of Lebanon's devastating civil war in the 1970s, sectarian tensions have remained high, most recently escalating among Sunnis and Shiites. Even the Christians are divided. Yet the Lebanese people consistently identified themselves in relation to their country, rather than as Muslim, Arab, Christian, or Druze. At the core of Lebanese identification is a fear for the state: None of its people want to be submerged in any surrounding state, and Lebanon is too small to be divided into multiple viable states. They are in it together. But one can feel deeply Lebanese and at the same time assert that identity as a point of difference with other sects—as in "We are the true Lebanese" or "We are more Lebanese than you are." There is also a rallying effect: When sectarianism risks civil war and "Lebanon" is endangered, they all become even more Lebanese. This may be one reason why, despite civil war, sectarianism, and the multiple foreign hands intervening in a country of only 4 million, it has remained intact.

Shifts and trends in Arab self-identification are bound to be affected by the Arab uprisings. We might assume that free elections would give governments an air of legitimacy, and that this would eventually reduce the need to

---

6. Zogby, "What Arabs Think." In the 2002 Zogby poll, which included eight Arab countries, Arabs were asked to express how they would identify themselves to other Arabs and also to Americans. The choices they were given included "country," "religion," and "Arab" as well as "other" such as family. "Religion" and "Arab" scored highest and, in both questions, trumped country identification.

FIGURE 1.7 Identity Change in Lebanon, 2004–2011, First Choice

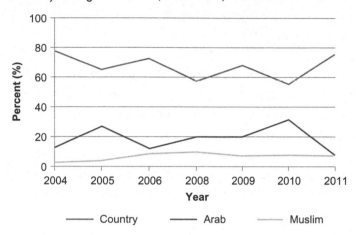

FIGURE 1.8 Identity Change in Lebanon, 2004–2011, First and Second Choices Combined

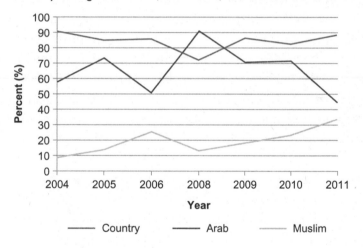

look for external validation of legitimacy. Although elected rulers may become unpopular, the fact that they are elected and can be removed means that a subtle differentiation emerges between a given unpopular government, on the one hand, and the legitimacy of the state and the system, on the other. In the era of authoritarians, the rulers *were* the state. My poll conducted after the revolution in October 2011 showed upward bumps in the identification with country and in those identifying themselves as "citizens of the world," perhaps a result of the broad international empathy Arabs felt after the first year of the uprisings. But any lasting effect will take years to measure and will continue to depend on the outcome of the revolutionary changes taking place across the region.

Identity and the Role of Media

One more factor strongly affecting identity across the Arab world is the rise of a transnational Arab media. In the next chapter we will look at how Arabs use their media and how it affects public opinion. A decade of polling and analysis shows that the Pan-Arab media, which rose in prominence particularly after the rise of Al Jazeera in 1996 just as satellite TV equipment became affordable, reinforced Arab and Islamic identity at the expense of the state. Since 2004, for example, those watching transnational media outlets like Al Jazeera have tended to shift away from a country identity toward an Arab identity, while Muslim identity has mostly remained about the same.

Similar trends have also been evident for those watching two other transnational media outlets, MBC and Al Arabiya, with some notable differences. Those watching MBC have exhibited more dramatic shifts upward in their primary identity as Arabs and have tended to identify with their countries even less. At the same time, their primary Muslim identity has remained relatively constant. Those watching Al Arabiya exhibited a similar downward trend on their identification with country, their primary Arab identity remained relatively flat, but they have shown a slight uptick in their primary identity as Muslim.

Is it possible these shifts were not primarily the result of watching transnational media? Certainly. A self-selection process takes place when viewers choose a particular station to watch for news. People give attention to issues, and opinions on issues, that are connected to their core aspirations. In fact, Al Jazeera viewership itself varied somewhat from year to year even as overall viewership generally expanded over the decade. Not surprisingly, it spiked during the most important crises that captured the public's imagination and attention: The 2003 Iraq war, the 2006 Lebanon war, and the 2008 Gaza war. These events themselves are what most affected the public mood—even if the coverage of them might have been an important reinforcing factor.

In fact, the history of the decade tells the story of Arabs rallying behind common aspirations, regardless of the particular media outlet they watch. In a region where fear of foreign domination and anger with Israel have been the dominant forces affecting collective political consciousness, the decade was full of galvanizing and destructive events. It started with an American tragedy that increased the tension between the West and Muslim-majority countries, and moved from one destructive war to another. All the while, unelected Arab rulers at best seemed inept and helpless, and at worst were seen as collaborators with the public's enemies. In the era of an Arab awakening, aspiring leaders will surely need to provide answers to the daily needs of ordinary life, but none will succeed, no matter what ideology they champion, without understanding the broader aspirations of their public. These broader aspirations are at the absolute core of how Arabs define themselves.

CHAPTER 2

THE INFORMATION REVOLUTION AND PUBLIC OPINION

W HEN THE REVOLUTIONS in Tunisia and Egypt rapidly swept away two entrenched regimes, most observers understandably focused on the role of social media in mobilizing the predominantly young revolutionaries. Indeed, the fact that the Arab uprisings began in 2010, and not, say, in 2005 or 1995, is almost impossible to explain without reference to the information revolution.

The long-standing anger that propelled Arabs to the streets and public squares had been documented and discussed for many years, especially in the decade following the 9/11 tragedy. My own public opinion polls over the past decade have shown a consistently widening gap between governments and publics in the region, fueled both by official repression and by increasing access to modern tools of communication and information.

In fact, many theories about the rise of Al Qaeda and terrorism more broadly have held that the absence of opportunities for legitimate political expression could lead some to violence. The overwhelming majority of experts on the Middle East counseled aggressive reform, particularly given the rising percentage of unemployed young people in many parts of the Arab world. But it is one thing to recognize pervasive public anger and another to hypothesize that the public is capable of acting collectively to force its will on authoritarian rulers.[1]

---

1. In an editorial cartoon I published in the *Los Angeles Times* in 1997 about Arab public anger over the 1991 Iraq war and the subsequent sanctions on and isolation of Iraq, I highlighted the dilemma of not knowing when upheavals would come. Fearful of making inaccurate predictions

Most analysts assumed, however, that translating public anger into mass political mobilization requires effective political parties or social institutions, or at least charismatic leaders. Tunisia and Egypt had none of these at the outset. Instead, inchoate resentment at decades of repression gathered in what amounted to a massive Arab public chat room, where it assumed its own order and cohesion and soon found its way back to the street and into action. And by "soon," I mean very, very soon.

One reason so many, including governments, were taken by surprise by the scale of the uprisings and by the media tools that enabled them is that social media spread at an astonishing speed, almost too fast to analyze its impact before it hit. "During the week before Egyptian president Hosni Mubarak's resignation, the total rate of tweets from Egypt—and around the world—about political change in that country ballooned from 2,300 a day to 230,000 a day. Videos featuring protest and political commentary went viral: The top twenty-three videos received nearly 5.5 million views. The amount of content produced online by opposition groups, in Facebook and political blogs, increased dramatically."[2]

My polling data didn't begin to show significant Internet use subject to meaningful analysis until 2009, and usage wasn't high enough to be comfortably analyzed until later. By 2011, my six-country Arab poll illustrated how rapidly the use of the Internet had spread—and by implication, how little we understood about its impact. A quarter of all Internet users said they had acquired access only in the previous year. Five years earlier, in a sample of 4,000, so few respondents said they relied on the Internet for news that it was not possible to conduct meaningful statistical analyses. The years 2008 to 2010 brought a dramatic increase in those reporting Internet use (Figure 2.1). By 2011, 20 percent of respondents in our poll indicated that the Internet was their primary source of international news, in contrast to only 8 percent in 2009 (Figure 2.2).

and being dismissed, an analyst grows complacent about the brewing storm, which finally blows up in everyone's face. "U.S. Iraqi Policy Alienating Arab Allies," Los Angeles Times, November 30, 1997.

2. Catherine O'Donnell, "New Study Quantifies Use of Social Media in Arab Spring," September 12, 2011. Available online at: www.washington.edu/news/2011/09/12/new-study-quantifies -use-of-social-media-in-arab-spring/.

FIGURE 2.1 Use of Internet, 2008–2010

How often do you use the Internet, if at all?

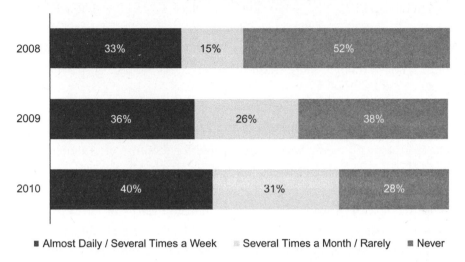

■ Almost Daily / Several Times a Week ■ Several Times a Month / Rarely ■ Never

FIGURE 2.2 Primary Source for International News, 2009 and 2011

What's your primary source for international news?

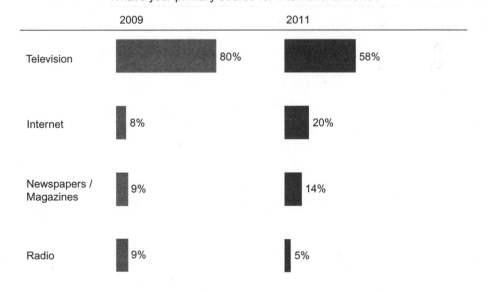

Bottom line: Even though analysts had understood that the information revolution, including the rise of the Internet, was bound to have an impact on regional politics, the expansion took place so rapidly that we lacked a full understanding of the consequences. Cybermedia, in short, were not the *cause* of the revolts but the *tools* that enabled them. As Figures 2.1 and 2.2 show, though, more traditional broadcast media also played a key role.

Political Consequences of the Information Revolution

The rise of social media was indispensable for the kind of organizing that enabled the mass Arab uprisings. But the seeds of public empowerment had been planted through a broader information revolution that centered primarily on the spread of satellite television. Indeed, even with the new instruments provided by social media, portable cameras, and phone devices, satellite television remained the principle instrument of broad dissemination of information across the Arab world. In places like Syria, for example, despite government censorship, individuals could easily film horrific scenes of bloodshed and mass revolt in remote areas of the country. But it was primarily the airing of those scenes on television stations like Al Jazeera and Al Arabiya that brought them to almost every home in the Arab world and beyond. We'll look at Al Jazeera in much greater depth in Chapter 3. For now, the focus is on its role as one of multiple information sources—albeit the leading one—influencing Arab public opinion.

A decade and a half ago, most Arabs received their news from government-controlled media within their own borders. By 2010, Arabs in every country I polled got their information from sources that originated outside their borders. This fact alone has had huge effects: When former Libyan dictator Muammar Qaddafi was trying to blame the 2011 uprising against him on Al Qaeda, the West, or Israel, his public had access to media sources it trusted that reported on the true nature of the revolt, and his narrative was simply dismissed.[3] In Egypt, a country whose media once dominated the Arab information market, the public had long sought answers from Al Jazeera and other Arab satellite networks, even as the government continued to invest heavily in the local media that it mostly controlled.

---

3. "Gaddafi Blames al-Qaeda for Revolt," *Al Jazeera*, February 25, 2011.

This is not to say that satellite media outlets such as Al Jazeera and Al Arabiya did not have their own particular editorial line or that at some level they did not reflect the short- or long-term interests of their sponsors, including the Qatari government, which funds Al Jazeera,[4] or members of the Saudi royal family, who sponsor Al Arabiya television. But the new media environment brought competing information sources, with consequences not only for how Arabs viewed the world but also for how they defined themselves and their relationships with their governments.

The Impact of Media on Opinion

Measuring the impact of the media on public opinion is not a straightforward proposition. Although we have considerable data on media preferences in the Arab world, both for news and for entertainment, Arabs channel-surf just as others do. Moreover, mere correlation between viewership and opinion does not tell us if people's opinions are a direct consequence of watching the media, or if those who hold particular opinions are simply attracted to stations that agree with them. In general, though, we can assume that the media outlets that matter are the ones viewers specify as their primary sources for news. In my annual poll in the Arab world, I ask what medium is a respondent's primary source for news (television, radio, Internet, newspapers, or other sources). From 2000 until 2010, nearly 90 percent of respondents said that television was their most important source of news. I follow up by specifically asking which television station is the respondent's first choice for "international news" and which is their second choice. In my measure of the relationship between viewership and opinion, I focus on the television stations identified by the public as the most important source of news.

Over much of the past decade, up until the Arab uprisings, Arabs in the countries I polled consistently identified Al Jazeera TV as their first choice for news. Al Jazeera commands about half of total viewership. If one includes that segment of the public who identify Al Jazeera as their second choice for news, the total viewership increases to over 80 percent. This large share of the market for news makes it a little harder to measure differences in the influence of the media across the population. We can assume that

---

4. Note that in 2011 Al Jazeera's ownership was transferred to a privately held company but it continued to be funded by the Qatari government.

nearly everyone watches Al Jazeera, even if they don't all identify it as their first or second choice for news, because presumably people often watch what their spouse or friends or neighbors watch.

One thus has to be particularly innovative to devise measures that test the effects of viewership, if any, on opinion. Beyond that lies the issue of whether people choose media that reflect their own opinions or whether their opinions are shaped by the media they choose. Recognizing that this is a two-way street with many stops along the way—and acknowledging that the same questions could be asked about viewers of, say, Fox News and MSNBC—I nonetheless offer four related propositions, based on my two decades of probing the region, and then provide some reflections based on the evidence from the data.

First, although news content obviously matters for opinion formation, the biggest change that occurred in the Arab world is not so much the content of Al Jazeera (or any other station) as the availability of multiple sources of information from outside state boundaries. This has made it impossible for the rulers of the region to hide inflammatory information from their publics. If one station fails to reveal it, others are more than happy to exploit the opportunity.

We see, for example, that viewership of Al Jazeera in Egypt reached its climax during the Israeli war in Gaza in 2008–2009 when Egypt's population wanted to follow every detail of the war next door. Meanwhile, government-controlled television, fearing anger over the Egyptian government's friendly relations with Israel, offered far less information. In the same way, when Al Jazeera offered only limited coverage of the 2011–2012 uprisings in neighboring Bahrain, other stations, ranging from Hezbollah's Al-Manar TV to BBC Arabic TV, gladly filled the gap. As the people of the region have been exposed to more perspectives, the governments and media outlets have lost full control of the narrative, as other media provided alternatives.

Second, on issues related to core identity on which the public already has deeply held positions—such as Palestine, Israel, the United States, or the Iraq war—people watch international news on the TV channel that best reflects their views and abandon those channels that go against them. This is particularly true in times of crisis and conflict that bear directly on core issues of identity. The success of Al Jazeera, Al Arabiya, and other such outlets has been largely due to their catering to public opinion on these core identity issues. Al Jazeera coverage of the wars in Iraq, Gaza, and Lebanon was very much in harmony with prevailing Arab public sentiments, and Al Jazeera gained viewer support at the expense of other stations. For example, Egyptian television, Al Arabiya, and other local television channels in the Arab world were demonstrably less sympathetic to the Palestinian Hamas and the Lebanese Hezbollah; they bucked the prevailing public sentiment, which was well captured by Al Jazeera.

Understanding the Arab and Islamic identities of its viewers, Al Jazeera hosted important symbols of both. An icon of Arab nationalism and one of the most celebrated journalists and political writers in the Arab world, Muhammad Hassanein Heikal, was invited to host his own program,[5] which reminded people of his links to the most beloved Pan-Arab leader, Egypt's Gamal Abd Al-Nasser. Al Jazeera also aired a program hosted by one of the leading popular Islamic scholars, Yousef Al Qaradawi,[6] who had the honor of giving the keynote speech at the victory celebration in Tahrir Square, following the toppling of President Hosni Mubarak. So, even aside from the content and coverage, the symbols were hard to miss.

Third, on secondary issues on which viewers may have little information or unformed opinions, public opinion is directly affected by the content of information from the media sources they trust in the first place. In this area, outlets like Al Jazeera have considerable ability to influence opinion. This is not surprising. In a viewer's opinion, a station is credible to the extent that its coverage matches what the viewer believes is accurate information on issues about which he or she feels competent. Once their initial trust is established, viewers are likely to also trust the station's coverage of issues that the viewer has no independent way to confirm.

Arab opinion regarding life in China illustrates this phenomenon. Early polls in 2002 and 2003 began to show that China was rising in Arab public opinion as a preferred strategic counterweight to the United States, but few Arabs envisioned living or studying in China. Chinese living standards, culture, and level of development seemed well below those of Western countries.

---

5. For more about Heikal and his Al Jazeera show, see Amira Howeidy, "Enter Heikal," *Al-Ahram Weekly*, July 8–14, 2004.
6. Al Qaradawi's Al Jazeera program is called *ash-Shariah wal-Hayat* (Shariah and Life) and it has an estimated audience of 60 million worldwide.

In a question in 2005, for example, Arabs in my six-country study were asked in which country of seven named (United States, United Kingdom, France, Germany, China, Pakistan, and Russia) they would prefer to live if they had to live outside their own country. In that poll, only 2 percent of those who identified Al Jazeera as their first choice for news selected China, in contrast with 6 percent among those who identified other networks. Soon thereafter, however, Al Jazeera ran a long series of favorable programs highlighting the significant development taking place in China, and in my 2006 poll in the same countries, the share of Al Jazeera's viewers choosing China increased to 8 percent while the share of non-Al Jazeera viewers choosing China remained constant.

Fourth, although identities and views on core issues related to identity do not change quickly, they do evolve over a long period of time as identities are reinforced or undermined. Therefore, in the long term, media does have an impact on the evolution of identity in the Arab world, particularly as media influences public opinion on the core issues of regional identity, both Arab and Islamic. Put briefly, in the short term, identity influences media selection; in the long term, media also influences identity.

Two additional criteria are essential for any news media outlet to command interest and long-term trust: the availability of fresh and timely information on issues the public cares about most, and the credibility of that information over time.

To see how all these issues play out in the Arab world, we turn next to the controversial eight hundred-pound gorilla of its regional media: Al Jazeera.

CHAPTER 3

THE NETWORK AMERICANS LOVE TO HATE: AL JAZEERA

T HE ARAB MEDIA EXPLOSION that recently has culminated in uprisings across the region springs from two interrelated sources: the growth of satellite television and the affordability of the receivers to the Arab masses, and the common language that Arabs share across state boundaries. Arabic unified a media market of some 350 million people in twenty-two countries and beyond.

Even before television, in the 1950s and 1960s there had been a dramatic increase in radio usage across the Arab world, especially after the rise of transistor and short-wave radios and their availability to the masses. The most striking and influential example was Sawt al-Arab Radio ("Voice of the Arabs"), sponsored by Egypt to spread Nasser's Pan-Arabist message in the 1950s and 1960s. This station was so popular across the region that it presented real challenges to Nasser's political opponents among the conservative Arab rulers in places like Saudi Arabia and Jordan, who attempted to jam the broadcasts.

Even Israel exploited the medium, especially after the 1967 Arab-Israeli war, when its Arabic radio began broadcasting programs specifically aimed at Egyptians. Knowing that Nasser had prohibited popular songs and even soccer games following the war in favor of martial music and a more somber focus on preparation for a new war, the Israelis made sure to air the Egyptians' favorite songs as a way of luring listeners to their political perspective. Radio, of course, was relatively easy to jam and governments worked to block threatening broadcasts, but its ultimate undoing as a primary source of news came with television's power of visual imagery.

By the early 1990s television had become king of the media, and each state had made sure it had its own TV stations as a way of building local identity and loyalty and as a means of controlling the flow of information to the public. In those days, average Arabs in most countries received their news from national nightly news broadcasts entirely controlled by the government. Viewers had to endure lengthy coverage of routine events, such as visits of rulers to a hospital or a village, before they got to serious news, which was filtered to protect the rulers and advance their immediate interests.

This would all begin to change before the twentieth century was out, but although Al Jazeera has become synonymous with a new world of Arab media change, it was not the pioneer. In the 1980s and 1990s, Saudi Arabia and wealthy members of the Saudi royal family took the lead by purchasing popular Arabic newspapers and distributing them across the region, and hiring some of the region's most prominent journalists. They understood that their broader Arab consumer needed more news and more diversity, and they allowed greater coverage of Arab and international issues—although critical coverage of Saudi Arabia and its royal family remained taboo. They also pioneered new satellite stations, beginning with one called MBC, in the early 1990s; these reached mostly the elites, as satellite technology was expensive at that time. The overall effect of this Saudi-sponsored media was to show the potential for a larger media market and also the potential threats other governments could face from transnational media. This simultaneous sense of inspiration and threat is likely what inspired the emir of Qatar, Sheikh Hamad Bin Khalifa Al Thani, to start Al Jazeera ("Peninsula" in Arabic, referring to the Arabian Peninsula, of which both Qatar and Saudi Arabia are parts) in 1996.

Coming to power only a year earlier after a palace coup that replaced his father as emir, Al Thani and Qatar were often criticized by the media, including the Saudi-controlled transnational newspapers. The criticism was directed not only at the circumstances of his takeover but also at independent policies he pursued that were not fully in harmony with Saudi policy, including warming up to Israel and taking the lead in helping to normalize relations between Israel and Arab countries. The emir didn't appear to have an especially progressive or a Pan-Arab agenda; still, by creating a station that reached not just the 250,000 Qatari citizens but as many as possible of the region's 350 million Arabs, he hoped to take away viewership from stations critical of him and of Qatar. There was another service that Al Jazeera provided to Qatari rulers: As a welcome voice viewed by Arabs as reflecting their own aspirations, Al Jazeera helped protect the Qataris from intense criticism for being a pro-American emirate that hosted a base for American airplanes attacking Iraq in the unpopular 2003 Iraq war. And given the competition, Al Jazeera's mission wasn't that difficult.

Now, instead of having to view lengthy footage of the royal family meeting foreign guests, viewers were exposed to programming that most Arabs hungered for, from opposing opinions to more information on issues they cared deeply about as Arabs and Muslims. This included live footage of bloodshed in Israeli confrontations with the Palestinians—footage that Arab national television broadcasts limited so as not to awaken their public's passion. Al Jazeera further broke taboos in the 1990s by reporting from the Israeli Knesset (parliament), showing open debates, including sharp criticism of the Israeli government by Arab members of the Knesset. One Arab nationalist member of the Knesset heavily covered by Al Jazeera, Azmy Bishara, later settled in Qatar and became a regular Al Jazeera commentator.

The result was a remarkable ascent: In just five years, by 2001, Al Jazeera had succeeded in becoming the most watched Arab television station for news, and within ten years more than three-quarters of Arabs identified Al Jazeera as being either their first or second choice for news. The station's success also spawned competitors, from a transformed Abu Dhabi TV, to Al Arabiya, BBC Arabic, Iran's Alalam, French and Russian Arabic stations, and many other country-based stations available on satellite.

With great success, though, came great criticism, at first from outside the Arab world and later from within it.

Mirroring, Not Leading, an Audience

In the years after 9/11, particularly in the aftermath of the Iraq war, many American commentators and politicians blamed the Arab media, especially Al Jazeera, for stoking Arab anger against American foreign policy. One of the ideas presented to address this perceived bias of the Arab media was to back an alternative American TV station, called Al Hurra, that would compete in the marketplace and offer a more "objective" view of events. Like other American attempts to win hearts and minds in the Arab world, this was an idea doomed to failure from the outset.

To be sure, there is room for outside views, whether from East or West, in the crowded Arabic media market. And there are plenty of models—from BBC to Russian and Iranian Arabic TV. But while one can make a strong case for having an American Arabic TV station such as Al Hurra TV, there never was a significant possibility that it would supplant or even seriously challenge Al Jazeera or other popular Arabic stations. It seems clear that the popular Arabic outlets succeeded because they *reflected* the hearts and minds of the region on core issues, not because they *shaped* them.

To test this thesis, I set out to study two somewhat unique cases that have small but diverse populations: Lebanon, and the Palestinian/Arab citizens of Israel.

In the case of Lebanon, the politically consequential diversity of the population—multiple Christian sects, Sunni and Shiite Muslims, and Druze, with no single sect constituting a majority—provides some guidance to the self-selection involved in media viewership. Given that Lebanon had a competitive media market even in the days of government monopoly in other parts of the Arab world, the viewing habits of the various segments of its population are telling.

Polls I have conducted over the past decade make it clear that sectarian identity is a significant predictor of television news selection. In the 2011 poll, 52 percent of Shia Lebanese, for example, identified Al Manar TV of the Shiite group Hezbollah as their first choice for news, compared with only 4 percent of Sunnis and Druze and 1 percent of Christians. Similarly, 58 percent of Druze, 49 percent of Christians, and 46 percent of Sunnis identified the liberal Lebanese TV station LBC as their first choice, compared with only 15 percent of Shiites.

Al Jazeera's viewership in Lebanon varied more than in other parts of the Arab world, particularly among Sunnis and Shiites as Lebanon became entangled in divisive internal politics after the 2006 Israeli-Hezbollah war. Before that war, viewership of Lebanese TV stations still broke down along sectarian lines, but Al Jazeera was identified by a good number of Lebanese as their first choice for news—in part because its reporting focused more on regional issues, particularly the Iraq war and its consequences. In 2006, for example, just prior to the Lebanon-Israel war, 43 percent of Lebanese Shiites, 33 percent of Sunnis, 25 percent of Druze, and 16 percent of Christians identified Al Jazeera as their first choice. By 2011, with Al Jazeera seen to be taking sides in favor of Sunnis, only 7 percent of Shiites identified it as their first choice for news.

The point is that while there are multiple reasons audiences view a particular station for news, the most critical factor is the extent to which a station reflects their views on issues that matter most to them and to their identity. When a station fails to do this, viewers look for alternatives.

In a more nuanced case, I conducted polls among Palestinian/Arab citizens of Israel. This segment of the Arab population exists in a democratic state with a relatively free media environment. Among this population the first language is Arabic, but most are also fluent in Hebrew. Arabs in Israel are thus able to watch media from both Arab and Israeli sources.

In the first two decades of Israel's existence, Palestinian Israelis primarily listened to Arab radio stations for news, especially Egyptian, Syrian, and Jordanian stations. When they wanted to hear outside views, they typically listened to the BBC in Arabic, the French Radio Monte Carlo, or the Voice of America. Most of them were not yet fluent in Hebrew and thus did not closely follow Israeli TV and radio in significant numbers. The Israeli government had its own Arabic radio programming, which was listened to by some, but always with suspicion, given the ongoing conflict between Israel and the Palestinians. More than any station, however, Arabs in Israel, like Arabs elsewhere, listened to Sawt al-Arab Radio, which reflected the views of Egypt and Gamal Abd Al-Nasser. So high was their trust in Nasser's narrative that even when it became abundantly clear by the end of the 1967 war that Arab armies, including Egypt's, had been badly defeated and that Israel was now occupying what had been Egyptian, Jordanian, and Syrian territories, some Arabs in Israel continued to believe that this was merely a trap set by Nasser.

It didn't take long, though, for the narrative to begin shifting, and soon the credibility of Sawt al-Arab and other Arab media collapsed in response to ongoing and mounting evidence that the balance of power in the region rested overwhelmingly in Israel's favor. By then more Arabs had become fluent in Hebrew, and while they saw Israel's Arabic media as propagandistic, they saw the Hebrew media as more credible. I do not have polling data on the trends and viewership in the 1970s and 1980s, but anecdotal evidence suggests that more and more Arabs in Israel were getting their news from Hebrew sources and viewing Arab sources with suspicion.

But with the rise of the Pan-Arab media in the 1990s, viewership trends shifted yet again. As happened in much of the region, these stations, especially Al Jazeera, came to dominate the news media market in ways not witnessed before. Like Nasser's Sawt al-Arab, Al Jazeera first and foremost catered to Arab hearts, but unlike Sawt al-Arab it provided more timely information and far more diversity of views.

In polling I conducted from 2009 to 2011, I sought to understand the trend in viewership among Israeli Arabs. Overall, roughly the same portion of Arab-Israelis as Arabs elsewhere in the Middle East—roughly half—identified Al Jazeera as their first choice for news. This finding has been relatively robust for the three years studied. At the same time, roughly one-quarter to one-third say Israeli TV is their first choice for news, but what is more interesting is the sectarian habits among Muslims who constitute more than 70 percent of Arabs in Israel. Only 17 percent of them identified Israeli TV as their first choice, while 53 percent identified Al Jazeera. In contrast, among the Druze—who, unlike other Arabs, are required to serve in the Israeli military—68 percent identified Israeli TV, while 15 percent identified Al Jazeera. Among Christians, 46 percent identified Israeli TV, while 31 percent identified Al Jazeera.

That identification is critical, for the selection of news media can also be seen in evidence from beyond the sectarian divide. In the 2010 poll, I broke down the Arab-Israeli population into two groups: those who had relatives who became refugees in 1948, and those who didn't. Roughly 53 percent of those polled said they had relatives who were refugees. Of those, 60 percent identified Al Jazeera as their first choice for news, whereas 60 percent of those who didn't have refugee relatives identified Israeli television as their first choice. This trend seemed to apply to all sects, again suggesting that preexisting and identity-defining attributes provide a good predictor of media selection.

The Power Behind the Media

Why does Al Jazeera continue to thrive despite increasing competition? And what fuels the expanding Arab media without realistic prospects of profit?

It is impossible to answer these questions without reference to the political aims of the sponsors and the aspirations of the consumers.

Al Jazeera has been successful largely because it understands the media market and its consumers.[1] But it's unlikely Al Jazeera would have succeeded without the billions of dollars in resources committed to it by the Qatari rulers over the past decade and a half. Viewers want a station that reflects their core identity and positions on central issues, but they also want timely and extensive information, which is expensive to provide.

Because Al Jazeera is well funded and doesn't need to make a profit, it can provide extensive coverage where others have failed. In the 2008–2009 Gaza war, for example, no station anywhere in the world could match Al Jazeera's coverage, with multiple reporters in Gaza itself, in Israel, in the West Bank, and in Egypt. In fact, no other television station had live coverage from Gaza or Israel during the war—an advantage that many stations, including American, tried to overcome in the November 2012 Gaza fighting by sending reporters to Gaza. And even though Al Jazeera is often accused of bias or of an ideological bent, it has been bold in ensuring presentation of multiple views, including presenting Israeli views dating back to the 1990s, when few other Arab stations dared do so, as well as airing Bin Laden tapes, Iranian views, and hosting or covering speeches and news conferences of American officials—including then-secretary of defense Donald Rumsfeld, American military commanders and spokesmen, and White House and State Department officials—during the Iraq war. So while Al Jazeera officials understood and catered to their audience, they also made sure they always aired views that challenged, sometimes even offended their audience.

There was also a price to be paid for Al Jazeera's extensive coverage. Almost every government in the region was offended by Al Jazeera at some point, which resulted in significant pressures on the Qatar government. The United States accused Al Jazeera of incitement, and even China in 2012 was angered by Al Jazeera coverage, taking action against Al Jazeera English.

---

1. It is important to note that, while the discussion in this book is primarily about Al Jazeera's Arabic news station, which is most influential, Al Jazeera is increasingly a media empire that includes sports stations, children's programming, live events (similar to C-SPAN), a station (Al Jazeera Mubasher Misr) specifically dedicated to covering Egypt, and the expanding Al Jazeera English that initiated major expansion plans in the American market by purchasing Current TV in 2013. In its coverage, Al Jazeera continues to cater well to its market: Al Jazeera English is very different from the Arabic station and caters to the international market.

The question is, for what purpose does Qatar support Al Jazeera? What does Qatar gain?

One cannot completely rule out an ideological position of the emir. Al Thani once described himself to me as a "Nasserist," or an admirer of the Pan-Arabist Gamal Abd al-Nasser, and Al Jazeera has indeed hosted Arab nationalists as regular commentators, including Egypt's most prominent analyst, Muhammad Hassanein Heikal. But the network also hosts prominent Islamists, such as Sheikh Yousuf Al Qaradawi. Beyond any progressive or pan-Arab aspiration of the leadership, the strategy is simply seen to be in the long-term survival of the Qatari leadership and of the emirate itself.

To begin with, Qatar is a small, ultrawealthy state across the Gulf from Iran and neighboring a larger and more powerful fellow member of the Gulf Cooperation Council (GCC), Saudi Arabia, with which it has not always had an easy relationship. Qatar considers the United States its primary strategic ally and hosts a major American base on its soil—not something popular in the Arab world. After the 1993 peace agreement between Israel and the Palestine Liberation Organization, Qatar was among the most forthcoming of Arab states to reach out to Israel. For that reason, and for its propensity to pursue a policy independent from Saudi Arabia, the dominant Saudi-owned media, as well as the Egyptian media, made Qatar their favorite target of criticism.

Al Jazeera became an instant counterweapon. First, by merely overtaking the Saudi and Egyptian media, it deflected criticism against the emirate and its leaders. Second, by providing a credible fresh news outlet that focused on Pan-Arab issues, it gained accolades that balanced the perception that it was a key American ally and friendly to Israel. Third, the success of Al Jazeera provided Qatar an instrument of leverage in dealing generally with its detractors. Better to be close to one's rival when the rival is funding the primary media source in the Arab world.

But the Arab uprisings created both new opportunities and new challenges for Al Jazeera. On the one hand, Al Jazeera seemed on the right side of history: It was a central part of the information revolution that enabled the uprisings, and the uprisings themselves created new opportunities for coverage as Arabs everywhere tuned in to the story. On the other hand, the Arab uprisings seemed nearly unstoppable. Could they sweep the Arab world all the way to the doorsteps of the Gulf monarchies, including the Qatari rulers themselves?

Potentially facing common threats, Qatar found itself increasingly closer politically to its GCC partners, especially its senior partner Saudi Arabia, despite their sometimes uneasy, even competitive relations. In the coverage of the uprisings in Libya and Syria, Al Jazeera and the Saudi-funded Al Arabiya took closer positions than ever. On GCC partner Bahrain, where a Sunni monarchy ruled over a revolting Shiite majority, Al Jazeera covered the story but only to a limited degree. Al Jazeera's explanation focused on the lack of access allowed by Bahraini authorities, but it was hard to miss the Qatari dilemma, and hard to convince critical commentators that politics were not an important consideration. But Al Jazeera's biggest challenge in pleasing its audiences was in the Syrian uprisings, to which Al Jazeera dedicated significant resources and made them its priority story for months. While Arabs were overwhelmingly sympathetic with the Syrian people against the Assad regime, they were heavily divided on the wisdom of external intervention, which Al Jazeera seemed to favor, increasingly reflecting the foreign policy position of the Qatari government on this issue.

In stark contrast to 1996 when Qatar's role in regional politics was relatively modest, by the time of the Arab uprisings, Qatar itself had become a significant player in the geopolitics of the region: from leading the arming and funding of Syrian rebels, mediating among Palestinian factions, funding the reconstruction in Lebanon after the 2006 war, and providing more aid to Egypt than anyone else after the revolution, to sending military support for the campaign against Muammar Qaddafi in Libya. To the extent that Arabs were divided on many of the issues in which Qatar was involved, both Al Jazeera and Qatar were bound to come under greater scrutiny.

This opened Al Jazeera up to some criticism from some former admirers on the left. In an article for the Lebanese newspaper *Al Ahkbar* titled "Al Jazeera's Autumn: The Fall of an Empire,"[2] columnist Pierre Abi Saab conveyed a feeling shared by a sizable minority who had previously admired Al Jazeera:

> After the spread of satellites in the 1990s, Arabs came to know
> two types of liberation. The first is social . . . and the second was
> political, with Al Jazeera, which imposed itself in a short time,

---

2. *Al Akhbar*, March 28, 2012 (my translation). Available online at: www.al-akhbar.com/node/61098.

regionally and internationally. It is the story of Alice in Wonderland. In a small rich state [Qatar], an exciting new information experiment was started, and bet on difference, courage, and professionalism. From covering the story to carrying the flag of the opinion of the other, an alternative media took shape that viewers of official television could never imagine, from the [Atlantic] ocean to the Gulf.

This surprising innovation became a source for the Arab individual who hungered to uncover what was unsaid, and to follow the political debate, even if in passing. How is it possible for a political regime that differed little from those around it to create this progressive opening, which made many ignore the strange mix of political constituents for the TV station: from the Iraqi Baath to the liberalism that legitimized Israel during one period, to an Islamist current that swallowed those who opposed it? Who cares? Arabs now had their equivalent of CNN that looks from another angle at events, from the British-American war on Iraq to the Israeli assaults on Lebanon and Gaza, ending up in the Tunisian and Egyptian revolutions—history was taking shape live on Al Jazeera. Then the Qatari regime discovered a new hobby, and decided to become a sponsor of the Arab revolution. The station rolled over the Manama [Bahrain] spring like the Saudi tanks in order to "lead" the movement for change in Syria. Quickly professionalism began to slip, turning into intended deviations, then systematic lies, as is proven by documents and statements that have leaked out in recent weeks. Not that the Syrian regime is beyond tyranny and repression, but the media conversation took the revolt away from the people. On the rock of the Syrian tragedy, the kingdom of delusion was shattered. The station returned to its natural size. Suddenly viewers noticed that they are watching an official medium akin to those we see in all the authoritarian systems. It even surpasses the latter by virtue of its experience and reputation and claims of independence and objectivity. Today, scandals and resignations continue, leaving in the memory of the contemporary Arab media a deep wound named Al Jazeera.

Al Jazeera Faces the Future

Despite such blistering criticism from within the Arab world, there is no evidence yet that Al Jazeera has lost significant viewership. On the one hand, its predilection (reflecting its funders) against the Syrian regime and its reserved coverage of Bahrain play well among the mostly Sunni Muslim population of the region. About 90 percent of Arabs also share Al Jazeera's support for the rebels in Syria. But the push for international intervention in Syria is a source of deep division among Arabs, and this has opened Al Jazeera to criticism as the number of its media competitors has increased. Two other factors could play a role in determining Al Jazeera's dominance: the emergence of alternative free media in newly democratizing countries, especially Egypt, and the increasing number of Arabs, especially among the young, who now get their news not from TV but from the Internet.

It is already clear that the open environments in Egypt and Tunisia have generated media that are far more attractive both to local audiences and to Arab audiences outside. In Egypt, whose population constitutes nearly one-quarter of the entire Arab world, there are many people with considerable journalistic talent and skill who have been stymied by the political control of state-supported media—indeed, so stymied that many of the most talented journalists left the country to work for the likes of Al Jazeera, Al Arabiya, and the BBC. The overthrow of Mubarak has brought far more diversity to the pages of newspapers and on television, both private and public networks, and a clear display of previously hidden talent. Popular television host Hafiz Mirazi, who had become a star first on Al Jazeera and later on Al Arabiya, has now returned to Egypt to host his own show on Egypt's Dream TV. Muhammad Hassanein Heikal left Al Jazeera and joined Egypt's private television station, CBC. Others will follow.

Egyptian media has the potential to eventually put pressure on other Pan-Arab TV stations. But the problem for any aspiring media competitor is not simply putting forth a credible product but also having the significant resources required to provide the kind of timely coverage of international and regional issues that Arab viewers now expect.

This alone is a potential barrier to objectivity. As yet there is simply not enough advertising revenue in the Arab world to sustain a competitive station, and the most substantial funds available for advertising come from governments and the elites around them, or from parties that do not want to alienate ruling elites, particularly in the Gulf region. Egypt's new government, like its old, may want to invest heavily in state-sponsored media, but that will inevitably infringe on its freedom of expression, even in a more democratic Egypt. Local private stations that have proliferated may do well locally, but they will not have the resources to cover regional and international news competitively. And government regulators may try to limit the influence of private media, as they did in November 2012 by requiring Dream TV (a privately owned Egyptian station launched in 2001) to relocate its headquarters.

This resource dilemma for the Arab media means that even as the market grows more frustrated with existing stations like Al Jazeera, the scale of the enterprise dictates that there will be limited numbers of possible competitors and that those competitors will likely come with their own political baggage.

The same resource dilemma will ultimately affect Internet news as well, although to a lesser extent. Even now, as TV is losing news-market share to the Internet, all the successful TV stations have Internet sites, some of which are among the most popular sites in the Arab world, including Aljazeera.net. Inevitably, those sites that have the resources to provide the freshest information and to constantly update the news will likely do best in the marketplace. These emerging sites have to compete with websites with no geographic tie to the region, including popular news sites in the West and elsewhere—newspapers such as the *New York Times* and the *Washington Post*; news websites such as Foreign Policy and the Huffington Post; TV sites such as CNN, the BBC, and Fox; and even comedy news icons like Jon Stewart and Stephen Colbert—but as my polls show, the majority of Arabs who use the Internet go principally to Arabic-language websites.[3] And those with resources—and agendas—will strive to use their resources to influence the new market of information and ideas.

---

3. 2011 Annual Arab Public Opinion Survey. Anwar Sadat Chair for Peace and Development, University of Maryland. Available online at: http://sadat.umd.edu/ViewsArabs_Oct11_graphs %20FINAL.ppt.

CHAPTER 4

INCITEMENT, EMPATHY, AND OPINION

A FTER 9/11, AMERICANS DISCOVERED pervasive anger with the United States among Arabs and Muslims globally, even among those who had no sympathy for those attacking American soil. As Americans sought to understand what would cause such resentment and whether or not it was connected to the terrible act, many focused on the idea that media incitement was behind Arab and Muslim sentiments. In the years since, this concern with Arab media fomenting regional anger has led to further objections to material aired by Al Jazeera and other Arab media. Among the examples cited: speeches by Osama bin Laden, including those that specifically called for violence against the United States; graphic pictures of Arab and Muslim victims of the American-led wars in Afghanistan and Iraq; Palestinian victims of Israeli offensives in the West Bank and Gaza; provocative images of torture in Abu Ghraib prison; and stories of American soldiers flushing Qurans down the toilet.

Without the excessively provocative images and stories, or at least with lighter emphasis on them, less anger might have been directed toward the United States. One can certainly argue that in many instances Arab media have been "biased" in reporting about conflict, in that a viewer is left with no doubt whose side the media are on. (The same argument, of course, could be made with regard to Israeli media reporting on conflicts involving Israel, and American media reporting in the weeks after 9/11.) But to argue that incitement is a primary cause of conflict, or that it could be significantly reduced through diplomatic or educational efforts while conflict rages, is to confuse symptoms and causes.

To begin with, the information revolution encourages controversial coverage, even as more objective information is also aired. If there is an event the public would have an interest in seeing, someone is likely to cover it, and those who do will gain in market share. Photographs from Abu Ghraib showing American soldiers taking pleasure in torturing and humiliating Iraqi prisoners initially appeared in the American media, before Arab outlets picked up the story. And the inability of American Al Hurra TV to air speeches by Hezbollah's leader Hassan Nasrallah during the Israel-Hezbollah war of 2006—congressional funds would have dried up if it had—meant that few Arabs were watching Al Hurra. Certainly there is room for more responsible journalism, always a factor in public perceptions, but in an era of intense media competition and unprecedented availability of information, someone is likely to air any story that gets public attention.

Media coverage, though, is *not* the core problem; the issue goes to the orientation of people's hearts in times of conflict and pain. Positive coverage of "the other side" is often dismissed. Negative coverage reinforces, but does not cause, preexisting perceptions. Soon after 9/11, for example, the Bush administration understood that there was a serious problem of perception for the United States, not only in the Middle East but elsewhere in the world. Part of the prescription was to appoint a highly accomplished advertising executive with no foreign policy expertise, Charlotte Beers, as America's public diplomacy czar to craft America's message to the world. Needless to say, the strategy failed and her tenure didn't last long. Rather than improving, Arab public opinion toward the United States grew still more unfavorable in the following months.

This should not have been a surprise. A commission mandated by Congress and appointed by the Bush administration to explore effective American public diplomacy noted that perceptions of America in the Muslim world are principally a function of substantive American foreign policies, not of public relations, even if the latter can help at the margin.[1]

---

1. *Finding America's Voice: A Strategy for Reinvigorating U.S. Public Diplomacy* (New York: Council on Foreign Relations Press, 2003). Available online at: www.cfr.org/us-strategy-and -politics/finding-americas-voice/p6261. I was a member of this committee.

Empathy in Conflict

One question is whether airing material that highlights the suffering of the other side actually provokes more resentment than empathy in conflict. I designed polls to gauge Arab attitudes toward positive media coverage of Israelis and Israeli attitudes toward media coverage of Arabs. Of Arabs I asked: "When you watch a movie or program about the Jewish Holocaust, which of the following is closest to your feelings?" (of Israelis, I asked about the suffering of Palestinian refugees). Respondents could then choose from these options: I feel empathy for the Jews who suffered under the Nazis; I resent the airing of the program, as I feel it brings sympathy toward Israel and Jews at the expense of Palestinians and Arabs; I have mixed feelings; and other. Based on the weighted average results from the five countries, 11 percent expressed empathy, 53 percent resentment, and 21 percent mixed feelings (Figure 4.1). These results were parallel to Jewish Israeli attitudes toward Palestinian suffering (as we will see, only 10 percent expressed empathy). Note that my questions did *not* measure empathy directly—only if empathy is trumped by other feelings. The bottom line is that, in conflict, empathy is superseded by fear of giving advantages to the enemy—which is why, in extreme conflict, such as on the battlefield, where one either kills or is killed, demonizing the enemy is partly a survival strategy. It's less about Arabs and Jews than about endless conflict.

There were variations among respondents. Moroccans were least likely to be resentful (34 percent) and most likely to be empathetic (24 percent) or to have mixed feelings (30 percent). Egyptians and Saudis were less empathetic, with a bit more than half being resentful. About one-third of Saudis either expressed empathy (5 percent) or mixed feelings (27 percent), and about one-quarter of Egyptians expressed empathy (7 percent) or mixed feelings (20 percent).

About two-thirds of Jordanians and Lebanese were resentful (65 percent), while about a fifth of each was empathetic or had mixed feelings. Finally, Emiratis[2] were very resentful (89 percent), with only about 1 in 10 indicating empathy or mixed feelings.

Those who were statistically less likely to be resentful tended to be women and the less educated—with the two categories overlapping because the rate

---

2. It should be noted that the sample of 500 people in the United Arab Emirates included 350 citizens and 150 noncitizen resident Arabs.

FIGURE 4.1 Empathy with Jews over Holocaust, by Country, 2011

When you watch a movie or a program about the Jewish Holocaust, which is closest to your feelings: I feel empathy for Jews, I have mixed feelings, I resent it because it brings sympathy to Israel.

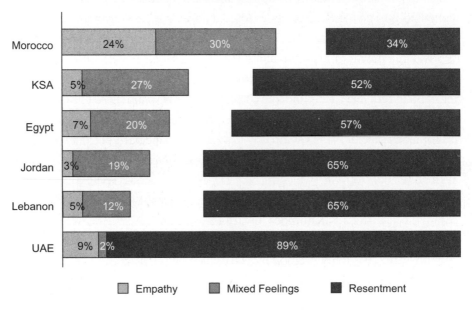

Empathy   Mixed Feelings   Resentment

of education among women tends to be lower. Media usage was also quite interesting. Those who primarily watch the Lebanese Hezbollah's Al Manar TV (64 percent), the Saudi-owned Al Arabiya (60 percent), and the United Arab Emirates' Abu Dhabi TV (59 percent) were most resentful, while those who watch the American Al Hurra TV (43 percent) were least resentful. Contrary to Western accusations, those watching Al Jazeera were slightly less likely than average to be resentful—although one should not be quick to draw conclusions about cause and effect.

Significant differences were not evident either between different age groups or between the employed and unemployed, but knowledge of certain languages had a stark effect on empathy. Strikingly, those who spoke French were a lot more likely to be empathetic (20 percent to 7 percent) or to have mixed feelings (31 percent to 20 percent) and a lot less resentful (40 percent to 56 percent) than were those who did not. Similarly, those who spent the most time on French-language Internet sites reported much more empathy (24 percent) or mixed feelings (39 percent) and were much less likely to be resentful (31 percent). This is largely explained by the fact that the greatest number of French speakers in the sample live in Morocco, where there was far more empathy across the board. Moroccan French speakers were still a little more empathetic than non-French speakers, but only by 25 percent to 21 percent. The opposite was true for those who also speak English. English speakers were more likely to be resentful (56 percent to 49 percent), less likely to be empathetic (7 percent to 13 percent), but also more likely to have mixed feelings (24 percent to 21 percent). Reading English-language Internet sites had no meaningful effect on empathy or resentment.

The difference between English and French speakers appears to be related to frequency of use. Many of the French speakers, especially in Morocco, are more fluent in French than in Arabic and for many of them French is a first language. Thus, they tend to watch French TV and media more frequently, and this creates some identity separation from other Arabs. The overwhelming majority of English speakers learned English as a second or third language and generally use Arabic in their daily lives.

Identity and Empathy

The way people ranked their identities mattered for the degree of empathy they expressed. Not surprisingly, those who identified themselves primarily as "citizens of the world" tended to be most empathetic and least resentful, while those ranking Muslim identity highest tended to be the least empathetic and the most resentful. Those with Arab identities were more resentful than those who identified with their own country (Figure 4.2).

For example, those who said that their own government's decisions should be based on what was best for the world were the most empathetic (20 percent empathetic, 27 percent mixed feelings) and the least resentful (40 percent) of Arabs polled, whereas those who said decisions should be based on what was best for Muslims were the least empathetic (2 percent empathetic, 17 percent mixed feelings) and the most resentful (63 percent).

Similar results were obtained when respondents were directly asked about their primary identity (Figure 4.3). Those who identified themselves as "citizens of the world" first were significantly less likely to be resentful than those with a primarily Muslim identity (34 percent to 61 percent). In addition, they were more likely to be at least somewhat empathetic than those identifying themselves as Muslim first—52 percent (17 percent empathetic)

FIGURE 4.2 Basis for Government Decisions Versus Empathy, 2011

When you watch a movie or a program about the Jewish Holocaust, which is closest to your feelings: I feel empathy for Jews, I have mixed feelings, I resent it because it brings sympathy to Israel.

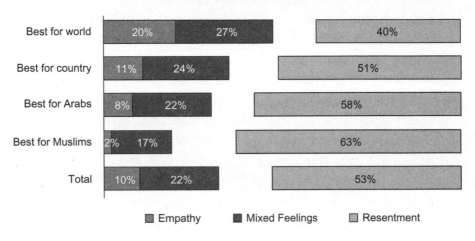

FIGURE 4.3 Primary Identity Versus Empathy, 2011

When you watch a movie or a program about the Jewish Holocaust, which is closest to your feelings: I feel empathy for Jews, I have mixed feelings, I resent it because it brings sympathy to Israel.

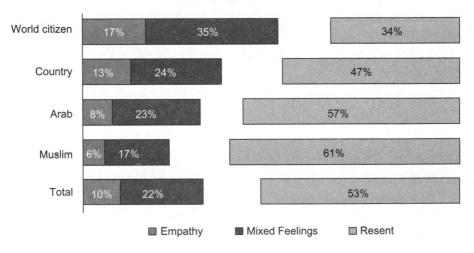

versus 22 percent (6 percent empathetic). Those identifying themselves as Arab first (57 percent) were more likely to be resentful than those identifying with their country first (47 percent).

Women in the Workplace

Attitudes toward the right of women to work outside the home were also correlated with the degree of empathy expressed. Those who said that women should always be allowed to work were significantly less likely to be resentful than those who said "only in times of economic stress" (45 percent to 61 percent), though it is interesting that they were only slightly less resentful than those who said "never" (53 percent). Tolerant respondents were also more likely to have at least some empathy (43 percent), with 15 percent saying they empathize and about one-quarter having mixed feelings. Those saying "women should never have the right to work outside of home" were as likely to be empathetic as those who said "women should work only in times of economic need" with about 3 in 10 saying they have at least some empathy.

Contrasting Questions Among Israeli Jews and Israeli Arabs/Palestinians

In November 2011, a month after the six-country Arab public opinion poll, I conducted an opinion poll among Jewish Israelis, fielded by the Dahaf Institute in Israel. Among other questions, I asked one pertaining to the suffering of Palestinian refugees: "When you watch a movie or program about the suffering of Palestinian refugees, which of the following is closest to your feelings?" Respondents were given the following four options: I empathize with the suffering of the refugees; I resent it as I feel it brings sympathy toward the Palestinians and Arabs at the expense of Israelis and Jews; I have mixed feelings; and other.

Only 10 percent of Jewish respondents expressed empathy with the suffering of the refugees, while 49 percent expressed mixed feelings and 30 percent expressed resentment (Figure 4.4).

One of the clues to attitudes on this issue comes from a third poll I conducted in November 2011, among Arab citizens of Israel only. In that poll, 44 percent of Arabs in Israel expressed feeling empathy when they watched a movie or program about the Holocaust, 21 percent expressed mixed feelings, and 33 percent expressed resentment. Obviously, that segment of the Arab public is most familiar with Jewish Israelis in their daily lives and as

FIGURE 4.4 Jewish Israeli Empathy for Palestinian Refugees, 2011

When you watch a movie or a program about the suffering of Palestinian refugees, which of the following is closest to your feelings?

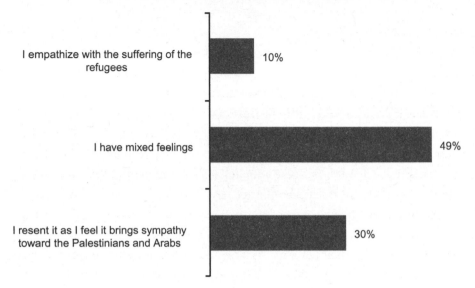

friends. In fact, when I broke down the data demographically, the Druze, who serve in the Israeli army, were most empathetic (84 percent) while Muslims were least empathetic (36 percent). These seemingly sectarian divisions were partially explained by the "identity" attitudes of Arabs who had relatives who became refugees in 1948 (least empathetic) and those who didn't, including the overwhelming majority of Druze (most empathetic).

The two questions asked of Arabs and Jews are of course not identical, not only with regard to the nature of the suffering but also with regard to those responsible. In the Holocaust, Arabs were not a party; in the creation of the Palestinian refugee problem, Israeli Jews were a party in the conflict. Thus, in the latter case there is the possible fear of bearing responsibility, on the one hand, or a sense of guilt, on the other. On the Arab side, the feeling of asymmetry of power favoring Israelis and of Western support for Israel could also be a factor in the assessment of the impact of television programming.

Note, too, that these questions are not intended to measure the capacity to empathize, only whether television coverage of the other's suffering generates sympathy or resentment. The issue here is the fight for public support, the ability to sustain the urge to continue the conflict—particularly when majorities of both Arabs and Jews believe that the conflict is unlikely to be resolved any time soon. Majorities of Arabs in the five countries polled in 2011 and majorities of Israelis polled in a November 2012 poll inside Israel said they didn't believe that peace between them would ever happen.

Empathy with Civilian Casualties

Questions about the Holocaust and the suffering of refugees require a leap of the imagination for many respondents. To bring the issue of empathy down to a more immediate and personal level, I asked a comparable set of questions in all three polls about the respondents' most important feelings when they see Israeli or Palestinian civilian casualties of the conflict. The results revealed a dramatic lack of empathy across the great divide of Arabs and Israelis.

Only 19 percent of Israelis ranked empathy as one of their top feelings when they watch Palestinian civilian casualties, compared with 57 percent who feel Palestinians brought it upon themselves (Figure 4.5). Similarly, only 9 percent of Arabs in Egypt, Morocco, Jordan, Lebanon, and the United Arab Emirates reported empathy with Israeli civilian casualties as one of the

FIGURE 4.5 Israeli Sympathy for Palestinian Civilian Casualties, 2011

When you see Palestinian civilian casualties in the conflict with Israel, which TWO of the following best describe your feelings:

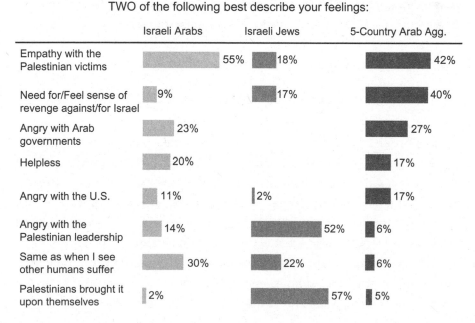

	Israeli Arabs	Israeli Jews	5-Country Arab Agg.
Empathy with the Palestinian victims	55%	18%	42%
Need for/Feel sense of revenge against/for Israel	9%	17%	40%
Angry with Arab governments	23%		27%
Helpless	20%		17%
Angry with the U.S.	11%	2%	17%
Angry with the Palestinian leadership	14%	52%	6%
Same as when I see other humans suffer	30%	22%	6%
Palestinians brought it upon themselves	2%	57%	5%

FIGURE 4.6 Palestinian Sympathy for Israeli Civilian Casualties, 2011

When you see Israeli civilian casualties in the conflict with the Palestinians, which TWO of the following best describe your feelings:

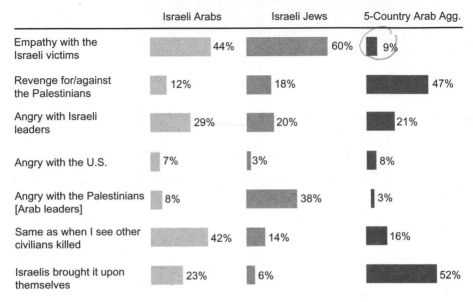

	Israeli Arabs	Israeli Jews	5-Country Arab Agg.
Empathy with the Israeli victims	44%	60%	9%
Revenge for/against the Palestinians	12%	18%	47%
Angry with Israeli leaders	29%	20%	21%
Angry with the U.S.	7%	3%	8%
Angry with the Palestinians [Arab leaders]	8%	38%	3%
Same as when I see other civilians killed	42%	14%	16%
Israelis brought it upon themselves	23%	6%	52%

top two reactions they have—dwarfed by their feelings that Israelis brought it upon themselves (52 percent; Figure 4.6). Given their unique situations of being both Palestinian and Israeli, Palestinian/Arab Israelis were alone in expressing higher degrees of empathy with both Palestinian and Israeli civilian victims, but they reported greater empathy for Palestinians.

The Effect of Friendship on Empathy in 2011 Poll of Arab and Jewish Israelis

Friendship clearly affects the degree of empathy, but not equally across groups. Among Arab Israelis, having Jewish friends strongly affects the level of empathy with Israeli victims of the Arab-Israeli conflict, as does recent contact with those friends. Thus, those most likely to empathize with Jewish Israeli victims were Arabs with Jewish Israeli friends (54 percent) followed by those with Jewish friends but without visit exchange over the previous two years (43 percent); the least empathetic were those without Jewish friends (37 percent), but these were still far more empathetic than non-Israeli Arabs are toward Jews and than Jews are toward Palestinian casualties.

FIGURE 4.7 Effect of Friendship on Empathy, 2011

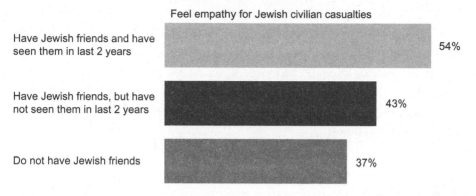

Do you have Jewish friends, and how does that affect your empathy toward Israeli Jewish civilian casualties?

Feel empathy for Jewish civilian casualties

Have Jewish friends and have seen them in last 2 years — 54%

Have Jewish friends, but have not seen them in last 2 years — 43%

Do not have Jewish friends — 37%

These feelings of empathy are not as powerfully expressed by Israeli Jews, for whom friendship with Arab Israelis has a less consistent effect on empathy. Israeli Jews with Arab friends tended to be somewhat more empathetic with Palestinian civilian casualties (24 percent) than those who don't have Arab friends (17 percent). But most Jewish Israelis (69 percent) do not have any Arabs friends, whereas only 46 percent of Arabs don't have Jewish friends. Why the friendship gap? Probably because Arabs constitute about 20 percent of the Israeli population and tend to be dependent economically on the Jewish majority; Arab Israelis thus have more motivation to interact with Jewish Israelis than do Jewish Israelis to interact with Arab Israelis. That said, it is also clear Jews who do have Arab friends express less empathy than do Arab Israelis who have Jewish friends. This is probably due mainly to two factors.

First, while most Arab citizens of Israel consider themselves to be also Palestinian, the Jewish Israeli public differentiates them from Palestinians under occupation when they hear the question about "Palestinian civilian casualties." Second, Palestinian Israelis themselves have sometimes been victims of the same violence that killed Jewish civilians, and many had Jewish friends who were victims.

The impact of contacts and friendship on attitudes is almost inherently asymmetrical. There is rarely full symmetry in any conflict, and there is increasing evidence that asymmetry of power and conditions result in different public responses. One recent experiment in social psychology is particularly telling. Professors Rebecca Saxe and Emile G. Bruneau conducted an experiment among Palestinians and Israelis to find out how each reacted to telling its narrative to the other. Palestinian attitudes toward Israelis improved, not from hearing the Israeli narrative but from having the Israelis merely hear the Palestinian story. There was no measurable impact on Israelis. And a month after the experiment, its effect on the participants disappeared altogether, as participants reverted to old attitudes. The scholars' conclusion was that the asymmetry of power, perceived and real, is a factor in the way each side reacts.[3]

The Incitement Issue and the Prospects of Peace and Conflict

Incitement obviously undermines peacemaking efforts. At the extreme, though, incitement also has behavioral consequence—although this is harder to prove. Incitement is often employed as a tactic to undermine reconciliation efforts, but its resonance in society is broader, including among those who in principle may be open to reconciliation. This is often a function of (a) pessimism about the prospects for peace and (b) the emotional preparation for what seems like inevitable conflict, which is easier if the enemy is demonized. Thus, incitement can be self-defeating: The more the enemy is demonized, the more difficult it is to convince people to make peace with the enemy. But if conflict is seen as inevitable, incitement is an effective public mobilization tool.

One reason education and public relations alone cannot address pervasive incitement and provocation in conflict situations is that they often serve strategic aims—sometimes deliberately and sometimes unintentionally. Just as empathy with the enemy is difficult to find, partly for fear that it could diminish the will to fight a seemingly inevitable fight, so incitement is a strategic tool often used by a weaker party to muster the will to sustain the fight.

---

3. Emile G. Bruneau and Rebecca Saxe, "The Power of Being Heard: The Benefits of 'Perspective Giving' in the Context of Intergroup Conflict," Massachusetts Institute of Technology, Department of Brain and Cognitive Sciences. Available online at: http://saxelab.mit.edu/resources/papers/Bruneau%26Saxe_inpress.pdf. Also see Emile G. Bruneau, Nicholas Dufour, and Rebecca Saxe, "Social Cognition in Members of Conflict Groups: Behavioral and Neural Responses in Arabs, Israelis and South Americans to Each Other's Misfortunes," *Philosophical Transactions of the Royal Society*, 367, no. 1589 (March 2012): 717–730. Available online at: http://rstb.royalsocietypublishing.org/content/367/1589/717.full?sid=250c4b7e-8e2f-462e-96a4-0e59 5e55fd69.

Provocation, by contrast, is often the tool of the stronger party, pushing for an earlier fight while it maintains a strong hand.

Arabs believe that "normalizing" relations with Israel diplomatically and through social, business, and academic interactions would serve to legitimize Israel's occupation of Arab lands and take away the biggest card Arabs have with Israel: acceptance of Israel (officially and in practice), especially in the absence of serious Arab military leverage. In times of optimism about peace, such as following the 1993 Oslo agreements between Israel and the Palestine Liberation Organization, in Arab countries—ranging from Tunisia and Morocco to Qatar and Oman—there was far more openness to dealing with Israel and Israelis. After the collapse of Israeli-Palestinian negotiations in the summer of 2001—which was followed by a violent Palestinian intifada and bloody Israeli operations in the occupied Palestinian territories—Arab public pressure increased to limit exchanges with Israel.

Attitudes of Arabs and Israelis toward each other—and the extent of empathy, incitement, and provocation—have been a function of how they both assess the prospects of peace and conflict. Following the 1993 Oslo agreements between Israel and the Palestine Liberation Organization—which fostered a general belief that the long-standing conflict was on its way to resolution—only a tiny portion of Israelis endorsed the idea of "deportations," or expulsion of Palestinians from their homes. But that number grew to over 40 percent after the collapse of the negotiations and a marked increase in suicide bombings against Israeli civilian targets. Similarly, only a small minority of Palestinians endorsed suicide bombings in the early days of optimism after the Oslo accords, but this segment became a majority after the collapse of the negotiations and after the harsh and bloody measures imposed by Israel. The point is that attitudes are not fixed and can shift dramatically. This shift is less a function of the incitement of those who oppose peace (they existed even when people were hopeful about the prospects of diplomatic solutions) and more a function of people's daily reality and their assessment of the odds of peace.

The Palestinians and the Israelis first addressed the question of incitement during negotiations in the mid-1990s, particularly in the Wye River negotiations headed by the Palestinian Authority president, Yasser Arafat, and the Israeli prime minister, Benjamin Netanyahu, and mediated by U.S. president

Bill Clinton. We can see from those early days that many aspects of the incitement issue were political and tactical.

When Netanyahu first became prime minister of Israel in 1996, he was reluctant to proceed on the same path of peacemaking with the Palestinians that had been started by his assassinated predecessor, Yitzhak Rabin, and for the first time raised the issue of incitement as a central one for the negotiations. The Clinton administration worked tirelessly to persuade him to engage and finally was able to put together a major peace conference at Wye River, in Maryland, in 1998. The Palestinians, and to some extent the United States, viewed Netanyahu's focus on incitement as a way to avoid serious negotiation. But they agreed to make the issue of incitement a negotiations topic, even as they proceeded to tackle topics more important to them, such as Israeli withdrawal from occupied Palestinian territories.

The leaders of the Israeli and Palestinian teams were political appointees who dominated the discussions in full meetings, had a contentious relationship with each other, and were clearly driven by political agendas and scoring points. The other members of the Israeli and Palestinian teams, however, were mostly professionals in areas ranging from law to media and education, and they were much more genuinely open to the idea of finding ways to reduce incitement.

In the full meetings of the Anti-Incitement Committee, of which I was a member, the conversation was hardly fruitful. The first meeting began with a discussion of how to define incitement, but we quickly discovered that there can be no agreement on this. Instead we operated on the assumption that "we know it when we see it." Among members of the American team there were few disagreements, but Israelis and Palestinians could never agree even on the examples presented. The Israelis would put forth examples of Palestinian incitement—say, a statement by a Muslim religious figure against Jews or Israel—and the Palestinians would respond with a charge against the Israelis, usually Israeli actions or statements pertaining to settlement expansion or Israeli rights to the occupied territories. And so it went—with each side downplaying the examples given by the other side or simply rejecting them as not constituting incitement.

Part of the problem was that many of the examples that Palestinians provided—such as confiscation of Palestinian lands, building settlements, or declarations by Israeli officials of Jewish rights to the West Bank ("Judea and Sumeria")—were about acts and statements that Palestinians saw as provocations but that Israelis did not see as being within the mandate of the committee. This debate about what is worse—using Israel's dominant power to change life on the ground for the Palestinians, or inciting statements in the Palestinian media—was never settled, and indeed it could not be settled in the absence of a degree of mutual trust.

The only constructive meetings were conducted by the media and education committees, especially when the political delegation heads were not present. These professionals definitely had grievances against each other, but when the subject turned to actual steps that each side could take in an environment of peacemaking, both sides agreed that there was much to be done to minimize incitement, including the need for both sides to revise their textbooks. But even then, trust was minimal, and everyone understood that these issues couldn't be separated from the broader political picture. There was always a sense that this was a side exercise and a tiny part of a bigger strategic game. Incitement can aggravate conflict, and peacemakers should resist it, but its prevalence and resonance across society are more the products of intense and seemingly hopeless conflict than real causes of the conflict.

In the end, even with focused attention on incitement and provocation by well-meaning and competent Israeli and Palestinian experts, and with the help of an independent American delegation, little progress emerged, either within the group or, certainly, in Israeli and Palestinian societies. For the most part, incitement, provocation, and lack of empathy remain symptoms of a deep conflict and the seemingly limited prospects of its resolution—much more than being primary causes of conflict that can be addressed on their own.

In fact, as soon as Netanyahu was defeated in the 1999 Israeli election and replaced by Ehud Barak as prime minister, the full Anti-Incitement Committee never met again, replaced by infrequent and lower-key local meetings. Barak, who was more committed than his predecessor to negotiating peaceful settlements with Syrians and Palestinians, saw this committee as less relevant and as something that Netanyahu requested for tactical reasons. Had the negotiations succeeded in shaping a durable Israeli-Palestinian peace, incitement would probably still exist, though to a lesser extent, but those who pay attention to it would be far fewer. Conversely, the collapse of negotiations in 2000, the advent of more violence, and gloom about the prospects for peace would have negated much of what would have been agreed on.

As it was, even the limited steps that seemed acceptable to both sides on media and education were forgotten as soon as casualties started to mount. Rather than resolution, the ongoing Palestinian-Israeli conflict continued to provide the prism through which Arabs see the world.

THE ARAB PRISM OF PAIN

T HE PALESTINIAN-ISRAELI CONFLICT ISSUE remains the prism of pain through which most Arabs view the world.

It is not uncommon for a people to have a collective historical experience, or repeated experience, intense and painful enough to help shape perceptions. For Jews, the Holocaust remains a collective atrocity that inevitably shapes perceptions, fears, and aspirations, even for those who had no relatives affected directly by the Holocaust. By itself the Holocaust is an extreme case, even in human history, but precisely because of its intensity it is inevitably linked to more persistent fears many Jews have had, even before and since, about persecution and anti-Semitism. It is hard to understand the global perspectives of Jews in the late twentieth and early twenty-first centuries without some reference to the Holocaust. Even as the issues of Israel and Israeli insecurity have themselves become a contemporary prism, these issues cannot be easily decoupled from the Holocaust past.

Collective experiences need not be a single tragic event, however. For African Americans, slavery and the subsequent history of persecution and discrimination have provided a prism that has shaped the outlook of generations. It isn't that an African American wakes up in the morning thinking about ancestors suffering as slaves and all the injustice and inhumanity that this entails, or that many African Americans have not moved beyond these experiences. It is that even in this case, where the experience is merely a memory, the impact on society, including the continuing economic lag between blacks and whites, is always present.

In Palestine, there was neither holocaust nor slavery. But for Arabs, the Palestinian-Israeli conflict still embodies collective historical and psychological experiences that are integral to the way they view the outside world. The conflict represents not only the painful experience of Arabs losing Palestine in 1948 and facing another devastating defeat in the 1967 war; it is also a reminder of a contemporary Arab history full of dashed aspirations and deeply humiliating experiences, usually tied to the West. Since 1967, Israeli control of East Jerusalem—a city that symbolizes an even older painful conflict dating back to the times of the Crusades—has added fuel to the fire. But what distinguishes the Palestinian-Israeli conflict from other painful experiences is that it is seemingly unending, with repeated episodes of suffering over which Arabs have no apparent control. This is an open wound that flares up all too frequently, representing the very humiliation that Arabs seek to overcome. If the Arab awakening is in the first place about restoring dignity, about raising Arab heads high in the world, then the Palestinian-Israeli conflict represents dignity's antithesis.

To whatever degree the Palestinian-Israeli conflict incites Arab publics, it is not one of the issues that Arab citizens identify as an immediate priority in their daily lives. Earning a living and feeding a family, the quality of schools for their children, personal safety and security in retirement—these are among the more pressing issues that Arabs constantly face, along with people everywhere. Moreover, some history might suggest that the importance of the Palestinian-Israeli conflict in the Arab world has been somewhat exaggerated. Most Arab governments, like others around the world, behave in a manner that advances their own self interest and their preservation of power—and the issue of Palestine is almost always trumped by, even sacrificed to, other priorities. Many Arabs, including those who profess to care about Palestine, have not done much for Palestinians. Indeed, in some cases, they've had conflict with them. Kuwait expelled thousands of Palestinians after its liberation from the Iraqi invasion in 1991, because Palestinians were seen as having sympathized with Iraq. Lebanon is the only Arab country to have allowed the Palestinians total operational freedom to wage military operations against Israel, but like other Arab states except for Jordan, Lebanon has never accepted its hundreds of thousands of Palestinian refugees as citizens or provided basic services to them. Instead these Palestinians continue to live in isolated and poverty-stricken refugee camps. And even

Jordan, the only country to provide citizenship to Palestinian refugees, confronted militant Palestinian groups in bloody events that amounted to a Jordanian-Palestinian civil war in 1970.

There is also another side to the story: Arabs did fight over Palestine. In 1948, Arab states, rejecting Israel's declaration of independence, launched a failed war that has left lingering wounds of humiliation. In 1956 Israel joined Britain and France in a tripartite attack on Egypt. The attack had many aims, but for Israel it had most to do with Egypt's support for Palestinians. In 1967 a devastating war with Israel brought humiliating and economically disastrous consequences for Egypt, Jordan, and Syria. This war broadened the Palestine question, as it involved territories from other Arab states: Egypt lost its Sinai Peninsula and control of Gaza; Jordan lost control of the West Bank, including East Jerusalem and Bethlehem; and Syria lost the Golan Heights, which to this day remain occupied. Less than seven years later, in 1973, Arabs were fighting Israel again as they sought to regain control of lost territories and avenge their prior defeat. While Egypt and Syria launched the actual fighting, there was considerable financial and political support coming from oil-rich states, particularly Saudi Arabia and Algeria, and also military backing from other Arab countries. After the war, Arab petroleum producers imposed an unprecedented oil embargo on the United States and other countries that supported Israel—an embargo that had major economic consequences, including the quadrupling of oil prices.

Israeli invasions of Lebanon in 1978 and 1982 were directed against the Palestine Liberation Organization and succeeded in forcing the PLO to leave the country, but not without devastating consequences for Lebanon that created tens of thousands of refugees, especially Shiites—providing the seeds for the rise of Hezbollah, which has remained focused on confronting Israel.

Every Arab generation since 1948 has witnessed wars and bloodshed connected to Palestine. And every major regional political movement has made Palestine and Jerusalem a central theme of its ideology and narrative, including the Islamic revolution in 1979 in non-Arab Iran. Iran's interest shouldn't be surprising. The Palestinian issue remains central to Muslims as well as Arabs. Jerusalem is Islam's third holiest site, after Mecca and Medina. It's also part of the central narratives of Muslim confrontation with Crusaders and the Muslims' ultimate success in expelling the Crusaders from Jerusalem in the battle of Hattin in 1187. For Iran, there is yet another reason: Iran's drive to influence Arab public opinion entails catering to the prism of pain of the Arabs they are trying to reach.

Hundreds of millions of dollars continued flowing to the PLO throughout the 1980s from Arab states, especially the oil-rich ones, and most especially after the onset of the first Palestinian intifada, even as Arabs were preoccupied with a destructive and costly war in the Gulf between Iraq and Iran. Iraq's invasion of Kuwait in 1990 and the subsequent American-led war to dislodge Iraq from Kuwait took a toll on Palestinians, not only in distracting Arabs from the Israeli-Palestinian conflict but also because of the reduced support from oil-rich states for the PLO, due to its support for Iraq. But even during the Iraq-Kuwait crisis, bloodshed between Palestinians and Israelis in Jerusalem and elsewhere nearly derailed the American effort to maintain a coalition against Iraq, and the Bush administration had to promise Arab states that it would turn to addressing the Palestinian-Israeli conflict as soon as the war ended.

The 1990s were peacemaking years, beginning, after the Gulf War, with the Madrid process, the American-led effort that brought Arabs and Israelis to the negotiating table. After the 1993 Oslo agreements between Israel and the PLO, most people assumed that the Palestinian-Israeli conflict was on its way to resolution, despite the ups and downs of the negotiations. The historic mutual recognition between Israel and the PLO and the sight of the two parties negotiating possible peace had the effect of lowering the Palestine issue in Arab public priorities, which was sometimes misinterpreted to be an indicator of reduced interest.

The collapse of the Palestinian-Israeli negotiations in July 2000 and the onset of the Palestinian al-Aqsa intifada, which included suicide bombings in Israel and harsh Israeli measures devastating to Palestinians in the West Bank and Gaza, generated considerable anger across the Arab world, including among Arab governments that had not acted forcefully in the past. In one important episode in 2001 the crown prince of Saudi Arabia, Abdullah Bin Abd al-Aziz (who later became king), turned down President George W. Bush's invitation to visit the White House and made it clear that the cause was his anger with American policy on the Palestine issue. A month later George H. W. Bush found it necessary to phone the crown prince to assure him that his son was not too pro-Israeli. This forced the Bush administration to reassess its policy in the summer of 2001,[1] and indeed the administration seemed much more inclined to push for diplomatic initiative, just before the tragedy of 9/11 reshuffled all its priorities.

The Iraq war took much of the Arab attention during that decade, but as we will see from the polling data, the Palestine question remained prominent. Hardly a day went by when Arabs were not reminded that most Palestinians continued to struggle both as refugees since 1948 and under the humiliating conditions of occupation that started in 1967. In April 2010, U.S. secretary of state Hillary Clinton described the global importance of the Palestinian-Israeli issue this way:

> One of the striking experiences that I had becoming Secretary of State and now having traveled something on the order of 300,000 miles in the last 15 months and going to dozens and dozens of countries is that when I compare that to my experience as First Lady, where I was also privileged to travel around the world, back in the 1990s when I went to Asia or Africa or Europe or Latin America, it was rare that the Israeli-Palestinian conflict was raised. Now it is the first, second, or third item on nearly every agenda of every country I visit. What does that mean? Well, it means that this conflict has assumed a role in the global geostrategic environment that carries great weight. And it also means that there is a yearning on the part of people who have never been to Israel and never met a Palestinian that somehow, some way, we create the circumstances for this to finally be resolved.[2]

Even though the Palestinian-Israeli conflict is certainly not the primary cause of regional ills—it is not the cause, for instance, of sectarian conflict

---

1. During that period of reassessment, I (along with one other expert and two former ambassadors to the Middle East) was invited for a consultation session with National Security Advisor Condoleezza Rice; her deputy, Stephen Hadley; the vice president's chief of staff, Scooter Libby; and several other White House officials. Rice made it clear that the approach they had taken on this issue "was not working" and that they were open to suggestions that would give the conflict higher diplomatic priority, something that Secretary of State Colin Powell was pushing.
2. Hilary Clinton, speech presented at the S. Daniel Abraham Center for Middle East Peace, Washington, DC, April 15, 2010. Available online at: www.centerpeace.org/highlights_detail .php?id_high2=3.

in Lebanon, Iraq, or Bahrain, or of the region's failed educational institutions and teetering economies—and is not the priority subject of their daily lives, for most Arabs and many Muslims it remains the prism of pain through which they see the world.

Exploring the Importance of the Palestine Issue

Over the decade preceding the Arab uprisings, I probed Arab public views of the Palestine issue on multiple levels. To begin with, I explored how important the Arab-Israeli conflict was in Arab perceptions. Certainly Arabs rank the issue high in their priorities during times of crisis, especially bloody crises involving Israel. But over the decade, I measured change, and the issue remained consistently high in perceived public priorities.

In 2002, for example, a Zogby poll asked respondents to express how important the Palestine issue was as compared to other central issues. In Saudi Arabia, 85 percent identified the Palestinian issue as being extremely important (and another 11 percent identified it as somewhat important). In comparison, 59 percent identified the economy, 62 percent identified health care, and 75 percent identified civil rights as being extremely important. In Morocco the expressed importance of the Palestine question also superseded all other issues. In Egypt, where 72 percent identified the issue as extremely important (and another 17 percent as somewhat important), it was ranked higher than the economy (51 percent) but was slightly superseded by civil and personal rights (75 percent).

To be sure, 2002 was a year of focus on foreign-policy issues, coming after the tragedy of 9/11, and there was intense bloodshed on the Israeli-Palestinian front that was the subject of daily media coverage, but my findings did not vary significantly in subsequent years.

Even in the intense years of the Iraq war, Arabs continued to rank Palestine high in their priorities. In polls I conducted in six Arab countries between 2002 and 2008, those who ranked the issue to be at least among the top three issues to them personally ranged from highs of 89 percent in 2004 and 86 percent in 2008, to lows of 69 percent in 2005 and 73 percent in 2003, 2004, and 2006.[3] It was 76 percent in 2009, 83 percent in 2010, and 78 percent in 2011. In comparison with other pressing issues, the "resolution of

---

3. Available online at: http://sadat.umd.edu/new%20surveys/surveys.htm.

Palestinian-Israeli conflict"[4] was ranked relatively high in recent years in a number of Arab countries, including since the onset of the Arab uprisings. In polls carried out by Zogby International for the Arab American Institute (AAI) for example, it ranked second in Jordan, Saudi Arabia, and the United Arab Emirates among eleven issues[5] in 2011. Even in revolutionary states where the issue ranked low in 2011, such as Egypt (8th) and Tunisia (11th), there were other indications of importance.[6]

Bottom line: Arabs have consistently perceived the Palestine issue to be important in their priorities over the entire post-9/11 decade, even if there was some variation over time and space.

The Arab Prism of Evaluation

Sometimes indirect indicators can be more revealing than direct ones. One of the questions I have asked over the decade goes as follows: "Whom among world leaders do you admire most—outside your own country?" The question is not meant to be a popularity contest: Arabs know very little about specific world leaders, and they are not in a position to evaluate them on most dimensions. The logic behind such questions is to learn about the frame of reference Arabs employ when making an evaluation: The answers provide clues about the reasons they select a particular leader and thus about their central criteria of evaluation. With the exception of 2003, when I named specific leaders for respondents to evaluate, the questions have been open-ended, asking the respondent to name leaders on their own. The results shed interesting light on the relationship between foreign leaders' stances on the Arab-Israeli conflict and their popularity among Arab citizens.

---

4. Note that the AAI question referred to ranking "the resolution of the Palestinian-Israeli conflict" not the "Palestinian issue."

5. The 2011 AAI/Zogby poll asked respondents to rank the following eleven issues: terrorism, political reform, ending corruption, heath care, resolving the Palestinian-Israeli conflict, civil rights, education, women's rights, political debate, democracy, and employment. Available online at: https://mail.google.com/mail/u/0/?ui=2&ik=d33e9e6dd2&view=att&th=13b9a4e700a32006&attid=0.1&disp=safe&realattid=4a5fc70df2d164fe_0.1&zw.

6. In Tunisia, the proposed constitution contained language criminalizing normal relations with Israel, something that had wide support in society. Even among those who opposed including such a specific measure in the constitution, there was support for the measure independently. And in Egypt, President Mohammad Morsi used almost every major occasion to state Egypt's intent to deal with Palestine as a priority issue.

In 2004 and 2005, Jacques Chirac of France was most admired.[7] It is important to remember that during these intense years of the Iraq war, the discourse in the West was very much about a possible clash of civilizations between Islam and the West, so the very fact that you have a Western leader from a state with a colonial history was telling enough. But Chirac scored on two fronts simultaneously, even aside from giving more policy attention to the Palestinians than other Western countries did: He was seen to have played a role in denying President Bush a United Nations cover for the Iraq war. Also, when Palestinian leader Yasser Arafat mysteriously fell ill, Chirac received him in France as a head of state; Arafat died in France shortly thereafter. This was, of course, in sharp contrast to Washington's support for the Israeli policy of confining Arafat to his compound in Ramallah in the West Bank.

Chirac's outstretched hand to Arafat also played well among the many Palestinians who assumed that Arafat had been poisoned. In 2012 Al Jazeera TV, with the cooperation of Arafat's widow, Suha Arafat, hired a Swiss firm to examine the possibility of radioactive poisoning, which had also been suspected in the 2006 death in London of the former Russian spy Alexander Litvinenko. The Palestinian Authority later asked an international team to exhume Arafat's remains, which was done on November 27, 2012.

In 2006 Chirac polled second, behind Hezbollah's leader, Hassan Nasrallah. At this time the Iraq war was seemingly intensifying the Sunni-Shiite divide. Sunni Muslims, who constitute the majority in the Arab world, worried about the rising power of Shiites in Iraq, Iran, and Lebanon, yet here were Arabs in mostly Sunni countries identifying a Shiite leader—a religious one at that—as the leader they admired most in the world, and certainly more than any Sunni leader. The reason was hard to miss: A few months before, Hezbollah was seen to have stood up to Israel in the 2006 war, in which, despite great devastation in Lebanon, Hezbollah was seen to have given Israel black eyes.

---

7. Ahmed Youssef, author of *L'Orient de Jacques Chirac* (Monaco: Éditions du Rocher, March 2003), argued that Chirac's policies made inroads with the Arab states: "As soon as the peace process between the Israelis and Palestinians deteriorated, Chirac appeared, in the eyes of Arab opinion, to be the only Western leader that could counter the unconditional support of the United States to Israel. Chirac then became more popular than certain leaders or kings in the Arab capitals" (cited by Olivier Guitta in *Middle East Quarterly* [Fall 2005]: 43–53).

A little more than a year later, in 2008, the Arabs I polled still identified Nasrallah as the most popular leader, despite a campaign to delegitimize him by several Arab governments worried about Hezbollah's popularity. To probe this issue a little more, I asked some questions that indirectly introduced the Sunni-Shiite issue.

In particular, Lebanon was in the middle of a painful political crisis that has endured. At the time the division was between a Sunni-supported government coalition and a Hezbollah-led opposition. Adding fuel to the fire was an ongoing investigation of the assassination of the popular Sunni Lebanese prime minister, Rafic Hariri, which pointed to possible involvement of Hezbollah's backer, Syria, and later Hezbollah itself. So I put the following question to the Arabs I polled in the overwhelmingly Sunni population in the six countries studied: "In the internal crisis in Lebanon, with whom do you sympathize most?" The results were again telling: Those who expressed sympathy for the Hezbollah-led opposition outnumbered those who expressed sympathy with the majority government led by Sunni prime minister Fouad Siniora by a ratio of 3 to 1 (Figure 5.1).

This is not to say that there are no Sunni-Shiite divisions in the region; it is simply that for most Arabs, this divide is generally trumped by the

FIGURE 5.1 Lebanese Politics, Six-Country Total, 2008

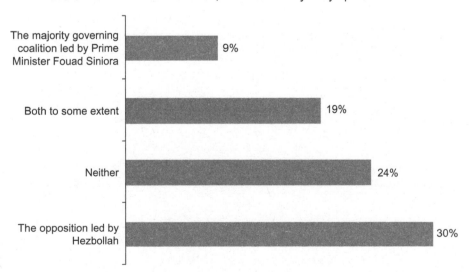

In the internal crisis in Lebanon, with whom do you sympathize most?

The majority governing coalition led by Prime Minister Fouad Siniora — 9%

Both to some extent — 19%

Neither — 24%

The opposition led by Hezbollah — 30%

Arab-Israeli conflict, especially in times of crisis. In fact, we can see the sectarian element of opinion in the way the Lebanese themselves were divided on the two sides: Shiites overwhelmingly supported the opposition, and majorities of Sunnis and Druze supported the government. Christians were divided, but more supported the governing coalition (Figure 5.2).

In my 2009 polling, Nasrallah dropped to second place, behind Turkish prime minister Recep Tayyip Erdogan. Here again, though, the reasons can be easily misinterpreted. Many believe that the rise of Turkey's and its leader's influence in the Arab world is principally connected to the attraction of its democratic system. That element has surely been consequential. But Turkey had been a democracy for some time, its prime minister and his party had been in power for years, and Turkey had taken an important position on

FIGURE 5.2 Lebanese Politics, by Confessional Group, 2008

In the current internal crisis in Lebanon, with whom do you sympathize most?

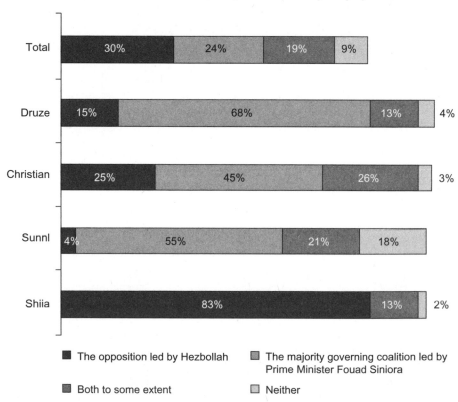

- ■ The opposition led by Hezbollah
- ■ The majority governing coalition led by Prime Minister Fouad Siniora
- ■ Both to some extent
- □ Neither

the Iraq war by denying American forces permission to operate from its territory, even though it was a member of NATO. None of that was sufficient to land Erdogan at the top of the poll, even when Arabs and Muslims seemed desperate for heroes. It took the Gaza war in 2008–2009 for Erdogan to capture the imagination of the Arab world, when, despite Turkey's historically cooperative relations with Israel, he was more critical of Israeli action and more supportive of Gaza Palestinians than many Arab governments were. Though Erdogan was briefly surpassed in 2010 by Venezuela's late president, Hugo Chavez, who had been outspoken in his own pro-Palestinian and anti-Israel stances, Turkey's prime minister returned to the lead after the first year of the Arab uprisings in 2011.

Arab Perceptions of the Arab-Israeli Conflict

In recent years Arab attitudes toward the Arab-Israeli conflict have remained consistent, even after the Arab uprisings. Generally a two-thirds majority of Arabs in the six countries I polled support the so-called two-state solution—the establishment of a Palestinian state in the West Bank and Gaza, with East Jerusalem as its capital, living side by side with Israel (Figure 5.3). Those who

FIGURE 5.3 Palestinian-Israeli Conflict, Prospects for Peace if Israel Returns Territories, Six-Country Polls, 2009 and 2011

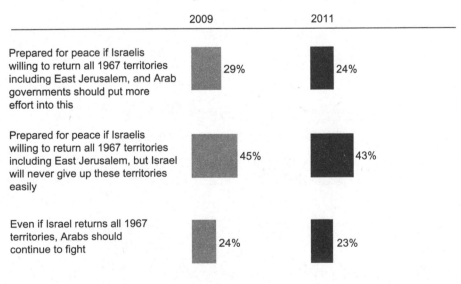

Which of the following statements is closer to your view?

	2009	2011
Prepared for peace if Israelis willing to return all 1967 territories including East Jerusalem, and Arab governments should put more effort into this	29%	24%
Prepared for peace if Israelis willing to return all 1967 territories including East Jerusalem, but Israel will never give up these territories easily	45%	43%
Even if Israel returns all 1967 territories, Arabs should continue to fight	24%	23%

reject peace with Israel even if Israel withdraws from Arab territories occupied in 1967 range from one-quarter to one-third of the population. The problem is, most Arabs have grown to believe that peace will never happen (Figure 5.4).

What's keeping the two-state solution alive is that Arabs don't see a good alternative. Aside from being angry with Israel—and sometimes with their own governments and with Palestinian leaders, for being, in their eyes, inept—they see few available options. When asked what the outcome for the Middle East would be if the prospects for a two-state solution collapse, most predict sustained conflict for years to come (Figure 5.5). One frequently mentioned alternative to the two-state approach is a one-state solution in which Arabs and Jews live as equals in the same territory, but the public in the Arab world sees little prospect of that succeeding either. About one-quarter of Arabs believe the status quo would continue. Part of the prism of pain is simply an agonizing resignation to what is, for Arabs, an untenable situation.

One question often asked is how Arabs believe they might attain their objectives, in this case the goal of establishing a Palestinian state in the West

FIGURE 5.4 Palestinian-Israeli Conflict, Prospects for Lasting Peace, Six-Country Polls, 2009 and 2011

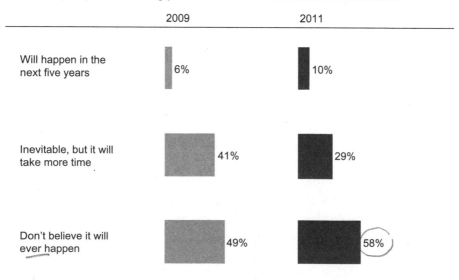

Which of the following statements is closest to your view about the prospects of lasting peace between Israel and the Palestinians?

	2009	2011
Will happen in the next five years	6%	10%
Inevitable, but it will take more time	41%	29%
Don't believe it will ever happen	49%	58%

FIGURE 5.5 Palestinian-Israeli Conflict, Likely Outcome if No Two-State Solution, 2009 and 2011

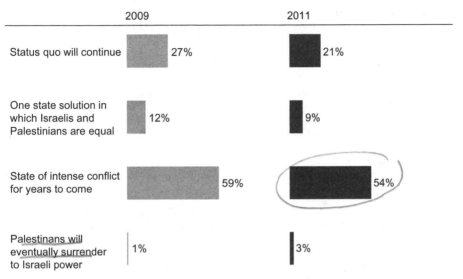

What do you believe is the likely outcome if the prospects of a two-state solution in the Palestinian-Israeli conflict collapse?

	2009	2011
Status quo will continue	27%	21%
One state solution in which Israelis and Palestinians are equal	12%	9%
State of intense conflict for years to come	59%	54%
Palestinans will eventually surrender to Israeli power	1%	3%

Bank and Gaza. Those who expressed the view that this outcome can be achieved through another war have been a minority, 14 percent in 2010 and 20 percent in 2011 (Figure 5.6). The biggest change from 2010 to 2011 was the decline in the percentage of Arabs who believed that a solution could be attained through negotiations—from 40 percent to 20 percent. In 2011 a plurality, 39 percent, expressed the view that there will be a solution only if it is imposed by either the United Nations or the United States.

Because the 1979 Egyptian-Israeli peace treaty—which ended a state of conflict between the two countries, which had waged four major wars from 1948 to 1973—has been central for the regional order and for American foreign policy for over three decades, this issue has been closely watched since the 2011 Egyptian revolution. In the October 2011 poll, we found Egyptians to be divided: 37 percent supported maintaining the treaty, while 35 percent wanted to cancel it, with 6 percent favoring its modification (Figure 5.7). But if Israel were to withdraw from occupied Arab territories and agree to a Palestinian state, the attitudes change slightly, with 41 percent supporting the treaty and 31 percent opposing it.

FIGURE 5.6 Palestinian-Israeli Conflict, What Is Required to Achieve Palestinian State, Six-Country Polls, 2010 and 2011

A solution to the Palestinian-Israeli conflict that leads to the establishment of a Palestinian state in the West Bank and Gaza, with East Jerusalem as its capitol, will happen only:

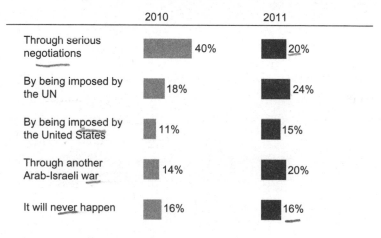

	2010	2011
Through serious negotiations	40%	20%
By being imposed by the UN	18%	24%
By being imposed by the United States	11%	15%
Through another Arab-Israeli war	14%	20%
It will never happen	16%	16%

FIGURE 5.7 Palestinian-Israeli Conflict, Egyptians' View on the Egyptian-Israeli Peace Treaty, 2011

With regard to the Egyptian-Israeli peace treaty, would you like to see Egypt: (EGYPT ONLY)

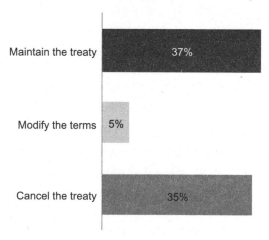

Maintain the treaty	37%
Modify the terms	5%
Cancel the treaty	35%

In the May 2012 poll in Egypt I also found the public divided on the treaty with Israel, with 46 percent favoring maintaining it and 44 percent favoring its cancellation. Parallel polls in Israel among Israeli Jews have been striking in indicating just how similar the opinion trends are, even if there are also meaningful differences.

To begin with, more Israeli Jews support the two-state solution than oppose it. Like Arabs, most Israelis are also pessimistic about its prospects, with a majority expressing the view that it will never happen. As with Arab attitudes, the level of Jewish Israeli support for a two-state solution remained stable from 2010 to 2011, but notably only 43 percent of Israeli Jews said they supported the two-state solution, compared with two-thirds of Arabs. About a third rejected withdrawing from occupied territories even if Arabs accept and recognize Israel (Figure 5.8). Israeli Jews are also pessimistic about the prospects of two states, with about a half saying it will never come about.

The most consequential trend in the attitudes of Israelis might be with regard to what happens if the prospects for a two-state solution collapse. A majority of Arabs continue to believe the outcome would be more intense

FIGURE 5.8 Palestinian-Israeli Conflict, Jewish Israelis' Views on Two-State Solution and Relinquishing Territories for Peace, 2011

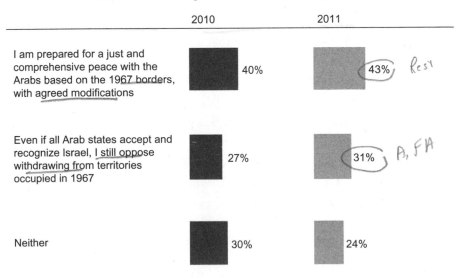

Which of the following statements is closer to your view:

	2010	2011
I am prepared for a just and comprehensive peace with the Arabs based on the 1967 borders, with agreed modifications	40%	43% Rest
Even if all Arab states accept and recognize Israel, I still oppose withdrawing from territories occupied in 1967	27%	31% A, FA
Neither	30%	24%

FIGURE 5.9 Palestinian-Israeli Conflict, Jewish Israelis' Views on Likely Outcome if No Two-State Solution, 2010 and 2011

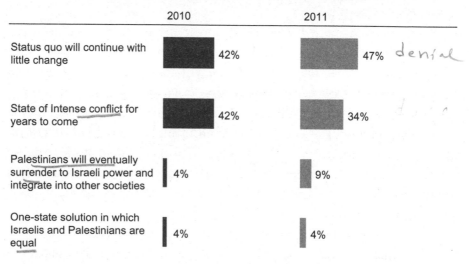

What do you believe is the likely outcome if prospects of a two-state solution to the Palestinian-Israeli conflict collapse:

	2010	2011
Status quo will continue with little change	42%	47% *denial*
State of Intense conflict for years to come	42%	34%
Palestinians will eventually surrender to Israeli power and integrate into other societies	4%	9%
One-state solution in which Israelis and Palestinians are equal	4%	4%

conflict for years to come, but Israelis have become less pessimistic on the subject: Nearly half now believe that the status quo would simply continue, while only 34 percent believe intense conflict would result (Figure 5.9). Though Israelis are divided on how good or bad the status quo is, there now appears to be less urgency to preserve the two-state solution, as Israelis appear comfortable with the status quo, given their relatively vibrant economy and the seemingly acceptable costs of occupation.

Arab Perceptions of Israeli Power

In the absence of serious prospects for peace, the prism of pain becomes a prism of conflict and competition for power and leverage. Arab (and Israeli) hopes for peace are transferred to gaining leverage, military and political, to address the pain by other means. Thus, Arab perceptions of Israeli power and of American support for Israel *and* of those who promise to stand up to Israel and the United States are a central part of the perceptions influencing their opinions.

Arabs see Israeli power as largely deriving from American power. Indeed, it's hard to find criticism of Israel in the past decade that didn't also include criticism of the United States. But one of the issues debated among Arabs is the logic of the American embrace of Israel. Certainly, the idea that support for Israel comes from domestic forces, particularly a pro-Israel lobby, has always been one popular interpretation. Another interpretation is that Israel is an instrument of American "imperialism." I sought to explore how Arabs view this relationship, especially after the 2006 Lebanon war when the Arab media was full of reports that the Israelis had wanted to stop the war earlier but that the Bush administration urged them on. In the 2008 poll, I asked, "What do you believe motivates Israeli policies in the region and American support for these policies?" The response: A plurality of Arabs believed that "the U.S. and Israel have mutual interests most of the time," while roughly one-quarter each supported the view that "Israel is a

FIGURE 5.10 U.S.-Israeli Relations, Six-Country Total, Arab View of Motivations for Israeli Policies and U.S. Support, 2008

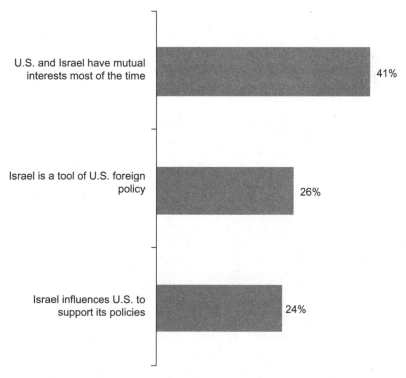

What do you believe motivates Israeli policies in the region and American support for these policies?

U.S. and Israel have mutual interests most of the time — 41%

Israel is a tool of U.S. foreign policy — 26%

Israel influences U.S. to support its policies — 24%

tool of U.S. foreign policy" or "Israel influences the U.S. to support its policies" (Figure 5.10).

Most of the Arab assessment about Israeli power, of course, has to do with
war episodes and interpreting their outcome. Some of the Israeli conflicts,
such as the 2006 Lebanon war and the 2008 Gaza war, were in part carried
out to "reestablish deterrence" as Israelis worried that their power was not
feared. Following both wars, I sought to see how Arabs read the results and
consequently interpreted Israeli power. It is important to keep in mind that
those polled in the six countries were not the ones who were directly on the
receiving end of Israeli power, except for the Lebanese.

In the 2006 poll, just a few months after the war, Arabs in every country,
including Lebanon but with the exception of Saudi Arabia, expressed the
view that the winner of the war was Hezbollah, not Israel (Figure 5.11).

FIGURE 5.11 Lebanon-Israel War, Arab Views on Who Won, 2006

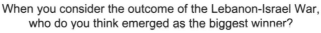

When you consider the outcome of the Lebanon-Israel War,
who do you think emerged as the biggest winner?

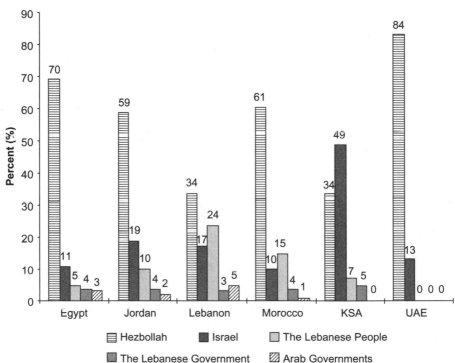

What is striking about the outcome of both wars is that despite the huge asymmetry of casualties and destruction favoring Israel, more Arabs expressed the view that Israel was weaker than said it was stronger. At the same time Arabs seemed to have more divided views of Israeli power (Figure 5.12).

These attitudes obviously reflect the mood of the public, but they don't necessarily reflect the views of governments and the leaders of Hamas and Hezbollah, who may draw different conclusions from the wars. In fact, since the 2006 war both Israel and Hezbollah in particular have been careful not to provoke each other, knowing that each would have to pay a price—even though both also assumed they will be fighting each other again and prepared themselves for the next round.

In this regard, it is noteworthy that the popular Hassan Nasrallah, even as he warns that his group has the capabilities to hurt Israel, makes it a point not to demean Israeli capabilities. In a speech he delivered in August 2012, for example, Nasrallah warned that he had the capability to kill tens of thousands of Israelis, if Israel were to attack Lebanon. But in order not to sound

FIGURE 5.12 Arab Views on Israel's Power, Six-Country Total, 2006 and 2008

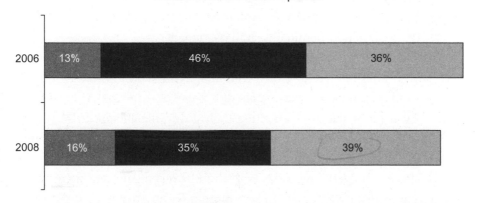

Looking at the recent violence in Lebanon and Gaza, describe your attitudes toward Israel's power:

2006	13%	46%	36%
2008	16%	35%	39%

■ Israel is very powerful and is likely to use that power to consolidate its position in the region even more in the future.

■ Israel is weaker than it looks and it is a matter of time before it is defeated.

▨ Israel has its strengths and weaknesses and no one can tell if it will get stronger or weaker relative to the Arab world in the future.

unserious to his audience, who have often witnessed Israeli power, he said, "We are more courageous than we have capabilities," and added that he knows Israel has enormous "destructive capabilities" and the demonstrated will to use them.

Factors Affecting the Arab Mobilization over the Palestine Issue

Are the Arab prism of pain and the opinions it helps explain simply a matter of "venting," without behavioral consequences? Under what circumstances are Arabs likely to act on them? These are far more nuanced questions than one might expect.

Although Arabs have continued to say that the Palestinian issue is central to them, their level of mobilization behind it is much higher in times of war and crisis, and much more muted in times of peacemaking. But there is a problem for most Arabs: the internal Palestinian divisions between the two largest factions. The fact that the PLO controls the West Bank while Hamas controls Gaza (both territories remaining technically under Israeli occupation) makes it difficult for the Arab public to decide what course to advocate and behind whom to rally—except when it comes to opposing Israel.

In my 2008–2010 polling, I found that Arabs in every country surveyed wanted to see the Palestinians come together in a national unity government and did not offer strong support for either side of the Palestinian divide. However, more Arabs in every country polled supported the militant group Hamas over the U.S.-backed Palestinian Authority, which is dominated by the secular PLO and its dominant Fatah movement.

Over the past few decades, even before conducting polls was possible, it was hard to miss the fact that the Arab people ranked Palestine higher in their priorities than their governments did. Some of the anger Arabs feel in times of war has come from watching their governments appear inept and subservient to the West, as happened all too frequently in the decade following the 9/11 tragedy. One consequence of the Arab uprisings is that the public will have a bigger voice in policy; even governments that manage to endure the uprisings will have to pay more attention to the people's will. This is already noticeable not only in Egypt but also in places like Jordan, where the pro-Western monarchy that maintains a peace treaty with Israel has to be more careful in its moves than in the past. But the big test will come if there is intense fighting between Israel and the Palestinians or Lebanese on the scale witnessed in 2006 and 2008, or if there is a new and sustained Palestinian uprising. Will the expressed public support for the Palestinians propel dramatically different consequences for state policies in the era of Arab public empowerment?

An early indicator might have been provided in November 2012 by new Egyptian president Muhammad Morsi. Following significant escalation of the violence between Israel and Hamas in Gaza, Morsi ordered an immediate withdrawal of Egypt's ambassador from Israel. Meanwhile, many within the Muslim Brotherhood who had backed him were calling for ending relations altogether with Israel. This took place very early in the conflict, when fewer than a dozen Palestinian and three Israeli deaths had been reported. Morsi then succeeded in mediating a ceasefire agreement between Hamas and Israel while helping Hamas attain some of its demands. By contrast, the government of Hosni Mubarak continued quietly cooperating with Israel during the three-week 2008 Gaza war during which about 1,400 Palestinians were killed.

The prism of pain through which the Arab public views much of the world, and certainly the United States, has been consequential even in the days when governments were more easily able to overcome public sentiment. In the era of public empowerment, enabled by an expanding information revolution, its impact on the behavior of both publics and governments will be more pronounced.

The Arab Awakening and the Prism of Pain

There is one other way in which the Arab awakening has raised the importance of the Palestinian-Israeli conflict in Arab public priorities. The Arab uprisings have been above all about freeing the Arab people from the domination of their rulers and of the outside world, the big powers. As suggested earlier, the conflict is itself an embodiment of the sense of humiliation and dependence. But this is not merely subjective and historical; there are some objective reasons for this outlook.

A good place to start is Israel's sense of deep insecurity. Without Palestinian-Israeli peace, Israelis know that war with Arab parties will remain ever possible. Some Israelis believe that even with Israeli-Palestinian peace, war would still be possible. For Israel, this means that it must plan for every contingency of war with the Arabs and even with non-Arab Muslim states such as Iran. Even Turkey, which in the past had cooperative strategic relations with Israel, is no sure bet. Souring relations in recent years have turned Turkey from an ally into a political foe. The net result is that Israelis feel that their security requires strategic and technological superiority over *any* combination of Middle Eastern states, especially Arab. On this they have the unreserved support of the United States and complete assurance from Congress and the White House that Israel will receive all the technological and military assistance it needs to keep its superiority and that Arabs will be denied similar capabilities. There is near consensus on this in Israel as well, regardless of the political outlook on matters of concessions to the Palestinians.

Seen from the Arab side, this Israeli imperative entails exactly the sort of dominance that they reject and are revolting against—the very essence of the prism of pain through which Arabs view the world. In an era of Arab awakening, a half a billion Arabs and Muslims in the Middle East and North Africa find it impossible to accept the strategic domination of a country of 8 million, especially when they don't accept the Israeli narrative for the absence of Palestinian-Israeli peace to begin with. And they see America, and to some extent other European countries, as providing the support to make this possible. This ensures that, at least so long as Palestinian-Israeli peace is absent, Israel and the Arabs are condemned to a relationship of confrontation and occasional war for years to come, and that American-Arab relations will always be caught in the middle.

CHAPTER 6

HOW ARABS VIEW THEIR UPRISINGS

How do Arabs themselves see the uprisings that have been sweeping through much of their world? The early days of revolution in Tunisia and Egypt captured the imagination in part because they were mostly peaceful and relatively successful, and encompassed many segments of the population, including liberals and Islamists. As the uprisings expanded to Libya, Yemen, Bahrain, and Syria, the degree of violence, at least in government responses to revolt, increased. And while in Tunisia and Egypt there was minimal foreign intervention, by the time the uprisings spread to Libya, foreign intervention was an important factor in determining the outcome. The views of ordinary Arabs are evolving in response to changing circumstances, but we can see emerging themes from polls, social media, and other commentaries that often track with the longer-term views that have come out of my surveys.

There is an ongoing debate in the Arab media on the nature of the uprisings and whether they are genuine public expressions of aspirations for dignity and freedom or simply instruments of foreign powers hoping to destabilize and weaken the Arab world. It was not surprising that ruling elites evoked the specter of foreign intervention every time they faced threats to their dominance. Thus, as the uprisings spread, former Libyan dictator Muammar al-Qaddafi claimed that Western powers were behind the revolt in his country or, alternatively, that Al Qaeda was behind it. The Assad regime accused Israel and the United States of causing the uprisings in Syria, and labeled regional powers working against the regime—such as Qatar,

Turkey, and Saudi Arabia—as simply taking orders from Washington. The Bahraini monarchy accused Iran of meddling and then invited Saudi forces to help quell the revolt.

One of the questions I asked respondents in an October 2011 Arab poll was about how Arabs interpret the uprisings: Are the uprisings being driven by ordinary people seeking freedom and dignity, or by opposition groups seeking control, or by foreign powers? By a solid but not overwhelming majority, most Arabs see the uprisings as the outcome of the plight of ordinary people, while 16 percent believed they are driven by opposition groups, and 19 percent see the hands of foreign powers at work (Figure 6.1).

And so there probably is some fear that foreign powers and opposition groups may be exploiting the genuine public drive for freedom. This did not, however, undermine the strong public support for the rebels against the governments. Attitudes also varied from country to country. Regarding the Syrian revolt, 86 percent of those polled in Egypt, Morocco, Jordan, Lebanon, and the United Arab Emirates said they sympathized with the rebels, while only 9 percent sympathized with the government. In Yemen, 89 percent supported the revolt and only 5 percent expressed support for the government. These trends tended to hold across the Arab countries studied, except in Lebanon, where the people were more divided on the

FIGURE 6.1 Arab Views of What Drives the Arab Uprisings, Six-Country Total, 2011

Thinking about the Arab Spring, is it mostly:

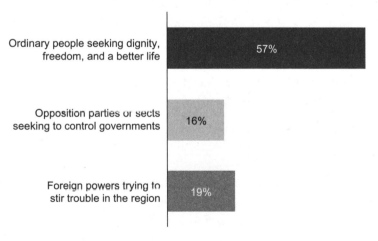

Syrian case, as might be expected because the two countries share a long border.

Regarding the uprising in Bahrain, only 64 percent expressed support for the rebels—less support generally than for rebels in other countries in our polling—while 24 percent backed the government. But there was a clear sectarian breakdown: Most people in the countries studied are Sunni Muslims, whereas most of the rebels in Bahrain are Shiites confronting a Sunni-dominated monarchical regime, where Shiites constitute the majority of the population.

In states where there is a significant Sunni-Shiite divide, attitudes appeared influenced by this divide. In Lebanon, attitudes were partly along sectarian lines, where Lebanese Shiites were far more inclined to support the rebels in Bahrain than the rest of the population. In Saudi Arabia, next door to Bahrain and the dominant member of the Gulf Cooperation Council that joins it with Bahrain, there was more support for Bahrain's Sunni monarchy than in the other states. Saudi Arabia has a Sunni majority (and a Sunni monarchy) but also a significant Shiite minority that had been restless as the Arab uprisings spread.

Sectarian divisions aside, it would be a mistake to conclude from the strong Arab support for rebels against governments that Arabs are equally supportive of foreign intervention, including from the West, to decide the battle against despised regimes. Mistrust of the aims of Western powers runs deep, and even as many Arabs were desperate to get help to stop the killing of innocents, their views of foreign intervention were ambivalent. There was one early exception to this ambivalence: Libya.

The Special Case of Libya

Libya offers perhaps the one exception to this distrust of foreign intervention. There were no scientific public opinion polls during the Libyan crisis, but a number of indicators suggested a degree of Arab public openness to Western intervention. There was also a surprising coincidence—especially in revolutionary times pitting governments against publics—of Arab public sympathy with the rebels in Libya, on the one hand, and Arab governments' hatred of Muammar al-Qaddafi, on the other. Several reasons account for this unique case.

First,[1] the timing of the Libyan uprising was significant, coming immediately after the initial euphoria of the Tunisian and the Egyptian protests (which captured the imagination of Arabs everywhere), and put the public decidedly on the side of the demonstrators in Libya. I was in Tunisia and Egypt as the Libyan uprisings were taking root, and the sympathy was clear in the streets as well as in the media. In Tunis, demonstrations on behalf of the Libyan revolt were taking place next to the demonstrations in support of the Tunisian revolution.

Second, as one revolution occurred after the other, people saw them as clearly "Arab," not just national in nature, and they expected that more change would be coming across the region. No one wanted the train to be stopped by Qaddafi.

Third, Qaddafi's brutality, but even more his extraordinary and graphic threats, were hard to ignore. Government brutality is hardly rare in the Middle East, but two things made this case particularly difficult for the Arab public to ignore: the noticeable use of the military (and mercenaries) against the demonstrations, in sharp contrast to what went on in the Tunisian and the Egyptian cases; and chilling, explicit threats, first by Qaddafi's son, Saif al-Islam, and later by Qaddafi himself, in which they called the demonstrators "rats" and threatened to "purify" Libya house by house, alley by alley, person by person.

Fourth, Qaddafi was the perfect prototype of the leader the Arab public wanted to dethrone. Perhaps more than any other Arab leader, he saw himself as above and beyond country—"God, Muammar, Libya." People believed he viewed himself as God's gift to Libya and to the Arabs, and that he encouraged others to believe it also. After the death of Egyptian president Gamal Abd al-Nasser in 1970, Qaddafi reportedly remarked that he was himself a leader without a country and that Egypt was a country without a leader—then called for unity with Egypt. In the Arab revolutions that were more about dignity and freedom, many saw Qaddafi as an embarrassment to their Arab identity.

Fifth, governments were sensitive to Arab public opinion from the outset. The unprecedented Arab League action of calling on the United Nations

---

1. Note this section about the Libya case is based on a short article I wrote for the *National Interest* on April 4, 2011: "The Striking Arab Openness to Intervention."

Security Council to impose a no-fly zone over Libya was in part out of defer-ence to pervasive Arab public opinion on this issue. No one wanted to be on the public's bad side in times of revolution.

Sixth, there was score settling that crossed even the Sunni-Shiite divide. Over the years, Qaddafi had managed to alienate, embarrass, and sometimes even directly threaten virtually every other Arab government. Even for many who would normally have been uncomfortable with the idea of foreign inter-vention against a sitting regime, Qaddafi was a greater evil. The Saudi posi-tion, for example, was partly due to specific animosity toward Qaddafi, who was accused of trying to assassinate the Saudi king. Even the popular leader of Hezbollah, Hassan Nasrallah, who had no kind words for the West or its intentions, reserved his strongest criticism for Qaddafi, with whom he had a long-standing feud over the disappearance of the Shiite Lebanese leader Mousa Sadr in Libya in 1978. Nasrallah also countered Qaddafi's preposter-ous proposition that the West was behind the Arab revolutions and defended them as indigenous and genuine.

Seventh, the position of key opinion shapers helped set up a receptive public mood toward intervention. Al Jazeera and Al Arabiya both immedi-ately took on a supportive tone about the revolution in Libya and gave the country considerable attention. Indeed, coverage of events in Libya quickly overtook the coverage of Egypt and Tunisia. Significantly, the Sunni cleric Sheikh Yousef Qaradawi, appearing on Al Jazeera, not only attacked Qaddafi and called on the Libyans to get rid of him, but also justified the international military intervention, even saying that under some specific circumstances collateral damage in such interventions can be justified.

Eighth, the seeming reluctance of the international community, especially the United States, to intervene made it hard to argue that Washington was itching to act. In fact, until UN Security Council Resolution 1973 was passed, imposing a no-fly zone over Libya, Arab commentaries, including headlines on Al Jazeera, were beginning to criticize the West for walking away from their "responsibilities." In some ways, one can say that the U.S. attempt to make the Arab revolutions not about Washington early on helped reduce the suspicion that Washington and the West were intervening for the wrong reasons.

Ninth, the speed of change in the Arab world, the surprisingly quick top-pling of President Hosni Mubarak in Egypt, and the Arab League's initiative to request UN intervention caught other foreign powers by surprise and forced them to make choices before they had made a full assessment of the changed strategic environment. France, which despite its colonial history in the region had been the most popular Western power in the Arab world, scrambled to recover from its early mistakes in the Tunisian revolution. As the uprisings in Tunisia started, the French foreign minister had continued to support despised Tunisian president Bin Ali, with whom the French had cultivated strong relations. Once Bin Ali was overthrown and France was blamed for supporting dictators, French president Nicolas Sarkozy quickly fired the foreign minister and decided to use intervention in Libya to show-case his support for the aspirations of the Arab people.

As for Russia and China, it was no secret that they opposed the intervention in Libya, as they both had good relations with Qaddafi and feared the expansion of Western influence in Libya at their expense, but they ultimately could not resist the pressure of the moment in authorizing the no-fly zone in Libya. This episode, however, made both China and Russia less willing to support similar UN action in Syria, because, among other things, they had felt that Western powers had gone beyond their UN mandate in their military intervention.

Finally, there was a pervasive sense in the Arab world that Arab and Muslim countries were incapable of intervening effectively, especially in times of revolution, because most lacked effective military power, and the one country that did, Egypt, was in the middle of its own revolution. This argument would be used often (including by Yousef Qaradawi) to justify inviting foreigners to intervene. At the popular level it was not even clear that the Arab publics seeking to remove regimes from power wanted to feel beholden to their rulers if they had done the right thing in Libya. They would have been happy to see revolutionary Egypt carry out the mission, but everyone understood that Egypt's transition made this impossible.

And so in the case of Libya, there was an openness to, though not necessarily an embrace of, international intervention. As the Qaddafi forces made use of their military superiority in the early weeks to reverse some of the rebels' gains, the pressure from a good segment of the Arab public was for more Western intervention, not less; most saw the survival of the Qaddafi regime to be the worst possible outcome. Yet even in this exceptional case of the absence of majority Arab opposition to Western intervention in Libya, the Arab public was divided. In the October 2011 Arab poll, I asked respondents if they believed that the international intervention in Libya had been "the right thing to do" or "the wrong thing to do." The results were still a reflection of ambivalence, but more leaned toward "the wrong thing to do" (46 percent) than "the right thing to do" (35 percent).

Foreign Intervention and a Divided Arab Public

So even the clearest case of Arabs desperately seeking to remove a dictator—Libya and Qaddafi—never translated into overwhelming Arab public support for Western intervention. My team and I conducted analyses of reader comments on popular Arab websites at the time, and we found that the Arab public was more receptive to Western intervention than in the past, but still largely ambivalent.

I studied reader comments on two of the region's popular websites, Aljazeera.net[2] and Alarabiya.net,[3] to try to discover the public reasoning on Libya. Not surprisingly, even with the hated Qaddafi, Arabs were caught between the sense that someone had to intervene to stop Qaddafi, on the one hand, and mistrust of Western powers, on the other. Ideally, they would have loved to see the Libyan story evolve the way of Tunisia and Egypt, but they sensed that this was not to be. Of the first twenty-five consecutive reader comments at the Al Jazeera website, 40 percent supported intervention, 28 percent opposed it, and 32 percent were neutral; of the first twenty-five consecutive reader comments at the Al Arabiya website, 48 percent supported intervention, 36 percent opposed it, and 16 percent were neutral.

Those who supported intervention varied in their logic. One comment said, "Was there an alternative? The man and his sons are crazy!" Another put it this way: "I have no problem with foreign military intervention to protect the people from getting killed by this dictator. Let this be a lesson for other Arab dictators." Some even defended the West: "Arab states are still condemning verbally and not doing anything. The result? The West has intervened. So don't blame the West"; and "Foreign military intervention is a necessary humanitarian intervention."

---

2. Al Jazeera reader comments are available online at: www.aljazeera.net/humanrights/pages/aa0f15a7-3bdf-4324-b9d2-de5575e1b69e.
3. Original Arabic comments are available online at: www.alarabiya.net/articles/2011/03/24/142774.html.

On the other side of the picture were the expressed fears of the West and the precedent that might be established by Libyan intervention: "Americans are smart with their plan, which is gradual colonialism. The Iraqi scenario is unfolding again." "The West only wants Libya's oil." "Arabs should have intervened, not Westerners." "I am against Qaddafi but I am also against foreign military intervention." Others questioned the legitimacy of intervention: "I personally think that this intervention violates the norm of sovereignty and noninterference in countries' domestic affairs."

These expressions of ambivalence became even more pronounced once the Western intervention resulted in many Libyan civilian casualties. Eventually the head of the Arab League, Amr Mousa, who had been in the forefront of securing UN support for the no-fly zone, began to criticize the Western powers for going beyond their international mandate. By the time Qaddafi was killed and his despised regime ended in Libya—something that the vast majority of Arabs wished for—the retrospective assessment of Western intervention was more negative than positive.

In a May 2012 poll, Egyptians were asked directly about their view of possible international intervention in Syria (Figure 6.2). At that time Arab media coverage continued to focus on the tragic death and destruction taking place, placing most of the blame squarely on the shoulders of the Assad regime in Damascus. Like other Arabs, 90 percent of Egyptians sympathized with the Syrian rebels against their governments, but their views on how to best address the Syrian wrongs were decidedly against Western

FIGURE 6.2 Egyptians' Views on Intervention in Syrian Conflict, May 2012

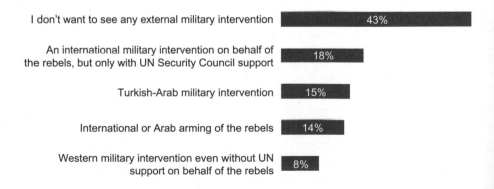

When you look at the crisis in Syria today, what would you like to see?

I don't want to see any external military intervention — 43%

An international military intervention on behalf of the rebels, but only with UN Security Council support — 18%

Turkish-Arab military intervention — 15%

International or Arab arming of the rebels — 14%

Western military intervention even without UN support on behalf of the rebels — 8%

intervention and certainly against international intervention without UN backing. The Egyptian people, like other Arabs, were at a loss when it came to ways of helping the Syrian rebels, for whom they expressed great sympathy.

The mixed views of the Arab public on international intervention were very much reflected in Arabs' assessment of the role of foreign powers in dealing with the Arab uprisings. Asked to specify which two countries they believe played the "most constructive role" in the events in the Arab world (Figure 6.3), half chose Turkey, followed by France (30 percent), the United States (24 percent), and China (20 percent).

The striking aspect is that the four top states identified had different approaches to the intervention in Libya and to the Arab uprisings broadly. Turkey initially was reluctant to support the intervention in Libya and was accused by the Arab media of having vested interests in the Qaddafi regime. France was most aggressive in its embrace of intervention, while the United States showed early reluctance but ultimately led from behind. China grudgingly backed the UN's resolution on Libya but was very much opposed to Western intervention and, together with Russia, became an even stronger opponent of international intervention in Syria. But as analyses in later chapters

FIGURE 6.3 Arab Opinions on Which Two Countries Played Most Constructive Role During Arab Uprisings

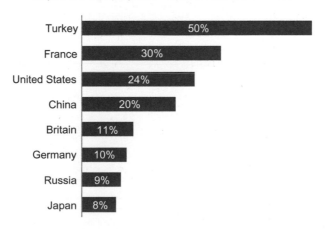

Looking at the international reaction to the events in the Arab world in the past few months, which TWO countries do you believe played the most constructive role?

- Turkey: 50%
- France: 30%
- United States: 24%
- China: 20%
- Britain: 11%
- Germany: 10%
- Russia: 9%
- Japan: 8%

will show, Arab attitudes toward these powers and the extent of trust in their intentions went beyond the Arab uprisings.

The notable thing here is that given the overwhelmingly negative views of the United States in the Arab world, the Arab verdict on the American handling of the uprisings is relatively positive. Despite some Arabs' criticism of the American role, the Obama administration's relatively early embrace of the public uprisings and the lack of any heavy-handed intervention in Egypt resonated with other Arabs. For France, although it received good marks from the Arab public, the positive ratings were smaller than the favorable assessment they had received in Arab public opinion in much of the previous decade. This was probably because Sarkozy's government was never as popular as Chirac's, and was seen to be friendlier to Israel than its predecessor had been. Moreover, the French erred early by sticking with Tunisia's president, Bin Ali. They then reversed course and tried to win favor by taking the lead in intervening militarily in Libya, but for many they managed only to seem excessively eager to get involved in the fighting.

With all the ambivalence about international intervention, Arabs maintained more positive attitudes about the public uprisings. Overall, Arabs polled in October 2011 expressed relative optimism about the future of the Arab world in light of the uprisings, despite the increasing complexity of the revolts in Yemen, Bahrain, and Syria. Fifty-five percent said they were more optimistic, 23 percent said they felt no change, and only 16 percent expressed pessimism—for a region in such ongoing turmoil, that's a strikingly *positive* result. They want change, freedom, and dignity, and are prepared to pay a high price for them. The United States would do well to stay on the right side of this historical tide.

CHAPTER 7

TRENDS IN ARAB ATTITUDES TOWARD THE UNITED STATES

IN EARLY 2010, a few months before the toppling of Hosni Mubarak, I appeared on a popular Egyptian television talk show—*al-Qahira al-Youm* (Cairo Today)—that addressed front-page stories in the press. One of the questions I was asked surprised me. The Egyptian press had apparently translated a *Washington Post* article about President Barack Obama's private spiritual life and his regular consultation with Christian ministers. Seemingly alarmed, the host asked me to comment.[1]

Immediately, I saw where the question was headed. During George W. Bush's presidency, there was considerable focus, at home and abroad, on the degree to which Bush's Christian faith and that of influential evangelicals influenced U.S. foreign policy, imbuing it with a crusading spirit. This played squarely into the hands of the minority of Muslims who prefer to frame foreign policy issues as a struggle between Islam and the "crusaders." At the beginning of his term, Obama had seemed to provide a fresh start, but was there a closet evangelical Christian waiting to come out?

I was able to put those concerns to rest fairly easily, but the very fact that this issue had to be addressed in the Arab media in 2010 was an indication of the decline in Arab public affection for a president who a year earlier had

---

1. Part of this chapter is based on my article, "Can Obama Please Both Arabs and Israelis?" in ForeignPolicy.com, August 25, 2010. Available online at: www.foreignpolicy.com/articles/2010/08/25/can_obama_please_both_arabs_and_israelis.

opened many hearts and minds even before he delivered a memorable and historic speech in Cairo in June 2009. These rumors reflected suspicion about the president's personal values, but Obama's rise and fall in popularity was primarily driven not by questions about his religious beliefs but rather, as my polls show, by his stated and actual policies toward the region. And despite the host's questions, the impact of Obama's personal values on Arab attitudes toward the United States and its presence in the region is much less consequential than is frequently thought.

Take, for example, the seemingly stark contrast between Presidents George W. Bush and Obama. For the several years previous to Obama's election, President Bush had been identified by Arabs in six countries as the most disliked leader in the world—even more disliked than any Israeli leader, including the hated former prime minister Ariel Sharon.[2] But this remarkably negative view of Bush was not driven by his personal religious views or reputed missionary zeal. Asked in the 2004 six-country poll what they thought drove Bush's policies in the Middle East, only 11 percent of Arab respondents identified his Christian faith; a majority identified his pursuit of the American national interest (Figure 7.1).

The same proved true for President Obama. His personal history—an African American whose father was Muslim and who spent part of his childhood in a Muslim country (Indonesia)—gave some optimism to many Arabs and Muslims (and pessimism to Israelis), but it was meaningful only as a possible indicator of future policy. So the question put to me on the talk show was driven by concern not so much about Obama's private religious beliefs as about the policies his beliefs might translate into—the template through which all U.S. presidents are judged. Arabs never embraced Obama simply because of who he was. They had been consistently reticent about the future president ever since his arrival on the global stage.

---

2. Arab detestation of Sharon dates back to 1982 when, as Israeli defense minister, he led the invasion of Lebanon and was later found by an Israeli commission to be indirectly responsible for the massacres of Palestinians at Sabra and Shatilla, which were carried out by his Lebanese allies. As prime minister, Sharon initiated some of the toughest actions against the Palestinians in the West Bank, especially after the outbreak of the Al-Aqsa intifada in 2000 brought a spate of Palestinian suicide bombings against Israel. So for Arabs to identify Bush first is extraordinary, except for the fact that they saw Bush as Sharon's enabler after expecting him to be "evenhanded." Additionally, in that period Arabs were focused on the hated Iraq war, for which they held Bush responsible.

FIGURE 7.1 Arabs' Views of What Drove George W. Bush's Policies in the Middle East, Six-Country Totals, 2004

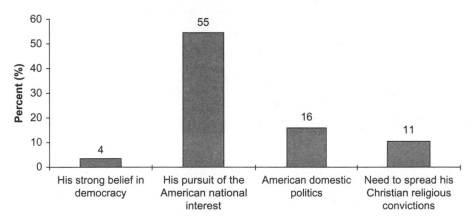

When you examine the Middle East policy of the American President, George W. Bush, do you believe his primary motivation is:

A Wary Embrace

In my annual six-nation Arab public opinion poll fielded by Zogby International in April and May 2008, I asked, regarding the three strongest candidates at the time (Obama, John McCain, and Hillary Clinton), "Who is best suited to advance Middle East peace?" Overall, there was little enthusiasm for any of the candidates. McCain, who spoke frequently of an "Islamo-Fascist" threat, received the nod from a mere 3 percent of those polled. Clinton was favored by 13 percent and Obama by 18 percent—separated by an amount not much above the margin of error. A plurality said "none of the above." These results don't indicate that Arabs ever saw Barack Hussein Obama as offering a great alternative to Bush, or that they bought into the notion that he was a "secret Muslim."

But early on this would change: By the time Obama delivered the Cairo speech in June 2009, my six-country poll was already showing remarkable openness toward the new U.S. president. Views of him personally were generally warm: 45 percent expressed positive attitudes, 28 percent neutral, and only 24 percent negative. There was also some optimism about American policy in the Middle East that we had not seen in previous polls, with 51 percent expressing hopefulness about American policy in the Middle East after a few weeks of the Obama administration. But though Arabs' embrace of Obama the person was inevitably tied to positive expectations for American foreign policy, the critical and overlooked dynamic is that the former was more a function of the latter—not the other way around. Arabs liked Obama's stated opposition to the Iraq war, his intent to withdraw U.S. forces from Iraq, and his opposition to torture and the Guantánamo Bay prison, which many in the region saw as evidence of targeting Arabs and Muslims. They also were heartened by his emphasis on the importance of the Arab-Israeli issue.

Even in those relatively halcyon days, though, there were clear signs that many Arabs were still only warily hopeful about Obama. In my spring 2009 poll, the overwhelming majority of those who had a favorable view of Obama expressed only a "somewhat favorable view," and in Egypt a significant number of those polled were neutral about him. In the annual open question "Whom among world leaders do you admire most?," Obama's name was not among the top choices. Additionally, the basic Arab public evaluation of the United States didn't dramatically change in 2009 from the previous year, with 77 percent expressing unfavorable views. My polls in 2010 found an even further decline, and the perception of Obama himself declined, with 51 percent expressing unfavorable views (Figure 7.2). True, far more Arabs had an unfavorable view of the United States than of Obama himself, but most of those who had a favorable view of the American president in 2010 also expressed the view that the "American system will not allow him to have a successful foreign policy." Bottom line: For Arabs, it is *always* about the issues.

FIGURE 7.2 Arab Perceptions of President Obama, Six-Country Totals, 2010

Which of the following is closest to your views in describing U.S. president Barack Obama?

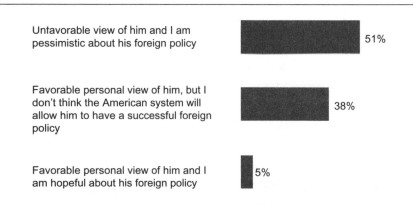

Issue One: Palestine

Like any other group of people, Arabs care about many things, but they view Washington in terms of a limited set of issues—and no single policy is more important than the Arab-Israeli conflict. To most Arabs, the United States is an anchor of a political order they do not like, in all its manifestations: authoritarianism, the declining global influence of Arab countries, the Iraq war, the war on terrorism, and the protracted Palestinian-Israeli conflict. But they don't rank issues equally when they evaluate U.S. foreign policy: The Palestinian-Israeli conflict is paramount.

A year after expressing openness to the new American president, my 2010 UMD/Zogby poll[3] showed that 61 percent of polled Arabs identified the Palestinian-Israeli conflict as the issue with which they were most disappointed in Obama's foreign policy. Obama's new tone toward Islam and Muslims was identified as the most positive policy issue, but only by 20 percent. The weight of this negative view on Obama's policy pulled the president's ratings down from 45 percent favorable in 2009 to only 20 percent favorable in 2010. Once again the Obama administration was being judged by the same yardstick as previous presidents.

President Bill Clinton's approval rating in the Arab world also yo-yoed during his term, a movement that tracked with his actions in regard to Israeli-Palestinian relations. It is something of a myth that Arabs ever embraced Clinton as much as Israelis did. Even in the early months before the Oslo agreements, Clinton was most often identified as "the most pro-Israel president ever." Clinton would continue to be viewed by Arabs as pro-Israel even in the most optimistic periods, including when he gave a historic speech to the Palestinian Legislative Council in Gaza. Arabs and others around the world simply assumed after Oslo that the Palestinian-Israeli conflict was on its way to a resolution.

Nonetheless, if Arabs hadn't been converted to Clinton himself, polls conducted internally by the State Department in the spring of 2000, near the end of the Clinton presidency, showed confidence in America to be relatively

---

3. University of Maryland with Zogby International 2010 Annual Arab Public Opinion Survey. Available online at: http://www.brookings.edu/~/media/research/files/reports/2010/8/05 %20arab%20opinion%20poll%20telhami/0805_arabic_opinion_poll_telhami.pdf.

high in parts of the Arab world, especially Saudi Arabia. This positivity was directly correlated to Arab optimism about the prospects of Palestinian-Israeli peace—and dropped substantially following collapse of the peace negotiations in late July 2000.

Issue Two: The Iraq War

By the time President George W. Bush assumed office in 2001, the bloom had gone off the rose. Anger with the United States intensified for multiple reasons: the collapsed Israeli-Palestinian negotiations in July 2000, the onset of the Palestinian intifada, and bloody Israeli operations in the occupied Palestinian territories. Arabs nonetheless hoped that the administration of the second George Bush would be more sympathetic to their grievances than the previous Clinton administration. But by the summer of 2001, talk out of Washington was making it clear that this Bush administration, unlike that of Bush's father, would be even more supportive of Israeli policies than Clinton had been. Soon thereafter, Bush was responsible for the most repeated and well-publicized conflation ever of Arab opinions about American values and U.S. foreign policy. Less than two weeks after the 9/11 tragedy, President Bush used a joint session of Congress to explain the attitudes of militants who launched the attacks—a description seen by many in the Arab world (and by some in the United States) as implicating Arab and Muslim people more generally: "They hate our freedoms."

A year and a half later, in March 2003, the U.S. military invaded Iraq, a decision that Arabs really did hate. In fact, the second Iraq war was more damaging to America's image in the Arab world than any single American policy since the end of the cold war. But the Iraq war example is also very useful in that it highlights the two issues that have defined Arab attitudes toward America more than any other—and the two issues that Al Qaeda sought to exploit to win broader public support beyond its fanatical ideological core.

The Iraq war was a reminder of the massive and unrelenting American presence in the Gulf region that followed the 1991 war. Unlike the earlier Persian Gulf War, the 2003 invasion of a sovereign Arab state was conducted without United Nations support and against the advice (and perceived interests) of some of Washington's closest friends in the Arab world. What made matters worse was that, despite overwhelming and passionate Arab public opposition to the war, the United States used incentives and threats to win the cooperation of Arab governments in Egypt, Jordan, Saudi Arabia, Qatar, the United Arab Emirates, Bahrain, and Kuwait. Seen from this perspective, the war represented utter collective Arab humiliation.

The Iraq war was also seen as a diversion from the Israel-Palestine question, which Arabs wanted to see tackled. Even more troubling, it was seen to strengthen the Israeli strategic position at the expense of Palestinians and Arabs.

It is not surprising, then, that unfavorable ratings of the United States in the six countries I studied (Egypt, Saudi Arabia, Morocco, Jordan, Lebanon, and the United Arab Emirates) peaked during the Iraq war. Between the beginning of the war in 2003 and the start of the Arab uprisings in 2010, Arab views of the United States were distinctively and consistently negative, averaging over 80 percent unfavorable. That public opinion levels didn't meaningfully change for the bulk of George W. Bush's term and the first two years of the Obama administration is a remarkable testament to the preeminence of policy—in this case, the Iraq war—above both personalities. The unmistakably different tone with which Obama approached both Arabs and Muslims simply made no difference in Arabs' views of American policy. It was only after Obama began winding down the war in 2011 that Arabs began to see the United States in a slightly more favorable light.

That same year Arabs were also consumed by the onset of an unprecedented public awakening. Arabs had mixed views about the role of outside powers in the uprisings, but in general the United States fared better than in the past—despite lingering criticism. It's noteworthy, though, that much of the improvement in attitudes toward the United States and the Obama administration happened in the middle—among those who shifted from "somewhat unfavorable" views to those who said they had "somewhat favorable" views. Trends were similar between those with and without access to satellite TV, with slightly more fluctuation among respondents without cable news (Figure 7.3). There were similar trends irrespective of satellite television access for the years 2009–2011 (Figure 7.4). The results speak clearly: Across the board, the proportion of Arabs who said they had "very favorable" views was generally constant and almost negligible during both the Bush and the Obama administrations.

By May 2012, Egypt was already providing evidence that the 2011 improvement might have been temporary. In a poll taken on the eve of the

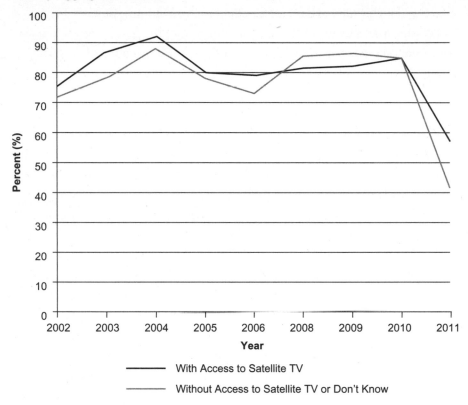

FIGURE 7.3 Unfavorable Arab Ratings of the United States, by Access to Satellite TV, Six-Country Aggregates, 2002–2011

With Access to Satellite TV

Without Access to Satellite TV or Don't Know

FIGURE 7.4 Unfavorable Arab Ratings of the United States, Without Regard to Satellite TV Access, Six-Country Aggregates, 2009–2011

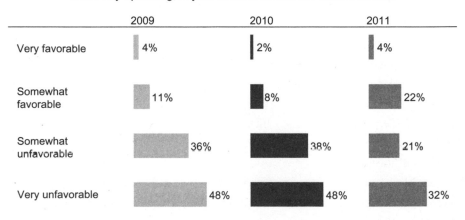

Generally speaking, is your attitude toward the United States:

	2009	2010	2011
Very favorable	4%	2%	4%
Somewhat favorable	11%	8%	22%
Somewhat unfavorable	36%	38%	21%
Very unfavorable	48%	48%	32%

Egyptian elections, 85 percent of those surveyed expressed unfavorable views of the United States. Part of the reason was a widespread perception that the United States would be intervening (through the Egyptian military) to prevent a democratically elected president from taking office or even being announced, but the Egyptian results were also consistent with prior trends. Ironically, of course, the United States actually tried to persuade the Egyptian military to accept whatever outcome emerged from the democratic vote, and when the Muslim Brotherhood's candidate, Muhammad Morsi, was declared the winner, former allies of Washington in Egypt turned the tables and started accusing the Muslim Brotherhood of being America's candidate. Thus, when Egyptians were in the middle of what was mostly an internal struggle, deeply held anger with the United States was an instrument used to gain advantage by those previously friendly to Washington (remnants of the Mubarak regime) against those previously hostile to it (especially Muslim Brotherhood). As the old saying goes, politics makes for strange bedfellows.

It Was Never About Values

Arab attitudes toward the United States were never at their core about values as such. It is true that "values" cannot be easily separated from policy, but opinions Arabs form about American values are based on policies, not slogans. Yes, Arabs admire the stated values of freedom and democracy, but their assessments of what America in fact stands for are formed by observing American policies and their consequences for Arabs themselves. It isn't that Arabs say, "We don't like American values; therefore we reject American policies." It is the opposite: They reject American policies and therefore question American values and whether America stands for what it professes. From Woodrow Wilson's time, America has championed self-determination, and that has long found resonance in the Arab world. But how does that square with America's seeming acceptance of Palestinians living under occupation? America champions freedom and democracy, but how does one reconcile that with U.S. support for Arab autocrats who repress their people?

It should not be surprising that every time I asked a question about the primary source of anger and disappointment with the United States, an overwhelming majority of Arab respondents specified U.S. policies, not U.S.

FIGURE 7.5 Basis of Arab Attitudes Toward the United States, Six-Country Totals, 2004–2008

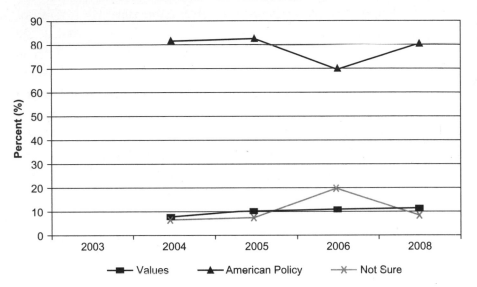

Would you say that your attitudes toward the United States are based more on American values or on American policy in the Middle East?

values. On average, roughly 75 percent chose "policy" while only 10 percent opted for values (Figure 7.5).

What Arabs Still Like About the United States

Egyptians, Jordanians, Moroccans—ordinary Arabs everywhere—do not wake up every morning thinking, "I am angry with America." They think of sending their kids safely to school, of putting bread on the table, of falling in love, of listening to their favorite music, of going to a party or a wedding. And many simply hope to get a job or a decent education. And throughout it all, American and European products are interwoven into their everyday existence.

Symbols of Western culture—fast-food restaurants like Hardee's and Pizza Hut, Coke and Pepsi, designer clothing like Polo Ralph Lauren, American sports jerseys and footwear labeled for icons like Michael Jordan, and American music and sitcoms, such as *Friends*—are hard to miss all over the

Arab world. Even in conservative religious countries like Saudi Arabia, American brands are well known, and restaurants like Kentucky Fried Chicken and McDonald's are sprinkled throughout its cities. What's more, the most unlikely-looking consumers—young women wearing the most conservative outer garments and veil—often wear fashionable Western clothes and cosmetics underneath.

Television is another area in which the United States maintains a huge, welcome presence in the Arab world. Though Arabs watch news frequently, they also watch lots of entertainment, and their thirst for American and other Western entertainment programs, and Hollywood movies and stars, is hard to quench.

In my 2009 Arab poll we asked respondents: "When you watch television, how often do you watch American or European movies, shows, or music videos?" On average in the six countries studied, 61 percent said they watch such programs at least five to six days every week (and another 12 percent said three to four times per week). While Moroccans were most likely to watch Western programs almost daily (79 percent), 46 percent of Saudis said they watch at least five to six days a week, while another 17 percent said they watch three to four times per week.

The popularity of Western products and brands doesn't mean there is no opposition to them as representatives of decadent Western values, but despite the complaints and influence of religious conservatism, Western cultural influence continues to grow. Though there were campaigns to boycott McDonald's restaurants in Egypt during the 2003 Iraq war and also during bloody confrontations between Israelis and Palestinians, according to an owner of multiple restaurants in Egypt (and a former Egyptian government minister), Muhammad Mansour, these efforts succeeded only episodically; sales declined by about half for a few months, then returned to normal. In fact, in a 2006 poll I asked how Arabs made their decisions when it came to buying products in the marketplace (Figure 7.6). On average, only about 18 percent said they base their decision on the politics of the product's country of origin. There were some important variations, however, with one-third of Saudis saying politics mattered for their choice, compared with only 5 percent in the United Arab Emirates, which has become a global trade and commerce center with hugely diverse populations of workers, suppliers, and buyers.

FIGURE 7.6 Arab Decisions About Purchasing Products, Six-Country Totals, 2006

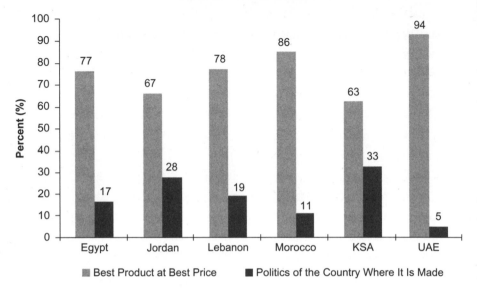

When you purchase any product in the market place how do you make a decision about what to buy?

■ Best Product at Best Price   ■ Politics of the Country Where It Is Made

How Much of the West Is Too Much?

In the face of increasing globalization in which Western symbols are dominant, the fact that there is concern about protecting Arab and Muslim culture and religion, even identity, is completely predictable. Most non-Western ethnic, cultural, and religious groups have some concerns about globalization's impact. Even representatives of Christianity, including popes John Paul II and Benedict XVI, have themselves expressed concern about a dominant part of contemporary Western culture: "consumerism."

This conflict between cultures is also not new. In the nineteenth century during the Napoleonic occupation of Egypt—some of the earliest Arab encounters with modern Europe—Arab writers were already grappling with ways to reconcile what Arabs admired about the West with their own culture and beliefs. By the turn of the twentieth century, the dominant Islamic thinkers in Egypt, such as Muhammad Abduh and Jamal al-Din al-Afghani, who often followed their rigorous religious education in Egypt with further education in Europe, were preoccupied with reconciling what they saw as good about the West with their own Muslim identities.

Even the founder of the now-dominant Muslim Brotherhood in Egypt, Hassan al-Banna, articulated a view that he hoped would reconcile his deep Muslim faith with a drive to modernize Egypt scientifically, learning from what the West had to offer. His model at that time was Japan as he saw it in the 1930s: a proud nation that managed to protect its culture and identity but wholeheartedly adopted scientific and technological advancement from the West. Some thirty years later, President Anwar Sadat, when he came to office in 1970, put forth a policy that he hoped would attract Islamists like many of the followers of the Muslim Brotherhood, labeling it *Al-Ilm Wal-Iman* (Science and Faith). Today many mainstream Islamists, including the Muslim Brotherhood, are struggling with the same issues.

The Fanatical Fringe

There are of course, elements, particularly radical Muslim elements, that eschew all Western influence and seek a totalitarian, Taliban-like Islamic rule, but they are still a minority. The Taliban government in Afghanistan was viewed as so fanatical by Arabs that all Arab states except two refused to have diplomatic relations with it. Radical Islamist groups must always be taken seriously, given the enormous danger that they might come to politically dominate a region or state, but contrary to popular opinion in the West, there is no evidence that such groups have a large number of adherents in the Arab world, and there is bountiful evidence to the contrary.

In one particular question in my 2004–2010 polls, I sought to discover Arab attitudes about Al Qaeda: "What aspect of Al Qaeda do you admire most, if any?" Of the choices presented, the most common aspects chosen every year were that Al Qaeda "confronts America" and that it "stands up for Muslim causes such as the Palestinian cause." Those who embraced Al Qaeda because of its aims to establish a Taliban-like Islamic state or because they liked the group's methods of operation were a small minority. For example, 36 percent in 2004 and 25 percent in 2010 identified its confrontation of the United States as the most admired aspect of the group; and 20 percent in 2004 and 31 percent in 2010 identified its "standing up for Muslim causes." Meanwhile, only 7 percent in 2004 and 3 percent in 2010 identified its methods; and 7 percent in both years identified its objective of an Islamic state. About one-quarter in both years said they did not admire any aspect of the group.

So Arab attitudes toward Western culture and Arab receptivity toward different aspects of the West vary across Arab societies, but only the radical fringe professes total aversion. These variations are also present, up to a point, in the Arab attitudes toward the United States and its policies.

United, but Not Monolithic

Egyptians' suspicions of American policy motives in 2011 reflected the fact that Egyptians' attitudes toward the United States are among the least positive in the Arab world. In a 2008 poll, only 9 to 16 percent of respondents in Egypt and Saudi Arabia expressed favorable views of the United States, while 73 percent in both countries said their attitude was "very unfavorable." In comparison, attitudes in Lebanon, Morocco, and the United Arab Emirates tended to be more favorable, even though only between 22 percent and 26 percent expressed favorable views. There are also similar divergences in opinion among subgroups within the larger Arab polity, though I did not find appreciable differences for gender, age, or marital status. Even education and income appear to account for only small, often statistically insignificant, differences.

But there are sectarian differences. Look, for example, at the three countries where I measured diversity: Lebanon, Jordan, and Egypt. One of the widest divergences in opinion was between two bitterly opposed Muslim groups in Lebanon. Sunnis in Lebanon approached almost a breakeven point in their attitude toward the United States (45 percent gave favorable responses), while Shiites were completely negative (all gave unfavorable responses). What made the difference? Quite possibly the fact that the pro-U.S. March 14 coalition was led by Sunni politician Saad Hariri—the son of Rafic Hariri, the former Lebanese prime minister who was assassinated on February 14, 2005.

In both Egypt and Lebanon, Christians and Muslims always differ in their level of unfavorable views toward the United States. In Egypt in 2008, 88 percent of Muslims and 77 percent of Christians had unfavorable views. (The difference was larger among those who held "very unfavorable" views: 75 percent of Muslims to 53 percent of Christians.) A year after the Egyptian revolution, in 2011, the ratio was 59 percent to 30 percent. Keep in mind, though, that Christians are only about 10 percent of Egypt's population, so their sample is always small. In Lebanon, where Christians are about one-third of the population, 20 percent of Christians had "very unfavorable" views of the United States in 2008 polling, compared with 75 percent of Muslims in 2008. Three years later, in 2011, that gap had narrowed to 38 percent of Christians to 56 percent of Muslims. The same trend in differences, to varying degrees, obtained in other years. Moreover, using my data, two scholars have conducted multiple-year statistical analysis and found significant differences between Christian and Muslim attitudes toward the United States.[4]

These differences in attitudes are often connected to local circumstances. Shiites in Lebanon have been in a power struggle with an increasingly stronger Sunni-led coalition and see the United States as taking their opponents' side and as the enemy of their leading group, Hezbollah. Not surprisingly, their attitudes toward the United States tend to be extremely negative. Christian Arabs are somewhat warmer toward the United States because a larger percentage of them have relatives in the United States and the West. For example, although fewer than 5 percent of Arabs are Christian, a majority of Arabs in America are Christian. Druze tend to change their attitudes depending on their alliances of the day, which often shift as they calculate how to assure their continued survival as a small minority. Egyptians' anger with the United States and Israel harkens back, in part, to their own vision of themselves as leaders of Arab causes, but the anger also reflects their enduring "guilt" that Egypt's 1979 separate peace treaty with Israel limited the country's ability to weigh in on the Arab side.

Despite these differences, however, there is no ignoring the fact that the overall attitudes toward the United States across the different Arab divides have been highly unfavorable.

What Do Arabs Think Drives American Foreign Policy?

Although American policy toward the Israeli-Palestinian conflict has been Arabs' long-standing, overarching concern, there is another issue to which they attribute American motivations in the Middle East. For decades Arabs have seen both Israel and oil as the two key forces driving American policy

---

4. Erik C. Nisbet and Teresa A. Myers, "Anti-American Sentiment as a Media Effect? Arab Media, Political Identity and Public Opinion in the Middle East," *Communication Research* 38 (2011): 684.

in the Middle East. Even though American discourse sometimes conveniently downplays these issues—particularly oil—Arabs do not. Since the collapse of the Soviet Union, the two American wars in Iraq and the invasion of Afghanistan have only reinforced the sense among many that the United States has been seeking to "weaken" the Muslim world partly to guarantee easy and uninterrupted access to oil. Furthermore, without the balancing effect of the Soviet Union, Arabs see American support for Israel growing.

Beginning in March 2003, just before the Iraq war, I began asking questions initially about the perceived motivation behind the war, and later about American policy in the region broadly.[5] The stated goals of the war were initially focused on Iraq's presumed weapons of mass destruction; after the war they were expanded to include spreading democracy in the Middle East. The results tell much of the story about Arab attitudes toward the United States.

Every year since 2003, Arabs ranked controlling oil and protecting Israel highest as driving forces of American foreign policy, followed by weakening the Muslim world and regional dominance. The percentage of those who believed that democracy and peace promotion were central factors were dwarfed by the percentage of those who identified the two leading factors (Figure 7.7).[6]

Respondents in the same six countries were asked to choose the two most important factors they believed to be driving American policy. Though these questions were asked during the first three years of the Obama administration, the results were similar, with oil and Israel leading the way and only single-digit percentages for peace and democracy promotion (Figure 7.8).

America Versus American Policies

Conventional wisdom about how Arabs (and many in the developing world, including Latin America) saw the United States used to hold that they liked

---

5. The selection of options in the questions was based on options that were widely referred to in both the West and the Middle East, ranging from aims to control oil and help Israel, on the one hand, to fighting terrorism, limiting the spread of weapons of mass destruction, and spreading democracy, on the other.
6. In the questions during this period, respondents were asked how important they believed each factor was individually. In 2004, the question was asked with different wording: "When the U.S. went to war with Iraq, how important do you think were the following motives?"

FIGURE 7.7 Arab Views of Most Important Factors Driving U.S. Policy in the Middle East, Six-Country Totals, 2003–2006

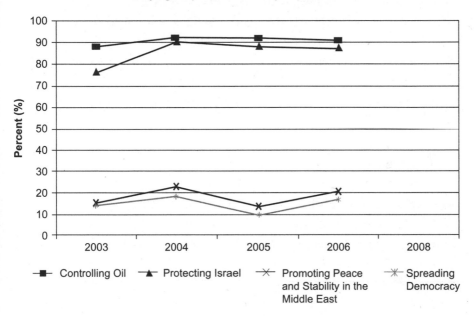

When you consider American objectives in the Middle East, how important do you think the following factors are to the United States?
Saying "Important" or "Very Important"

- ■ Controlling Oil   ▲ Protecting Israel   ✕ Promoting Peace and Stability in the Middle East   ✱ Spreading Democracy

FIGURE 7.8 Arab Views of Most Important Factors Driving U.S. Policies in the Middle East, Six-Country Totals, 2009–2011

Which TWO of the following factors do you believe are most important in driving American policy in the Middle East?

	2009	2010	2011
Controlling oil	39%	47%	55%
Protecting Israel	52%	50%	44%
Weakening the Muslim world	38%	34%	32%
Preserving regional and global dominance	25%	36%	29%
Promoting peace and stability	8%	6%	8%
Fighting terrorism	4%	5%	8%
Preventing spread of nuclear weapons	12%	13%	7%
Spreading human rights	4%	4%	5%
Promoting democracy	5%	4%	5%

its people but didn't like its government or its foreign policy. We did not measure this over time, but this certainly holds together anecdotally, as many Americans who have visited the Middle East over the years will attest. But in the past decade there has been a change. The first term of the George W. Bush administration brought a war in Iraq that appeared unjustified after no weapons of mass destruction were uncovered and that, at least for most Arabs, seemed a disaster for the region and for the United States. When Americans reelected Bush in 2004, Arab puzzlement was great, and questions grew over whether there really was a gap between government and the public in America.

Although I didn't have specific questions in the past about Arab views of the "American people" (as differentiated from an abstract "United States" whose polices they dislike), I decided to introduce this question in 2010 and 2011, to see if in fact there were differences in attitudes.

What I found is that attitudes toward the American people were indeed differentiated from attitudes toward "the United States," but on the whole they were more divided and, in 2010, more negative than conventional wisdom supposed: Only 28 percent had a favorable opinion of the American people in 2010. A year later, after the Arab uprisings began, that number grew to 48 percent.[7] Although I don't have longitudinal studies to compare these numbers with, other measures suggest continuing negative perceptions of America beyond foreign policy.

One question I've asked over the years is what country Arabs would consider as a possible place to live, if they had to live in one of eight countries named: France, Britain, Germany, Japan, Russia, China, Pakistan, or the United States. From 2005 to 2011, the United States ranked no better than fourth place among these countries, with only 5 to 11 percent saying they would choose America as a place to live. The United States fared a little better as a place to get an education, ranking second in 2005, but no better than fourth place in the following years, with 11 to 20 percent choosing it as a place to study. Because I don't have similar data for years before 9/11, it's hard to know for sure if these relatively low numbers are mostly a function

---

7. Note that in Chapter 11 there is a discussion of how American views of Arabs may have changed following the Tunisian and Egyptian revolutions, with American demonstrations, like those in Wisconsin, repeating slogans in Tahrir Square, which played back in the Arab media.

of reports following that tragedy of how difficult it had become for Arabs and Muslims to visit the United States.

Finally, I attempted to capture the way Arabs evaluate the United States ✓ through this question: "What two steps by the United States would improve your views of America most?" The top four answers all pertained to the Arab-Israeli conflict and the presence of American forces in the Gulf region (Figure 7.9). Even in the era of the Arab awakening in October 2011, there were only single-digit percentages for "working hard to spread democracy" and "increased economic aid." It is not that Arabs discount democracy and a strong economy—quite the contrary. Rather, they don't see the United States as the primary vehicle for these issues and don't trust U.S. intentions. In the end, everything is overshadowed by the heavy effect they feel from the American role in the Gulf and the Arab-Israeli issue.

After Egyptian president Muhammad Morsi appointed General Sedky Sobhi as the new chief of staff of the Egyptian army in the summer of 2012, it came to light that when Sobhi was a student at the U.S. Army War College in Pennsylvania, he "argued in a paper that the American military presence in the Middle East and its 'one sided' support of Israel were fueling hatred toward the United States and miring it in an unwinnable global war with

FIGURE 7.9 Top Two Steps United States Could Take to Improve Arabs' View of United States, Six-Country Totals, 2009–2011

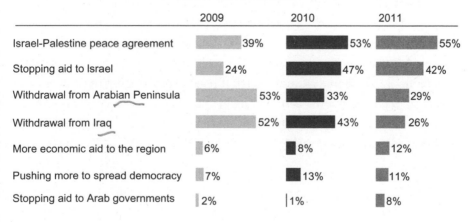

What TWO steps by the United States would improve your views of the United States the most?

	2009	2010	2011
Israel-Palestine peace agreement	39%	53%	55%
Stopping aid to Israel	24%	47%	42%
Withdrawal from Arabian Peninsula	53%	33%	29%
Withdrawal from Iraq	52%	43%	26%
More economic aid to the region	6%	8%	12%
Pushing more to spread democracy	7%	13%	11%
Stopping aid to Arab governments	2%	1%	8%

Islamist militants."[8] Sobhi's views are widely shared across the Arab world and certainly in Egypt. It is improbable that any charm campaigns by American officials, no matter how clever, well meaning, or expensive, will alter these key prisms of Arab perceptions—and certainly not in the era of a great public awakening and empowerment.

The Interaction of Arab and Israeli Opinions Toward Washington

Because the Israeli-Palestinian issue lies at the core of Arab attitudes toward the United States, it's hardly surprising that the relationship between America and Israel is a good predictor of Arab-American relations. In the absence of Arab-Israeli peace, this triangle is generally seen as a zero-sum game. For America to win support of one side, it generally must lose the support of the other. This was certainly the case for the Obama administration.

Like Arabs, Israelis judged Obama not personally but on their fears that his policies would undermine American support for Israel. They rooted against Obama in both elections. During the 2000 U.S. presidential campaign, Israelis rooted passionately for Gore/Lieberman and against Bush/Cheney—just the opposite of initial Arab instincts. Certainly both Arab concerns and Israel's embrace partly involved vice presidential candidate Joe Lieberman, who had been a strong supporter of Israel and was the first Jewish American to run for the office on a major party ticket. Then the dialogue flipped again. Bush supported the tough Israeli policies in the West Bank and Gaza and became a favorite leader among Israelis—and was well on his way to being the most reviled leader among Arabs.

If Obama had visited Israel early in his first term and delivered a powerful speech, it might have bought him a brief period of Israeli goodwill, just as the Cairo speech did in the Arab world. But sooner rather than later, acceptance would come back to policy, and Israelis found the entire foreign policy paradigm of the Obama administration threatening: stripping references to Islam from the war on terrorism; relying on multilateralism, international organizations, and law; and insisting that Arab-Israeli peace is an American interest. Israelis had grown comfortable and secure in Bush's world, which emphasized

---

8. David D. Kirkpatrick and Kareem Fahim, "In Paper, Chief of Egypt's Army Criticized U.S.," *New York Times*, August 16, 2012. Available online at: www.nytimes.com/2012/08/17/world /middleeast/in-paper-chief-of-egypt-army-criticized-us.html?pagewanted=all.

unilateralism, seemingly linked Islam and terrorism in the discourse, and, in practice, deemphasized the Arab-Israeli issue for much of the time.

Beneath all the tough talk, the nuclear weapons, the conventional superiority, and the occupation is a deeply insecure Israeli nation. This insecurity defines the outlook of most Israelis from right to left, especially in times of crisis. In the 1990s there was a sense—particularly after the Oslo agreement—that history had finally ended: The United States had won the cold war, and Israel, in effect, had won the Arab-Israeli conflict, with the Palestinian-Israeli conflict on its way to resolution. Most Arabs, Israelis, and others around the world, including those who didn't like the projected ending, still saw it as inevitable—which is why first lady Hillary Clinton was hearing few voices addressing the Arab-Israeli issue during that period. All that changed after the collapse of the peace negotiations in 2000, the rise of the Al-Aqsa intifada, and the fear that 9/11 generated for Israelis.

The escalation in violence not only brought destruction and death to Palestinians and Israelis; the Israeli body politic also saw in the escalation an "existential crisis." In large part this crisis was due to the increase in suicide bombings during that period and the Palestinians' ability to galvanize far more Arab, Muslim, and other support around the world than in the 1990s. As for 9/11, it above all raised real fears in Israel that perhaps the United States would conclude that the horrific attack on American soil should be blamed on U.S. support for Israel.

The emergent interpretation adopted by the Bush administration—"They hate us for our values"—was thus welcome music to Israeli ears. Whether Israelis fully believed this interpretation or not, it reassured them of U.S. support just as it alienated Arabs. In his 2009 Cairo speech, Obama attempted to unravel Bush's unyielding framework in order to reach out to Muslims and bring both Arabs and Israelis to the table to pursue a negotiated peace settlement.

Yet despite the U.S. mediation efforts from the start of the Obama administration, Arabs and Israelis not only weren't sold on a Middle Eastern adaption of Obama's "hope" campaign theme; they steadfastly remained in a zero-sum mood. Arabs polled at the time were very pessimistic about the outcome of the negotiations, with majorities expressing the view that the two-state solution will never happen. Yes, the message was, people would be happy to be surprised, but their bet was on failure. And when diplomatic failure occurs, conflict escalates and each side wants to prepare solid alliances for the morning after. The role of the United States is thus largely seen from that perspective: Whose side will the United States take when it all falls apart? And every signal the United States sends of reaching out to one side will anger the other.

Predictably, polling leading up to the 2012 American presidential elections once again reflected the diametrically opposed viewpoints between the Israeli and the Arab worlds. Polling in the spring of 2012 showed a complete reversal of fortunes for the Obama administration. Arabs believed that the administration had essentially given up on pressuring the Netanyahu government in Israel to talk peace, particularly after the resignation of presidential peace envoy George Mitchell in 2011. When the administration opposed the Palestinian bid for statehood at the United Nations in 2011, and President Obama followed this with a particularly pro-Israel speech to the United Nations General assembly in the fall of 2011, Arabs assumed that the soaring rhetoric of the Cairo speech at the start of the president's first term was just that: rhetoric, nothing more. In addition, American presidential candidates had made their typical pledges of fidelity to Israel in pursuit of the pro-Israel vote. The result?

According to a poll I conducted in Israel in February 2012, most Israeli Jews preferred Obama to every Republican candidate remaining in the field at the time: 32 to 29 percent over Romney, 34 to 21 percent over Rick Santorum, 31 to 27 percent over Newt Gingrich, and 34 to 24 percent over Ron Paul.

In sharp contrast, a poll I conducted in Egypt in May 2012, fielded by JZAnalytics, showed that Romney was preferred over Obama by a large majority of Egyptians polled—73 percent to 25 percent—a remarkable shift for Obama from the positive attitudes expressed in Egypt and elsewhere in the Arab world in the spring of 2009.

Of course, Egyptians and other Arabs knew little about Mitt Romney in May 2012, and they were bound to alter their views as they learned more, especially during and after his campaign visit to Israel in July 2012. Their initial verdict had predictably been more based on disappointment with Obama than support for Romney, but both Israelis and Arabs are quick to judge American presidents through the prism of their ongoing conflict. There is simply no way around this dilemma, and there never was.

Little, if any, trust existed between Israelis and Egyptians before Egyptian president Anwar Sadat undertook his historic visit to Jerusalem and before an actual agreement was signed. Even when Sadat and Israeli prime minister Menachem Begin went to Camp David in 1978, each side was prepared to leave with no peace agreement at all as long as they consolidated their relations with the United States at the expense of the other. Only after an agreement was reached did their attitudes toward each other and toward the U.S. role change.

The same could be said about the Oslo agreement. No public trust existed between Israelis and Palestinians, and no serious preparation to change attitudes was in place. But once an agreement was reached and backed by the United States, attitudes changed—and the Palestinians warmed up to Bill Clinton and U.S. mediation.

For any American administration, winning the Arab and Israeli publics at the same time is nearly impossible without a genuine diplomatic breakthrough. Whether Arab-Israeli peace will come through American mediation efforts, local initiative, crisis, or accident—or come at all—is beyond anyone's ability to predict. Both Arabs and Israelis expect conflict instead of peace, and this expectation will continue to drive the perceptions of both publics. America will inevitably be caught in the middle, especially in times of crisis, as Arabs will continue to see Washington as Israel's enabler, and Israelis will continue to fear any daylight between American and Israeli policies.

This will be especially true in times of fighting and bloodshed between Israel and the Palestinians. As Israel's principal backer, the United States will remain the target of anger and suspicion. It is for this reason that American policy must never waiver in its efforts to resolve the Palestinian-Israeli conflict in particular and the Arab-Israeli conflict more broadly.

CHAPTER 8

ATTITUDES TOWARD IRAN

T HE RISE OF IRANIAN POWER in the Middle East following the 2003 Iraq war has led American officials to try to rally Arab support for isolating Tehran. The arguments in favor of this initiative appear convincing at first glance. Beyond Persian-Arab rivalries, Iran's people are mostly Shiite Muslims, whereas Arabs are predominantly Sunni Muslims, so there is a religious divide that's consequential. Add to the mix that many of the Arab rulers who are allied with Washington, particularly in the United Arab Emirates and Saudi Arabia, regularly talk to American officials about Iran as a threat, which they genuinely feel.

Lost in this picture, though, is another reality altogether, captured by the way the Arab people polled in the past decade have responded when asked to identify "the two countries posing the biggest threat" to them. Without any prompting, the vast majority of Arabs, year after year, consistently identified Israel first and the United States second. Iran has ranked a distant third (Figure 8.1).

With these numbers in mind, American hopes for isolating Tehran seem less plausible. Why would the Arab people, in the midst of their own revolution, join an American effort against Iran when they see America and its key regional ally, Israel, as posing far greater threats? So even though this American initiative wasn't completely without basis, it failed to recognize that Arab attitudes toward Iran are far more complex than has been reflected in our public discourse. In fact, Arab attitudes toward Iran could never be separated

129

FIGURE 8.1 The Two Countries That Are the Biggest Threat, Six-Country Totals, 2009 and 2011

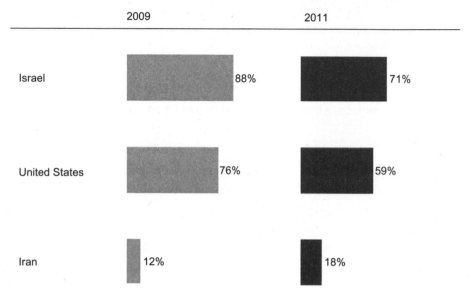

Name TWO countries that you think pose the biggest threat to you.

	2009	2011
Israel	88%	71%
United States	76%	59%
Iran	12%	18%

from other regional issues, especially the Arab-Israeli conflict, and any American policy aimed at avoiding this linkage will have limited prospects.

The complexity of the Iran issue in Arab eyes has been present for decades—it is not simply a function of the Iraq war, although the latter has intensified the dilemma of the issue for most Arabs—and it deserves more detailed analysis, starting with a little history.

Arab Conflict with Iran from the 1950s

Even skipping over centuries of ancient Arab-Persian rivalries, the past six decades have provided plenty of conflict. In the 1950s, Iran was one of the earliest and staunchest opponents of the Pan-Arab movement championed by Egypt. Tensions were further fueled by Iran's pro-Western shah, in particular for his close ties with Israel, with whom, like Turkey, he developed a warm relationship.

The shah also developed good working relations with pro-Western Arab states like Saudi Arabia and Jordan, and even Egypt after Anwar Sadat came to power in 1970, but Arabs despised his support for regional American policies—particularly the fact that, together with Israel, Iran became one of America's most important strategic allies in the Middle East, especially during the Nixon administration. It was on the shah's watch that Iran came to control three islands in the Gulf that are also claimed by the United Arab Emirates, and it was the shah who started the Iranian nuclear program.

On an official level, the animosity between Arabs and Iran did not end following the shah's overthrow by an anti-Western Islamic revolution in 1979. Iran's relationship with Arab governments would become even more tense as a result of the Iran-Iraq war, which began when Iraqi forces invaded Iran after accusing the new regime in Tehran of provoking Shiites against governments not only in Iraq but elsewhere in the Gulf region. (For more than three decades, Arab leaders have stressed the differences between Arabs and Iranians, in both ethnic and religious terms, although many Arabs never totally bought into this rhetoric. Following the 1979 revolution and the subsequent Iraqi invasion of Iran in 1980, rulers put particular stress on Arab-Persian differences.)

Saddam Hussein, in particular, was able to rally some Arab public support for his war effort by appealing to these differences. Other Arab governments in the Gulf rallied behind Baghdad despite their own long-held differences with Saddam Hussein. Saddam's war with Iran was bankrolled and supported by oil-producing Arab states in the region, particularly Saudi Arabia, the United Arab Emirates, Qatar, and Kuwait. The price of that eight-year war was steep: hundreds of thousands of dead and wounded on each side and devastation of the region's economies as the war plundered the enormous cash reserves that had flowed into the region in the mid-1970s when oil prices quadrupled.

Here, too, the Shiite-Sunni overtones of the war could not be ignored, with Iraq fearing that Iran would assist and help empower Iraq's Shiite majority against a secular government dominated by Sunni elites (but with many Shiites in the mix).[1] Likewise, Saudi Arabia and other Gulf Arab states feared that the success of the Iranian revolution could encourage their own

---

1. Although Saddam Hussein and many of those he trusted were Sunnis, especially those from his hometown of Tikrit, it is sometimes forgotten that many of those around him who were most wanted by the American forces during the 2003 war were Shiite. In fact, a majority of those in the so-called "deck of cards" of wanted Iraqi officials prepared by the U.S. military were Shiite.

Shiite communities to revolt. But the emphasis was principally on the Arab-Persian divide, not Sunni-Shiite, as the Iraqi government's source of legitimacy was secular Arab nationalism and many of its soldiers fighting Iran were Iraqi Shiites.

The following decade began with the Iraqi invasion of a neighboring Arab state, Kuwait, in 1990 and the subsequent American-led war to dislodge Iraq from Kuwait. As a result, throughout the 1990s the Arab public was less focused on Iran than on the international sanctions imposed on Iraq and the humanitarian conditions for Iraqi citizens. Concern over the plight of Iraqis was a sore point for the Arab public throughout much of the 1990s—an inevitable outcome, perhaps, of the expansion of the American military presence in the region, including in Saudi Arabia, the birthplace of Islam.

The fact that the American-led war against Iraq had seriously reduced Saddam Hussein's military capacity gave rise to a new dynamic. Arab governments that had rallied behind U.S.-led efforts to liberate Kuwait now worried more about an emergent Iran. Most had seen Baghdad as the key counterbalance to Iranian power during that period. That included the United States, which had imposed its own sanctions on Iran during the Clinton administration in what was termed "dual containment" of both Iraq and Iran, lest Iran gain from a weakened Iraq.

The 2003 Iraq war definitively changed this shifting strategic environment. The second U.S.-led invasion of the country completely eliminated Iraq from the region's military equation. In this new alignment, Sunnis in Iraq were seen to be the biggest losers. Meanwhile Iran gained influence in Iraq through religious and cultural ties with the country's newly empowered Shiite population—even as the American forces were in Iraq helping to consolidate a Shiite-majority government.

Arab Common Cause with Iran

Saddam Hussein had been able to convince many Arab governments to support and financially back his 1980 invasion of Iran and the subsequent war, but Arabs were conflicted. On the one hand, Saddam was the leader of an Arab nation that looked to be the most promising in the region, with large financial reserves from the oil boom, a vibrant industrial sector, and an educated and skilled population. Saddam Hussein also had reputable credentials on Palestine. He had led the Arab block that opposed Egypt's peace treaty with Israel at a time when the prevailing Arab mood was that Egypt had sacrificed Palestine to regain its Sinai Peninsula from Israeli occupation.

However, many Arabs had also hoped after the Iranian revolution that an anti-Israel, anti-Western Iran would join an alliance with similar-minded Arabs. In my many visits to Arab countries during the Iraq-Iran war, I frequently heard views, even among those in places like Jordan and Egypt who had hopes for Saddam Hussein, that they were disappointed that Hussein was "wasting" the resources of Arabs and Muslims in the wrong conflict. The bloody and devastating eight-year war forced choices, including on the Palestine Liberation Organization itself, which received immediate and valuable support from Iran but was highly dependent on Arab financial support. And that war distracted attention from the Palestine question; the first Palestinian intifada against the Israeli occupation in the West Bank, in 1987, can be attributed to the Palestinians taking matters into their own hands to refocus regional and global attention on their cause.

In the absence of rigorous public opinion polls, we can't know with any confidence how majorities of Arab citizens felt about Iran and its revolution. But we do know that after the overthrow of the shah in Iran, many Arabs were inspired by what Iranians were able to do and admired the leader of the revolution, Ayatollah Khomeini. Despite his Shiite religion, Khomeini's success in overthrowing a despised regime and standing up to Washington inspired Sunni Islamists across the Arab world.

From the outset, Khomeini had also championed the Palestinian cause, which captured the imagination of the Arab public. One of his first symbolic acts was to close the Israeli embassy in Tehran and turn it over to the secular PLO, Israel's nemesis. And he started an annual tradition that has since spread across many Muslim countries, *Youm Al-Quds* (Jerusalem Day), highlighting the importance of the city and the cause of Palestine, not only for Iranians and Shiites, but for Muslims everywhere.

Thus even in the years when the focus was on conflict between Arabs and Iranians and when the public narrative centered on Arab-Persian conflicts of interest and religious divisions among Shiites and Sunnis, Arab public attitudes toward Iran were quite complex. The issues of authoritarianism, Western domination, and Israel/Palestine were always there, sometimes trumping other divisions. This was certainly accentuated by the 2003 Iraq war, and it remains the case in the era of the Arab public awakening.

Why Is the United States Seen as a Bigger Threat?

For the decade following the 2003 Iraq war, polls conducted in Arab countries have consistently shown that the Arab public's anger with American foreign policy and with Israel trumps existing concerns about Persians and the Sunni-Shiite divide in the formation of attitudes toward important foreign policy issues, including Iran's nuclear program.

To begin with, there is the way Arabs identify threats, as seen from my annual six-country Arab public opinion poll. Many Arabs view Iran as a challenge to them and to their aspirations, but most see Israel and the United States as far bigger threats. At a minimum, there is an "enemy of my enemy" logic that has benefited Iran in direct proportion to how much of a threat it seems to pose to America and Israel. Poll results show that any sense that Iran threatens Arabs has been dwarfed almost to extinction by the extent to which Israel and the United States are seen as primary threats. For example, in 2008, 2009, and 2010, at least 88 percent identified Israel as one of their two biggest threats, and at least 77 percent identified the United States that way. In contrast, the percentage of those identifying Iran as a primary threat ranged from 7 percent to 12 percent.

Great variations can be found in public attitudes on this issue from country to country, particularly depending on proximity to Iran. In contrast to the averaged results from the six countries studied during 2008 through 2010 (weighted by population), Iran is seen as a considerably bigger threat by its neighbors across the Persian Gulf, like the United Arab Emirates and Saudi Arabia, than in North African states like Egypt and Morocco (which is farther from Tehran than is most of Europe). In 2010, 27 percent of Saudis and 24 percent of Emiratis identified Iran as a top threat, compared with an average of 10 percent for the six countries studied.

Still, it is noteworthy that Israel and the United States supersede Iran as a threat even among the people of Gulf Arab states, like the United Arab Emirates and Saudi Arabia, for whom the U.S. military provides vital protection.[2]

---

2. The only exception came in the United Arab Emirates in 2009 when Iran and the United States were tied as second perceived threats after Israel.

In the 2011 poll, in Saudi Arabia and the UAE, Israel remained the number one perceived threat, followed by the United States, but Iran was identified by 35 percent of Saudis and 45 percent of Emiratis as one of the top two threats; in comparison, Iran was picked as one of the top two threats by 15 percent of Egyptians and 18 percent of Moroccans.

Perhaps more telling were Arab attitudes toward Iran's nuclear program. Arabs have been divided among those who believe that Iran is pursuing only a peaceful program and those who believe Tehran is seeking nuclear weapons. In 2011 a slight majority said Iran is seeking nuclear weapons—indicating that they don't trust Iran's official position that its program is peaceful. Yet, consistently, year after year, polls also indicate that the Arab public does not support international pressure to curb Iran's nuclear program (Figure 8.2).

Remarkably, citizens of Israel who are Arab/Palestinian also share these attitudes (Figure 8.3). In contrast with Jewish Israelis who fear that a nuclear Iran would pose an existential threat to them, Arab Israelis do not want Iran pressured to curb its nuclear programs even though, if Iran were to use nuclear weapons against Israel, the devastation would hit Arab and Jewish Israelis alike (as well as Palestinians in the West Bank and Gaza, and many other Arab neighbors).

Driving Arab attitudes are not only more benign assessments of Iranian intent, but an even stronger sense of double standards: Most see in the effort

FIGURE 8.2 Iran's Right to Pursue Nuclear Program, Six-Country Totals, 2008–2011

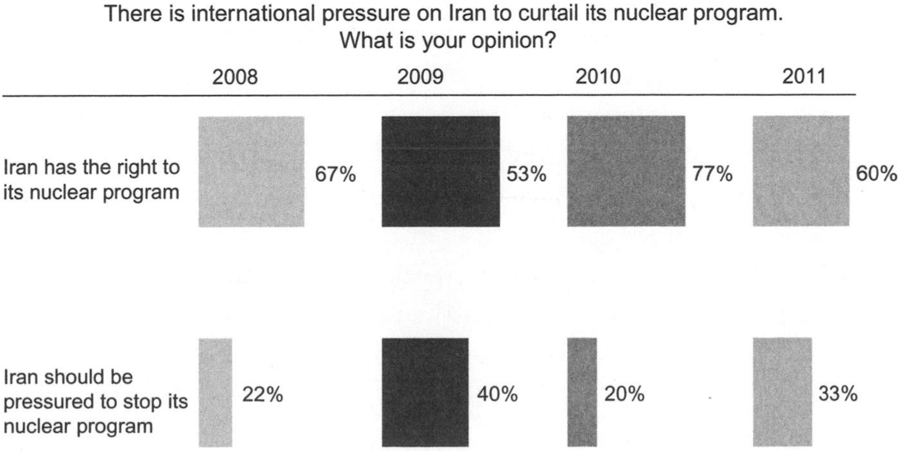

There is international pressure on Iran to curtail its nuclear program.
What is your opinion?

	2008	2009	2010	2011
Iran has the right to its nuclear program	67%	53%	77%	60%
Iran should be pressured to stop its nuclear program	22%	40%	20%	33%

FIGURE 8.3 Iran's Right to Pursue Nuclear Program, Six-Country Totals and Arab/Palestinian Israelis, 2011

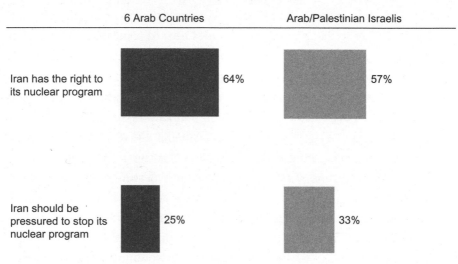

There is international pressure on Iran to curtail its nuclear program. What is your opinion?

6 Arab Countries — Arab/Palestinian Israelis

Iran has the right to its nuclear program: 64% / 57%

Iran should be pressured to stop its nuclear program: 25% / 33%

against Iran's program an unjustified targeting of another Muslim country, without raising questions about Israel's significant nuclear weapons capabilities. In fact, it is noteworthy that in 2009, there was a spike in the number of Arabs supporting pressuring Iran. This was largely a product of the optimistic mood that accompanied the first few months of the Obama administration, when many liked the tone of President Obama, his outreach to Arabs and Muslims, and his focus on international law and cooperation. The less focused Arabs are on their sense of "double standards" in the way the international community deals with the Middle East broadly, the more they are inclined to support pressure on Iran.

Arabs generally support an end to nuclear proliferation, and Arab governments, especially Egypt's, have pushed for turning the Middle East into a nuclear-weapons-free zone. But short of that, Arabs tend to be evenly divided on the question of whether a nuclear Iran would be better for the Middle East, although only a minority definitively say it would be worse. In the 2010 poll—taken shortly after Israel intercepted a Turkish flotilla headed for Gaza against Israeli warnings, and killed or wounded many on the ships—the urge to find a counterbalance to Israeli power may be responsible for the majority in that year saying that a nuclear Iran would be better for the Middle East. This is more a reflection of anger with Israel and the United States than a real endorsement of Iranian power, but the nuclear issue is not confined to Iran. In a 2012 Egyptian poll, a majority of Egyptians, 61 percent, said they wanted their country to develop its own nuclear weapons if Iran builds such weapons, and half said they wanted Egypt to get nuclear weapons even if Iran didn't develop them but Israel kept its own.

Arabs' Electronic Conversations on Iran

Because polling has consistently shown that Arabs have a complex relationship with Iran, it's hardly surprising that a range of these nuanced, varied, and surprising opinions often crop up in discussions I've had with Arabs everywhere. One obviously unscientific way to capture a little of the range and flavor of Arab opinion on Iran is to record and sort the comment streams on the two popular Arab news websites Aljazeera.net and Alarabiya.net.[3]

Note that these websites, like the popular TV stations they represent, are supported by Sunni governing elites in Qatar and Saudi Arabia who are very concerned about Iran's potential to incite Shia in the countries of the Gulf Cooperation Council, especially in Bahrain and Saudi Arabia. These media have been particularly critical of Iran, especially for its support of the Syrian regime following the start of the uprisings there. Certainly, the readers of these websites are diverse, particularly in the case of Aljazeera.net. Obviously, too, this sampling also excludes Arabs without access to the Internet— and those who simply don't care to comment online. So, although this exercise has no pretensions of broad authority, the comments do animate some of the individual opinions more drily captured by polling.

I conducted analysis of reader comments on three controversial events involving Iran that did not directly involve Israel or the United States. The first was a 2010 visit to Lebanon by Iran's president, Mahmoud Ahmadinejad,

---

3. These readers' comments do not necessarily represent the views of Arab majorities; for that we have the polls. What they do provide is a picture of the varieties of issues that are on Arab minds when it comes to Iran, the likes of which I typically hear on my visits to the region and read and hear about in the Arab media.

which was seen by many as exacerbating the internal tensions between the Shiite Hezbollah-led coalition, supported by Iran, and their Sunni-led opponents. My team and I translated and analyzed the first twenty-five consecutive comments from each of these websites. The results were telling: Of the total fifty comments from the two sites, 30 percent were negative about Ahmadinejad's visit, 10 percent were neutral, and 60 percent were positive. Alarabiya.net's readers were almost evenly divided between those who were positive and those who were negative, whereas 70 percent of Aljazeera.net's readers were positive about the visit.

Negative comments came from readers who were fearful of Iran or who see it mostly through the Sunni-Shiite prism. One reader on Alarabiya.net commented, "Lebanon will never be an Iranian colony! You are not welcome by the majority of the Arab Lebanese because you are coming as a colonizer, not as a friend." Even among the fans of the Lebanese Shiite leader of Hezbollah, Hassan Nasrallah, some worried about Iranian influence in the Arab world: "I love you, Mr. Hassan Nasrallah, but please don't let the Iranians have a presence in Lebanon." Another comment—"You are not welcome at all, only by the minority"—was an unsubtle allusion to the Lebanese Shiites.

The second group were those few neutral parties who saw the Iranian leader as simply conducting public relations stunts and deceiving his Arab audiences: "We are tired of bogus leaders who keep promising but end up doing nothing for the Palestinian cause."

The third and largest group of commentators expressed support for Ahmadinejad. One theme was that he was standing up to Israel and the United States: "The enemy of my enemy is my friend. Iran has always stood against Israel and with Arab rights." Another asked: "How can those who are against the visit call for the liberation of Palestine? How can you object to his visit when he is championing the Palestinian cause?"

More common were simple endorsements: "He is a hero who has given Arab societies what no Arab ruler has thanks to the Islamic Republic of Iran"; and "If Arab rulers were half as good as Ahmadinejad, we wouldn't be here."

Such comments flesh out what we already know about Arab views of Iran: They are diverse, and anger toward Israel and the United States engenders more positive feelings toward Tehran than one might otherwise expect, given a deep history of Persian-Arab conflict and Sunni-Shiite divisions.

The second comment stream we studied followed an article detailing Ahmadinejad's even more controversial April 2012 visit to an island in the Gulf, Abu Musa, in an archipelago Iran has controlled since 1971 but which the United Arab Emirates claims as its own. Though most Arabs support UAE claims to the islands, only a surprisingly small group expressed extreme negativity toward Ahmadinejad.

In this stream, we examined the first thirty-six comments on Aljazeera.net[4] on a story provocatively titled "Iran Confirms Claim over Abu Musa Islands and the Gulf Coordination Council Objects." Only three were outright hostile condemnations of Iran. One screed read, "Every time and at every event Iran confirms that it is more insidious and dangerous than the Jews. Every time things calm down a bit they aggravate it again. Iran is moving toward atrophy and destruction instead of its rulers trying to develop their people and modernize and provide open Internet for its people for exposure to the outside world. This is an indicator of the backwardness of the leadership that wants it[s] people to worship it without God."

But another, larger group of commentators mocked Arab condemnations and empty words. A tongue-in-cheek posting expressed skepticism: "We will liberate not only the three islands but we will liberate Jerusalem and we'll put Israel in the sea and Persians in the Gulf waters. Yes brothers we are the protectors, heroes, and glorious Arabs."

Many comments reflected alienation of the public from their rulers, a long-suppressed anger made more visible in the era of Arab public empowerment: "As an Arab citizen, do I care about returning these islands to UAE if the probability of my return is nil? I wanted to go now but the stakes are high even though I am a Sunni Arab. The Emiratis prefer Indians or Americans over Arabs. What is happening now is bringing foreigners to an artificial place in the Emirates"; and "I see the conflict between Iran and the rulers and it means nothing to me."

Finally, readers weighed in on Egyptian president Morsi's 2012 announcement that he would be the first Egyptian president to visit the Islamic Republic of Iran, in order to attend the Non-Aligned Movement summit. Tied to

---

4. "Iran Confirms Claim over Abu Musa Islands and the Gulf Cooperation Council Objects," *Al Jazeera News,* April 13, 2012. Available online at: www.aljazeera.net/news/pages/ae7a6562 -619f-4f55-b38d-d9dc7b150711.

the theme of Arab lack of action in the foregoing examples were comments related to the absence of Arab or Muslim unity, with some suggesting that Arabs unite to confront their enemies, while others proposed that Iran and the Arabs should come together in confronting enemies of Muslims.

Some comments counseled against Morsi's going: "This would be a failed visit; Iran is the reason for the rising sectarianism in the region and the leadership of the [Muslim] Brotherhood [from which Morsi hails] must understand this." Another warned, "I hope President Morsi is well informed about Iranian culture, religion, and aims . . . so that Iran accomplishes nothing and does not spread its faith and ideas in Sunni Egypt."

An attempt at coming up with a balanced view was expressed by another reader: "I think that the right stand is not to lend support to Iran, which is assisting in killing us in Syria . . . yet the West should understand that, even though we have differences with Iran, we will not permit a war against the Iranian people."

But the majority of comments were supportive, seeing good news, for various reasons, in possible cooperation between the two countries: "Iran and Egypt are Muslim countries, and those who don't want them to get closer to each other are allies of the Zionists and are still living in the [pre-Islamic era]." Another posted, "It is enough that this . . . visit is a thorn in the eyes of Israel and its agents"; a third wrote, "I have long awaited the rapprochement between Egypt and Iran, the moment of cooperation against imperialism and backwardness."

These comments offer an anecdotal window into some of the reasoning behind the seemingly puzzling attitudes we find in public opinion polls in Arab countries. Though varied, they generally confirm polling done in the region. Rather than finding clear cases of opposition to Iran, especially with regard to the first two events, which could have been seen mostly as provocative, the reactions were far more divided, and those in opposition were a minority.

Iran and the Arab Uprisings

The complex and conflicting relationship between Arabs and Iran has also spilled over into the Arab uprisings. Many Arabs have long hoped to see an Arab country that would be a model of inspiration to them. Instead, two non-Arab regional powers, Turkey and Iran, seem to have seized the stage. Iran, though, has a counternarrative: The uprisings in the Arab world were not "Arab" per se but constitute an "Islamic awakening" akin to Iran's in 1979. For Tehran, therefore, this awakening should be an occasion for increased Iranian-Arab cooperation. Significant numbers of Arabs support the Iranian narrative. Even among those who see the uprisings as an "Arab awakening," many see opportunities for Iranian-Arab cooperation against common declared enemies, particularly Israel and the United States.

This trend in public opinion would likely have been much stronger if Iran had not supported the ideologically secular but Allawite-led Syrian regime. An overwhelming number of Arabs—about 90 percent—expressed support for Syria's rebels, most of whom are Sunnis, and thousands of whom have been killed by government forces. As one of the few regional powers to support Assad—who has also been a lifeline for Shiite Hezbollah in Lebanon—Iran exacerbated existing Sunni-Shiite divisions, including concerns about the decline of Sunni influence in Iraq and Lebanon.

This sectarian divide in Arab opinions has also manifested itself in reverse when the rebel forces are primarily Shiites struggling against a Sunni regime. Sunni Arabs, particularly in the Gulf, expressed concern about possible Shiite empowerment in Bahrain. Although a majority of Arabs still supported uprisings in every country, the enthusiasm for rebels varied notably, depending on the country. In 2011 polling, over 80 percent of Arabs supported popular movements in majority Sunni Syria, Yemen, and Libya. In the case of majority Shiite Bahrain, over 60 percent voiced support for the rebels in October 2011—a majority, to be sure, but one muted by sectarian sentiments.

A strong indication that the Shiite-Sunni issue has risen in the priorities of Egyptians since the Arab uprisings came in the first televised debate among two then-leading presidential candidates in April 2012. One of the candidates, Abdel Moneim Aboul Futouh, considered a moderate Islamist with relatively liberal positions on social issues, was asked specifically about Iran. He expressed openness to possible cooperation but warned Iran against exporting the Shiite faith into mostly Sunni Egypt—reading some of his constituents' fears. An Egyptian Sunni Jihadist, who had been imprisoned multiple times beginning in 1981 when his group was found guilty of assassinating Egyptian president Anwar Sadat, put it this way in January 2013: "In the early 1980s, we were all inspired by the Iranian revolution and

FIGURE 8.4 The Two Countries That Are the Biggest Threat, Egypt, May 2012

Name two countries that you think pose the biggest threat to you

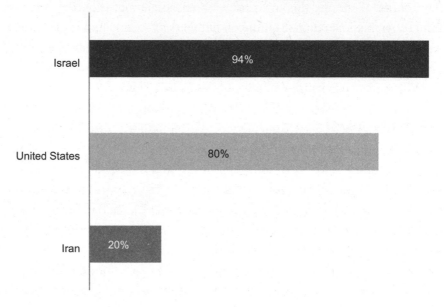

admired Khomeini and we still admire much about the Islamic government of Iran. But we are different and we don't want them to rule over us."[5]

This concern over the Shiite-Sunni divide—in particular as manifested in Syria—correlates with recent polls showing that Iran is rising in Arab perceptions as a primary threat. In comparison to 2009 when only 12 percent of Arabs identified Iran as one of the two top threats facing them, 18 percent identified Iran this way a year after the uprisings in October 2011. By May 2012, the proportion of Egyptians identifying Iran as one of the two biggest threats rose to 20 percent (Figure 8.4). Such numbers still pale in comparison to the perceived threat posed by Israel and the United States, but they are trending upward.

One more point to make: Even in this era of heightened tensions, neither the Sunni-Shiite nor the Arab-Persian divide is the most central factor in how Arabs view Iran. In the same May 2012 poll, Egyptians were asked to name the leaders they admired most in the world. Mahmoud Ahmadinejad

---

5. Meeting with author in Cairo, January 8, 2013, at the Ibn Khaldoun Center, arranged by Center director and leading intellectual and human rights advocate, Saad El Din Ibrahim.

was tied with Hezbollah's Hassan Nasrallah in second place, behind the prime minister of Turkey. In other words, despite the focus in the sectarian issues of the Arab uprisings, the increase in the number of Arabs who see Iran as a primary threat, and the fact that Hezbollah and Iran took the side of the unpopular Assad regime in Syria,[6] Arabs still showed a dramatic preference for strong regional leaders whom they perceived as willing to stand up to Israel and the United States. Arab opinions about Iran are complicated by historical ethnic and religious conflict, but most Arabs still evaluate threats primarily through the ever-present prism of pain.

---

6. According to a poll by the Arab American Institute released in February 2013, Iran's support for the Assad regime in Syria, and its roles in Iraq and Bahrain further increased negative views of Iran in the Arab world. Available online at: www.aaiusa.org/blog/entry/poll-release-arab-and-muslim-attitudes-toward-Iran/.

CHAPTER 9

ATTITUDES TOWARD DEMOCRACY, WOMEN, AND RELIGION

THE CHANT OF THE MILLIONS of demonstrators across the Arab world during the Arab uprisings left no doubt that, at the core, most were seeking dignity, freedom, and democracy. But much remained unclear: What do Arabs mean by "freedom" and "democracy," and how do they hope to reconcile these with other things they hold dear, especially religious beliefs? What role do they envision for Sharia religious law, and how do they reconcile that with democracy? And what are the consequences for constituents who could be affected by a system that sought to reconcile democracy with faith and traditions, particularly women?

One starting point for understanding Arab attitudes toward democracy is that, like most people, they also want other things beyond democracy. The Islamic faith, important in the lives of most Arabs, is one obvious value to be recognized, but there are others, including security and freedom from outside domination. Witness, for example, how Americans, for whom freedom and democracy are core values, are quick to accept violations of civil liberties and democratic process in the name of security, which too is dear to them. And most people, under fear of invasion or domination by an outside power, accept limits on their domestic freedom to confront an external enemy—which is why many rulers often exploit fears of outside threats to justify domestic repression.

One way to address this latter issue is by revisiting Arab reactions to the rhetorical push by the George W. Bush administration to spread democracy in the Middle East after the 2003 Iraq war. Was this the spark that lit the fire of democracy in the Arab world by inspiring reformers, or did it delay what was a natural course of change by giving democracy—through war and destruction in Iraq—a bad name? Or was the war itself, and the Arab regimes' acquiescence in it, the real spark for a public fed up with repressive rulers who not only limited their freedoms at home but also made their countries subservient to the United States?

This debate about the American role in the uprisings also took place in Washington. When the Arab uprisings started, some critics of the Obama administration faulted the president for having turned his back on the Bush administration's democracy-promotion agenda to focus on withdrawal from Iraq and the Arab-Israeli conflict. Obama had continued to speak of freedom and democracy, but his early trips, they noted, included visits to Saudi Arabia and Egypt—two countries whose regimes had been under rhetorical pressure from the Bush team to liberalize. This view, however, distorts a complex reality: Arabs never took the democracy policy of the Bush administration seriously—instead they saw Bush using it as a mechanism to justify indefensible policies, particularly the Iraq war.

If the American policies under George W. Bush had any effect on the Arab uprisings, it was, ironically, as a reminder of the widely perceived hypocrisy and cynicism of America and the Arab states it supported. To most Arabs, America's democracy promotion efforts were a fig leaf for wars designed to control oil and help Israel. Their leaders' support of these wars may well have provided further motivation to revolt. For Arabs, like most people, even though the notion of freedom immediately involved freedom from repressive rulers, it could not be separated from freedom from foreign domination.

There was never any doubt that Arab citizens across the region despised the absence of liberty, a fact doubted only by those who denied that Arabs had natural human aspirations. In fact, reform advocates in the region had pushed for change long before the Iraq war. Perhaps no one symbolized the Arab democracy movement more than Egyptian sociologist and leading intellectual, Saad Eddin Ibrahim. Ibrahim had made a lifelong mission of advocating human rights and democracy in the Arab world dating back to criticism of President Anwar Sadat in the 1970s. He captured a spirit among many Arabs, particularly among the young, in speaking out and in founding the Ibn

Khaldoun Center, which advocated for democracy and freer civil society. He championed the rights of women and minorities, but as a liberal, he also advocated for the rights of Islamists. He took on President Mubarak long before President Bush advocated democracy or even came to office, stepping over a red line when he publically challenged the prospect of Mubarak's son Gamal succeeding his father. He was imprisoned in 2000 and spent three years in and out of prison making international headlines embarrassing the Bush administration's democracy advocacy, forcing it to pressure Mubarak to release Ibrahim. Although he was acquitted and released in 2003, the cause of democracy for which he paid a price remained unaddressed. But the spirit that he and many younger reformers symbolized was a harbinger of things to come.

Notwithstanding these important efforts, a real promise of democracy and freedom didn't arrive before the Arab uprisings.

It is difficult to know how people understand democracy, especially those who have never experienced it, even if they may embrace it as the opposite of what they have and dislike. Veteran Middle Eastern diplomat and former assistant secretary of state Edward Djerejian once described what Islamists were seeking to achieve and pushing for reform as: "One vote, one man, one time."

My polls have always included questions designed to draw out respondents' views on democracy and to identify the states that come closest to their ideal. What emerges is a sense that the Arab definition of democracy is not as far from that of the West as one might think.

Despite admiration for Iran's perceived ability to stand up to Israel and the United States, that country has never been listed among the states with the most freedom and democracy and was not on the list of states Arabs want their country to emulate. Nor was any Arab or even Islamic state among the top five countries identified by Arabs as most democratic. Not only were all the countries on the list Western states, but the United States was always included—even in 2004, when talk of a civilizational clash between Muslims and the West was particularly fashionable and when Arab public anger over the Iraq war was at its height. By 2008 the order of Western countries changed slightly, and Japan appeared in the mix. But among these top nine countries identified, there was not a single Arab or Muslim country—nor any country that Americans would not recognize as democratic (Figure 9.1).

FIGURE 9.1 The Two Countries with the Most Freedom and Democracy for Their People, Six-Country Totals, 2004–2010

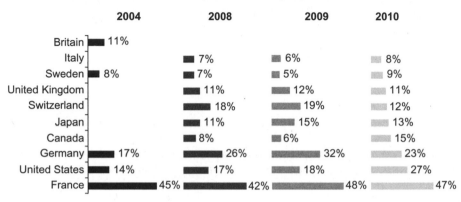

Name TWO countries where you think there is the most freedom and democracy for their own people

	2004	2008	2009	2010
Britain	11%			
Italy		7%	6%	8%
Sweden	8%	7%	5%	9%
United Kingdom		11%	12%	11%
Switzerland		18%	19%	12%
Japan		11%	15%	13%
Canada		8%	6%	15%
Germany	17%	26%	32%	23%
United States	14%	17%	18%	27%
France	45%	42%	48%	47%

The United States and Democracy

If, as these numbers suggest, Arabs believe that Western countries offer more democracy and freedom for their people than any Arab or Muslim states, and if Arabs have been seeking liberty in mostly repressive and unrepresentative systems, why was George W. Bush's policy to spread democracy in the Middle East so reviled?

To begin with, the Arab public never believed that the Bush administration's efforts to spread democracy in the region were sincere. On the eve of the Iraq war, in a poll I conducted in six countries, most Arabs said that the war was more about oil, Israel, and weakening Muslims than democracy; the percentages of those who believed that democracy was an aim were in the single digits. This same opinion trend remained the driving force in evaluating the issue of democracy in regional American foreign policy for every year since the war.

In 2005, for example, after the Bush administration began emphasizing the democracy issue in its Middle East policy, I asked in the annual Arab poll specifically about how Arabs perceived the stated U.S. policy on this issue. A large majority in each of the countries polled said they did not believe that democracy was a real American objective (Figure 9.2). Among the minority who believed it was a worthy objective, most believed the United

FIGURE 9.2 America's Professed Objective of Promoting Democracy in the Middle East, 2005

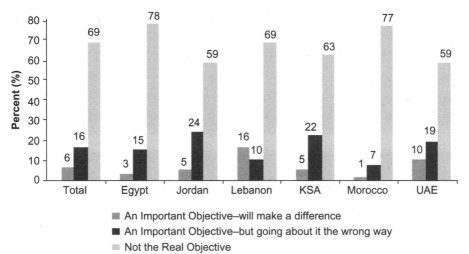

The United States has been actively advocating the spread of democracy in the Middle East especially since the Iraq war. Do you believe this is:

■ An Important Objective—will make a difference
■ An Important Objective—but going about it the wrong way
▨ Not the Real Objective

States was going about it the wrong way. These trends continued in all the following years in which we asked this question, most recently in 2008.

The distrust of American motives seen in these numbers was partially related to other priorities Arabs attributed to American policy, but it was also informed by the recent history of U.S. presidents hawking the virtues of democracy and then quickly ignoring their sales pitch as soon as other strategic priorities arose.

Case in point: In 1989 after the collapse of the Berlin Wall, at a time when many saw the end of the cold war as a victory of democracy over authoritarianism, President George H. W. Bush quickly stressed the advocacy of democracy as the new aim of American foreign policy. Some governments, including those of Jordan, Yemen, and Algeria, even responded with modest steps toward democratization. Months later, after Iraq invaded Kuwait, American priorities shifted to putting together and maintaining a war coalition, keeping American forces in the Gulf region, and ensuring the flow of oil in turbulent times. Rather than promoting democracy, the United States was in fact strengthening its ties with allied authoritarian rulers. Soon thereafter, Islamists who opposed American foreign policy objectives performed well in elections in Jordan and Algeria.

The story repeated itself when the Clinton administration came into office. Clinton's first secretary of state, Warren Christopher, not only spoke of the need for reform but was probably the first secretary of state ever to bring up the issue with an Arab leader, when he personally raised the question with Egyptian president Hosni Mubarak. But within months the PLO agreement with Israel shifted American priorities. The new objective—maintaining Palestinian and Israeli public support and securing the backing of Arab leaders for it—meant that democracy advocacy was again mere words.

As a result of this at best inconsistent recent history of democracy advocacy, Arabs viewed President George W. Bush's calls for democratic change

FIGURE 9.3 George W. Bush's Primary Motivation in Middle East Policy, 2006

When you examine the Middle East policy of U.S. president George W. Bush do you think his primary motivation is:

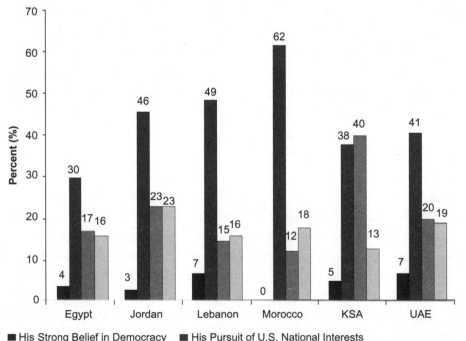

- His Strong Belief in Democracy
- His Pursuit of U.S. National Interests
- U.S. Domestic Politics
- His Need to Spread His Christian Religious Convictions

with jaundiced eyes. Given four possible motivations for President Bush's Middle East policy, few respondents selected "his strong belief in democracy." Across six countries in the 2006 annual Arab public opinion poll, that selection finished dead last, with between 0 percent (Morocco) and 7 percent. Far more credible to them was "his [Bush's] need to spread his Christian religious convictions," which garnered 13 percent to 23 percent of those polled. In five of the countries, far and away the largest group of respondents said that they believed Bush was pursuing U.S. national interests, just as the previous two administrations were believed to have done.

Reactions to American Democracy Advocacy

Reactions to the Bush administration's pressure for change varied between countries, but few of the developments seemed to arc toward democracy. Arab governments that were allied with the United States, particularly Egypt and Saudi Arabia, were annoyed by and sometimes a little worried about Bush's push for reform in their own countries. But overall, they, too, didn't take the efforts overly seriously, instead interpreting them in two ways: as an instrument of pressure to get them to support American strategic policies in Iran, the war on terrorism, and the Arab-Israeli issue; and as driven by an American administration desperate to justify an unpopular war, particularly at home.

To deal with the pressure, Arab rulers continued to cooperate strategically with the United States and moved to take cosmetic steps for reform, understanding Bush's domestic political need to claim accomplishments. They knew well that, once an American president claimed certain countries as proofs of success (as Bush did with Libya's Muammar al-Qaddafi), it would be particularly hard for him to turn around and claim them as failures the next day—even if the regimes he was touting made no further progress.

The net result was that only minor steps were taken, and these minor steps were often accompanied by further, sometimes less visible steps in the direction of more repression. Take Saudi Arabia. Despite holding municipal elections and national dialogue meetings and releasing numerous political prisoners, the old guard in the royal family felt threatened by the pace of democratization and instituted repression in the name of national security, especially after 2004 in parallel with the counterterrorism campaign in the kingdom. As a consequence, Arab public perception every year since the

Iraq war had been that the Middle East had become even less democratic than before, despite the talk of reform and progress.

As for those who welcomed American help to spread democracy among the public, they were divided into two categories. In one group were people like Ahmad Chalabi, the Iraqi anti–Saddam Hussein activist who was instrumental in building a Washington political coalition in favor of war. Chalabi, like many other Iraqis inside and outside Iraq, desperately wanted to topple a regime he despised by any method possible. In the other group were some genuine democracy advocates in the region, who had worked for reform long before the Iraq war or 9/11 and who wanted to believe that the Bush team's effort, with all its shortcomings, might help bring about change. While the former succeeded in urging war, the latter were eventually seen by their broader public as having been used by an administration whose strategic aims Arabs despised and whose democracy claims were never believed.

The vast majority of Arabs reacted cynically to the most recent U.S. push for regional democracy, noting the ongoing U.S. occupation of Iraq. Even as the United States made modest diplomatic efforts toward reform in the region, and provided modest financial resources for those efforts, the overwhelming efforts and resources of the American government went toward its military effort.

To secure the passage of American forces through Arab ports and passageways, such as the Suez Canal; to reach agreements with governments to safeguard American troops who were present in almost every friendly Arab country; to get essential Arab cooperation on intelligence in the daily war on Al Qaeda affiliates; to maintain relative stability on the Israeli-Arab front— for all these efforts the United States needed to work most closely not only with rulers in the Arab world but also with Arab militaries, security, and intelligence agencies on a daily, even hourly, basis. And much of the support, funding, and training went directly into these agencies—dwarfing the resources put behind democracy advocacy.

The net result was that parallel to the talk and modest efforts favoring reform were overwhelming efforts that strengthened the institutions of repression in the Arab world—key constituencies for every ruler whose strategic support the White House sought. This had consequences within the region that Arab citizens felt. When rulers are asked to support American foreign policies that are painfully unpopular, their fear of public opposition and revolt increases, and their instinct is to move behind the scenes to preempt unrest by limiting expression and rounding up potential opponents. The net result was more repression than democracy, and an Arab public perception that connects this repression at least partly to the United States.

Partly as a result of this dissonance between what American officials were saying and where American money was actually going, it was very hard to sell the Iraq war as a transition toward a model of democracy that would engender public demands for change. Instead it was seen much differently.

Americans tend to understand the Iraq war by focusing on our enormous losses: more than 4,000 troops dead, thousands wounded, and thousands more scarred for life, trillions of dollars in spending that by all accounts contributed to America's subsequent economic challenges. What's more, though the war's impact was hard to ignore at every level at home, it was still fought thousands of miles away from the American shores, by a volunteer army.

For many Arabs, even outside Iraq, the impact was direct, sometimes immediate and daily. American warplanes flew for their bombing runs from bases in neighboring Arab states, American ships passed through the Suez Canal in Egypt and docked in the naval base in Bahrain. Hundreds of thousands of Iraqi refugees flowed into poor neighboring states like Jordan and Syria. The devastation in Iraq itself was not only enormous but graphically covered in the Arab media. It is hard to know exactly how many Iraqis died in the war, but estimates range from 100,000 to several hundred thousand. Hundreds of thousands more were wounded. Over 4 million Iraqis were displaced, or more than 13 percent of the Iraqi population—half of them outside Iraq. This is aside from the deprivation, absence of personal security, and economic devastation.

To most Arabs, telling them that the invasion was good for Iraq is an insult of major proportions, even if many disliked Saddam Hussein and his regime. If this was democracy, Arabs wanted nothing of it. Starting with my very first poll after the Iraq war began, the overwhelming majority of Arabs in the six countries polled expressed the view that Iraqis were worse off than before the war. Certainly the Iraqi people had their own evaluations, roughly broken along sectarian lines, with Kurds positive about the change, Sunnis negative, and Shiites somewhere in between.[1] But beyond the shocking blood-shed and destruction in Iraq, Arabs outside saw a decline of an important Arab state, thus a weakened Arab world, and evaluated the state of affairs for Iraqi citizens largely through the prism of Sunni Iraqis. More important, polled Arabs consistently expressed the view every year that the Middle East had become less democratic than before.

Although the Arab uprisings that followed the Iraq war had a conve-nient timing for proponents of Bush administration polices, there is no evi-dence that those policies made democracy more attractive to Arabs. In fact, by contrasting a devastated Iraq with the relative security of their own countries, the war bought Arab autocrats some time. In the years immedi-ately following the start of the war, particularly in 2004 and 2005, Iraqi suicide bombings, sectarian conflict, and reports and images of torture and abuse helped Arab rulers from Syria to Jordan to Egypt. Faced with demands for increased democracy—or his own overthrow—a ruler could simply ask, "Would you rather live in Damascus, Amman, Cairo—or Baghdad?"

In fact, to the extent that the Iraq war helped rouse the Arab public into action, it was more in observing their utter helplessness during a decade that mattered most for the future of the people in the region. Their voices were never heard, and for that they blamed America as much as they blamed their own governments for being subservient to Washington. And to add insult to injury, they were being told that it was all for their own good, that democ-racy was on the way. Democracy *was* on the way, but for different reasons altogether.

What Type of Democracy Do Arabs Seek?

Arabs want freedom and democracy; they know democracy when they see it, and it mostly looks like Western-style democracies. But is this what they want for their countries? One clue can be found in Arab attitudes toward Turkey.

---

1. This is not particularly surprising, since the Kurds, who had been suppressed by Saddam Hussein, acquired more autonomy (and oil revenues) than ever before. The Sunni Arabs, who are a minority in Iraq, had a disproportionate share of the power, which they lost after the war. The Shiites, who constitute a minority, had limited influence and became the dominant power in the country after the war.

When I reviewed the results of my polls in 2011 and 2012, I noticed an apparent contradiction. On the one hand, Arabs greatly admire Turkey for its democratic government and leaders. On the other hand, Turkey was listed by almost none of our respondents as one of the top democratic countries in the world. My interpretation of this is that Arabs want democracy and freedom for sure, but they also hope to balance it with other things they want.

Despite not appearing on that list of favored democracies, Turkey is increasingly seen as a desirable *political* model across the Arab world. In October 2011, I conducted a poll of Egyptians asking, "If Egypt's political system looked like that of one of the following countries [France, the United States, Iran, Turkey, Saudi Arabia, Germany, China, Tunisia, Morocco, or the United Kingdom], which one would you prefer?" This polling came after the revolution when Egyptians' answers would have had a heightened sense of meaning. In the past, France had frequently topped this list. This time the number one answer by far was Turkey, with 44 percent (Figure 9.4).

Reinforcing the choice of Turkey were questions about the vision for a new Egyptian president. In the 2011 poll, Egyptians wanted their president to look most like Turkish prime minister Recep Erdogan. The Turkish leader

FIGURE 9.4 Country Political System Preference, Egypt, October 2011

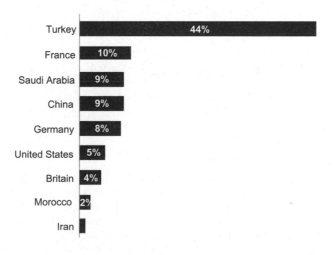

If Egypt's political system looked like that of one of the
following countries, which one would you prefer it to be?
(EGYPT ONLY)

Turkey	44%
France	10%
Saudi Arabia	9%
China	9%
Germany	8%
United States	5%
Britain	4%
Morocco	2%
Iran	

was also the preferred model for an Egyptian president among Arabs polled in the other five countries (Saudi Arabia, Morocco, Jordan, Lebanon, and the United Arab Emirates).

So why, if Arabs broadly view Western democracy and freedom favorably, do they not necessarily choose any of these Western countries as a model?

A second poll I conducted in Egypt, in May of 2012, pointed toward some answers. This time I asked about the most appealing role of religion in politics when they look at other Muslim-majority countries such as Saudi Arabia, Morocco, Tunisia, Turkey, Iran, and Malaysia. Once again Turkey was in first place by far, with 54 percent, followed by Saudi Arabia.[2] The choice of Turkey suggests that Egyptians and other Arabs are looking for a democratic model that incorporates aspects relevant for their identity, particularly the Islamic character of Turkey's democracy, and also Turkey's relative independence and ability to stand up to the United States and Israel—as indicated in Arabs' preference for Erdogan as leader. Iran also stands up to the United States and Israel but is not the model they choose, partly for sectarian reasons—Iran's population is mostly Shiite, while Turkey's is Sunni—but also because religion is generally seen to be too intrusive in the Islamic Republic of Iran. Saudi Arabia is both Arab and Sunni majority, and part of its attraction is its relative wealth, which many Egyptians experience as workers there and also during the Haj, the annual Muslim pilgrimages. Yet it still finished behind Turkey, largely because religion is seen as holding too much sway in that country as well.

The Egyptian resistance to religious extremism was seen in accusations that President Morsi, the candidate of Egypt's Muslim Brotherhood, took his orders from the *Murshed*, the spiritual guide of the Muslim Brotherhood. These not-so-subtle comparisons to Iran were meant to delegitimize the president. As a result Morsi has constantly tried to distance himself and his decisions from the Brotherhood, even as he continues to rely on their support.

---

2. Obviously there are differences between Turkey, a secular and democratic state in which a political party with an Islamist bent has been elected, and Saudi Arabia, a monarchy that applies a strict interpretation of Sharia Islamic law. Most Egyptians prefer Turkey, but a significant minority chooses Saudi Arabia, indicating an Egyptian divide, with many of the ultra-religious segments of the Egyptian public favoring a strict interpretation of Sharia law.

Most Arabs are Muslim, many are religious, and a significant number identify themselves as Muslim first. As noted earlier, Egyptians identify themselves as religious more than any other people polled on the subject globally.[3] And as Muslims, they care about Sharia, or religious laws and norms. It is hard to find a Muslim who says that Sharia is irrelevant. The debate is instead centered on the issue of compatibility of Sharia and democracy. On this there are many public opinion studies and a thoughtful book by Steven Kull analyzes some of the findings.[4]

As these questions stopped being theoretical in revolutionary Arab countries, particularly Tunisia, Libya, and Egypt, the debate acquired more consequential meaning—Arabs were actually envisioning the sort of system they wanted to have. It is noteworthy that almost all agreed that Sharia should be a basis for the constitution, including the pro-Western secularists in Libya who constituted the largest elected bloc in the Libyan parliament and many of the Egyptian candidates for president who were running against the Muslim Brotherhood. The issue was—and will remain so going forward— the extent to which Sharia should play a central political role and how people interpret Sharia as they build new political systems.

On the eve of Egypt's presidential elections in May 2012, I asked a question specifically about Sharia. Egypt has a strong Islamist movement, not only in the well-established Muslim Brotherhood but also in the ultra-religious Salafis, who surprisingly won more than a quarter of the vote in Egypt's first free parliamentary elections. Salafis are among those in the Arab world who want to impose strict Sharia law, including its harsh penal code, as the law of the land. In November 2012 the Salafis mobilized tens of thousands of Egyptian demonstrators demanding this Islamic law. But Egypt also has a strong Christian minority, mostly Coptic, constituting about 10 percent of the population, as well as many secularists who either don't want to see religion and politics mix together or want constitutional guarantees to protect the rights of minorities. Islamists themselves are also divided on how

---

3. In a 2007–2008 Gallup global poll in 143 countries and territories asking, "Is religion an important part of your daily life?," Egyptians ranked in first place. In fact, of the top ten most religious people, most were from Muslim-majority countries, including the most populous, Indonesia, and they were within the margin of error of Egyptians. Available online at: www.gallup.com/poll/114211/Alabamians-Iranians-Common.aspx.
4. Steven Kull, *Feeling Betrayed: The Roots of Muslim Anger at America* (Washington, DC: Brookings Institution Press, 2011).

much of a role religion should play in politics. These views were central in the debate about the nature of a new Egyptian constitution—whose content will ultimately be far more important than the results of the elections.

Indeed, it was the fights over the content of the constitution that generated the most intense confrontations in Egypt in 2012 and 2013 and revealed the emerging societal divide, particularly with regard to the role of religion. The constitution and the role that Sharia had in it—as well as the degree of presidential powers—motivated hundreds of thousands of Egyptian demonstrators in November and December 2012, divided between those who supported a strong role for Sharia and those who didn't. And although a constitution was ultimately drafted and was approved by over 60 percent of Egyptians voting, only about a third of Egyptians participated in the vote. In Cairo— which is not only Egypt's capital and its most populous city but also its economic, cultural, and political center—a majority rejected the constitution. In other words, the new constitution's legitimacy was immediately called into question and galvanized the opposition, which called for modifications.

The battle for the role of Sharia will outlive the debate on altering the new constitution, as interpretations and applications will continue to be debated for years to come. Even the 1971 constitution that was in force during Mubarak's era stated that "the principles of Sharia are the main source of legislation." The new constitution passed in December 2012 also cites Sharia as "the principle source of legislation." One key difference is that the latter gives the role of interpreting that law not to the courts, but to Islamic scholars at Cairo's al-Azhar University. This is critical, because in the end the battle is over interpretation and who has the ultimate authority to provide it.

But how does the public interpret the role of Sharia? The key is to try to understand how literally Arabs want to see Sharia applied in practice. My question in May 2012 attempted to gauge what the broader public wants and will tolerate with regard to Islam's role in the Egyptian government.

Although less than 10 percent of respondents said that the role of religion in politics is the most important factor in their voting in both the parliamentary and the presidential elections, two-thirds of respondents (66 percent) said they supported making Sharia the basis of Egyptian law. Significantly, of those who supported Sharia as the basis of law, only 17 percent said that they prefer applying Sharia literally, including the penal code, while 83 percent said they prefer applying the spirit of Sharia but with adaptation to modern times.

The meaning of "applying the spirit of Sharia but with adaptation to modern times" will always be subject to debate, but it is clear that the majority of the public, at least in Egypt, is opposed to strict implementation of Sharia. The Egyptian choice of Turkey as a model country when it comes to combining politics and religion further indicates the tough fight ahead for those aiming for more extreme views throughout the newly empowered Arab world. As in Egypt, much will obviously depend on how postrevolution Arab constitutions are written. That will be the biggest battle in the coming months and years as political systems in the region continue to evolve.

In Tunisia, for example, the dominant al-Nahda Islamist party has agreed to avoid invoking Sharia specifically in the constitution as long as there is a reference to Islam as Tunisia's religion. The group's leader, Rachid al-Ghannouchi, declared in September 2012 that the Islamist Salafis were a danger to Tunisia. These are obviously unsettled battles in a changing Arab world, but the authenticity of the popular uprisings has generated an authentic debate—and sometimes even determined action. In Libya, another North African country that deposed its leader, ultra-religious militants attacked the U.S. Consulate in Benghazi, in September 2012, killing four Americans, including the ambassador. At the time, anger was raging in several Arab nations over a provocative anti-Islamic film made in the United States, but soon after the attack Libyan demonstrators attacked Ansar al-Sharia, the Islamist activists accused of perpetrating the attack, and forced them to close their bases. So popular sentiment is likely to go back and forth, in country after country, as these issues are worked out.

Religion's Balancing Act

Because religion is such an important and complex part of how Arabs imagine an ideal political system, the questions I asked across six countries regarding the role of religion take on added weight. Although I shied away from questions that directly put the respondents in an uncomfortable position in authoritarian environments, such as asking directly about the popularity of their governments or of their rulers, or the degree to which they felt these rulers reflected Islamic values, I sought to find indirect indicators.

One of the questions asked over the decade regards the extent to which the Arab public wants to see clergy play a role in politics. And the results show that Arabs are widely divided over the issue, within each country and across countries (Figure 9.5). In some Arab countries a plurality of people wanted to see the clergy play a bigger role than they were perceived to be playing prior to the Arab uprisings. For example, in the last poll conducted prior to the Tunisian and Egyptian revolutions, in 2010, a plurality of respondents in four of the six countries studied, including in Egypt and Saudi Arabia, expressed the view that the clergy play too small a role in the politics of Arab countries. In Lebanon and the United Arab Emirates, however, more than 40 percent of respondents wanted the clergy to play a smaller role. Again the point needs to be made: Arabs are not homogeneous, on this issue or any other, even though they have strong shared identities.

FIGURE 9.5 Political Role of Clergy, 2010

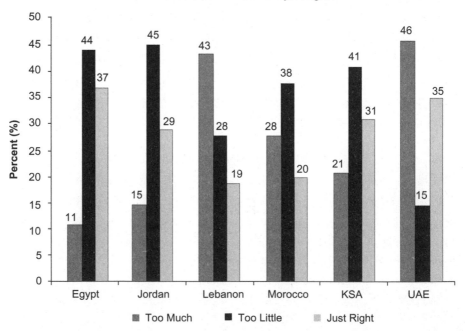

When you look at Arab countries today and think about government and politics, do you feel the clergy play too much of a role, too little a role, or is their role just right?

At the same time, respondents in the four countries that thought clergy played too small a role were divided when asked to choose which of two statements was closer to their views: "Religion must be respected but the clergy must not dictate our political system" and "Clergy must play a greater role in our political system" (Figure 9.6). Although the results were close, only respondents in Saudi Arabia thought clergy should play a greater role. The bottom line is that Arabs are split on the issue of the role of clergy, which reflects a broader division we found first in Egypt in the close results of the presidential elections in 2012—with the candidate supported by religious parties, Mohammad Morsi, winning by less than 4 percent over his opponent, Ahmad Shafik—and later in the intensity of the competing demonstrations over the role of Sharia in the constitution. It should be noted,

FIGURE 9.6 Political Role of Clergy, Question Rephrased

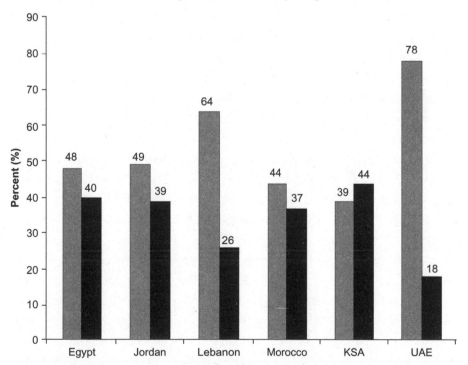

Which of the following statements would you agree with more?

■ Statement A: Religion must be respected, but clergy should not dictate the political system.
■ Statement B: Clergy must play a greater role in our political system.

however, that among those who want to see a larger role for the clergy are many who see the clergy as more moral than the politicians they know. The anticorruption mood among Arabs is very strong.

The relationship between the Egyptian public and the Muslim Brotherhood provided an early indicator of this public desire for a role for Islam in government, balanced by a wariness of extremism. A long-suppressed political party, the Brotherhood quickly emerged after the revolution as the best-organized group in the country, giving it a jump on the other parties, which had little time to get their acts together before Egypt's first free elections.

The Muslim Brotherhood did receive a majority of the vote in the parliamentary elections, but its subsequent heavy-handed attempts to dominate the writing of the constitution, and its decision to field a presidential candidate of its own after it had promised not to do so generated a public backlash and helped energize the disorganized opposition. The low turnout in the presidential elections—only 46 percent of the electorate voted—should have helped the Muslim Brotherhood because they were better organized, but their candidate, Muhammad Morsi, won only 26 percent of the vote in a field of eleven candidates. Although Morsi ultimately won the run-off election, the results were within 4 percentage points, despite the fact that his opponent, Ahmad Shafik, was a Mubarak appointee who was seen as backed by the military and the old-regime elites. In Egypt and in other Arab countries creating new political structures, a strong Islamist voice is all but certain to emerge, especially given the Islamists' superior organization. But unlike Iran after the 1979 revolution, when Islamists shut out secular voices and imposed a clerical regime, the Arab public empowerment in the information age and the diversity of views on the role of religion in politics ensures that authority will be widely contested. 2013 is not 1979. There may be attempts to monopolize power, as Egyptian opposition groups have accused the Muslim Brotherhood and President Morsi of doing. But the very forces that enabled Arab uprisings in the first place, without a need for political parties, will enable Arabs to contest any fresh attempts at imposing new dictatorships. Where democratic reform does not take hold, instability—with opposing forces pitted against each other—is more likely than new dictatorships, religious or otherwise.

Attitudes Toward the Role of Women

If democracy and freedom are the aims of most Arabs, those in the population who need them most—women—fear a setback, especially as Islamist parties ascend to power, as in Egypt and Tunisia. How do Arabs view the role of women in society and the workplace, and what are the prospects that women, too, will be empowered as the uprisings and political change continue across the region?

Women start with huge disadvantages. It is well known that Arab and Muslim societies broadly are behind the rest of the world when it comes to important measures of women's role in society. This fact has been established in numerous studies, including the 2005 Arab Human Development Report and studies by the World Bank. Despite important variations from country to country, the gender gap was wide in many dimensions, especially with regard to women in the workforce, political positions, and societal rights—including women's lack of the right to vote or even drive in Saudi Arabia, which that government only recently has begun to address.

Female activists have played a significant role in the Arab uprisings; they took to the streets and employed social media to spread information and organize demonstrators—often with risks that went beyond arrests or even tear gas. Many endured humiliating treatment, including "virginity tests" conducted by the Egyptian military on female demonstrators in Tahrir Square, and accusations of drug use, sexual promiscuity, and anything else that could shame them in mostly traditional societies. The efforts of these women activists were ultimately recognized when Tawakkol Karman, the charismatic female Yemeni activist, was included as one of the three women who were awarded the 2011 Nobel Peace Prize.

Yet the fact that women played important roles in the Arab revolutions does not guarantee that this can be translated into long-term gains for women's rights. After the Algerian revolution against French control in the early 1960s and the 1987 Palestinian intifada, women quickly reverted to more traditional roles.

The information revolution provides empowerment that knows no gender. And it has exposed women to the lives of women in other countries and connected them with international women's rights organizations. These factors could dramatically increase their expectations and their opportunities to organize and affect the public discourse. During a lecture tour in Saudi Arabia in October 2012, I visited the women's college in Dhahran. The director noted that the young women arriving from sheltered homes are at once taught to conduct research, especially on the Internet. Before the end of their first year, they start tweeting about politics and injustice.

But the societal barriers facing women remain great. On the one hand, there is overwhelming support in every country for more gender equality. In Arab Human Development Report polls[5] in Jordan, Lebanon, Egypt, and Morocco, 84 percent of those polled among the general population said, "Gender equality relates to your total concept of freedom." Over 90 percent said that girls and boys should have the same rights to education and to work, and 79 percent said that they should have the same right to "political action." On the other hand, only 46 percent of Egyptians and 54 percent of Jordanians said women had the right to assume the position of a government minister, and only 47 percent of Egyptians and 55 percent of Jordanians thought women should have the right to be judges. Overall, only an average 50 percent over the four countries—26 percent in Egypt and 39 percent in Jordan, 55 percent in Morocco, and 81 percent in Lebanon—thought that women should have the right to be head of state.

For now it is evident that the gap between men and women in the region remains wide. According to a World Bank study, the countries of the Middle East and North Africa have a lower participation of women in the workforce than any other region, including sub-Saharan Africa.[6] This gap tended to be particularly acute for less-educated women. For instance, 52 percent of women in Morocco and 48 percent in Yemen with postsecondary education earned wages, compared with only 10 percent of women with primary education in Morocco and 6 percent in Yemen.[7]

5. Arab Human Development Report, "Towards the Rise of Women in the Arab World," United Nations Development Programme, 2005. Available online at: www.arab-hdr.org/publications/contents/2005/annexes-e.pdf.
6. Talajeh Livani, "Middle East and North Africa: Gender Overview," The World Bank, 2007. Available online at: http://siteresources.worldbank.org/INTMENA/Resources/MENA_Gender_Overview_2007.pdf.
7. According to polls conducted by the Institute for Women's Policy Research (IWPR). See the IWPR reports, "Status of Women in the Middle East and North Africa." Available online at: www.iwpr.org/initiatives/swmena.

The correlation between education and employment in some countries is a hopeful sign, because more women are acquiring higher education. In a number of countries, including Saudi Arabia, women outnumber men as university students. This alone is potentially significant. But there are still huge cultural, political, and economic barriers to translating higher education directly into employment for women.

The cultural and religious norms that underlie many of the barriers to women's rights don't change quickly and may even be further emphasized in revolutionary environments, as has been the case in Tunisia and Egypt since their revolutions. In both countries, before the revolutions the largely secular ruling elites had opened space for women in the public square, but without truly addressing the core problems that have served as barriers to more meaningful women's empowerment.

The plight of religious women in the Arab world raises special issues and new opportunities. Many had been discriminated against before the uprisings. Veiled women in Tunisia, for example, were prevented from attending public schools or working in government jobs. Even in Egypt, veiled women were not allowed to work as announcers on state television. The first woman announcer wearing *hijab* took her place in August 2012, but secular women feared the imposition of restrictive religious norms and laws. In politics, the early picture for women was also mixed. Few women were elected to the new Egyptian Parliament, but about one-quarter of new parliamentary members in Tunisia were women, which was roughly double their percentage before the revolution. Of those, the highest percentage is to be found among the Islamist al-Nahda party's block.[8]

The debate about gender equality often takes the form of debating the "meaning" of equality, with some religious Muslims in the Arab world and elsewhere seeing women in the West as having fewer rights than meet the eyes and arguing that the emphasis on appearance and physical attributes has been demeaning to women and has reduced them to objects of male desire. These arguments may win over some among the most ardent supporters who want to prevent change—and unfortunately may provide a psychological

---

8. This was a function of an electoral law, endorsed by al-Nahda, that required every other candidate of each party's slate to be a woman. Many small parties started with a male candidate and won only one seat; by default, the party that won most seats, al-Nahda, had a greater percentage of women.

rationalization for being simultaneously in favor of women's rights and of placing limits on women.

Along with the diversity of views on women among Arabs and Muslims, there are also real differences across time and space in the status of women in Arab and Muslim societies. Nothing in Arab or Muslim culture or religion inherently prevents women's advancement. Religious scholars have debated these issues for over a hundred years, with several scholars arguing that the veil many Muslim women wear is a product of custom and culture, not religion. In the more recent debate in Egypt, one of the Islamist candidates and a former member of the Muslim Brotherhood, Abdul Mounem Abou Fatouh, expressed moderate, even liberal, views on the role of women, which he had written about earlier: "The woman is rational, spiritual, mental, and physical. Islam encourages her to advance herself in society with her reason, mind, and spirit, with all of her capacities and abilities. As for her body, society should not have a say in that issue and her appearance should not be a criteria to judge her as a human being."[9]

The diversity of Islamic opinions, the variation in the status of women from country to country, and the differences in expressed opinions are all indicative of the fact that there are other forces at work.

Women's Roles in Different Economies

One of the most important drivers of change, particularly when it comes to the rights of women in society, is earning wages, a key instrument of empowerment. There are certainly barriers to women's employment in most Arab societies, as some of the survey research on this issue has indicated. For example, in polls conducted by the Institute for Women's Policy Research (IWPR),[10] 64 percent of women in Yemen and 30 percent in Morocco said they are restricted from leaving the house, mostly due to family-imposed restrictions, but also because of potential harassment in the streets.

Yet these barriers may themselves be a function of economic needs and opportunities that vary across Muslim-majority countries. To understand the relationship between economic need and openness to women's mobility, I

---

9. Abdel Moneim Aboul Fotouh, "Islamist Views of Reform," in *Reform in the Muslim World: The Role of Islamists and Outside Powers*, ed. Shibley Telhami (Washington, DC: Brookings Institution, 2008).
10. See "Status of Women in the Middle East and North Africa."

have asked one specific question over the decade: "Do you believe women should have the right to work outside the home: always? only when economically needed? or never?" The results help illuminate the issue.

For every year and every country we studied (Egypt, Saudi Arabia, Morocco, Lebanon, Jordan, and the United Arab Emirates), we found that fewer than one-fifth of Arabs polled believed that women should never have the right to work outside the house; roughly a third or more said that women should always have the right to work outside the house. Not surprisingly, more men expressed the former and more women expressed the latter view. But the largest group, ranging from a plurality to a majority, said they believed women should have the right to work only when economically needed. There were variations among Arab states, but in all cases the number of people answering "never" was always a small minority, as in the result shown in Figure 9.7. In the United Arab Emirates, fewer people say "always" in comparison to

FIGURE 9.7 Right of Women to Work Outside the Home, 2010

Do you think women should have the right to work outside the home?

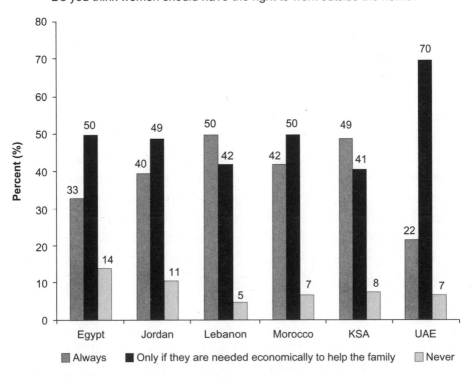

the others, likely because of the large number of female foreign workers (who outnumber the citizens and tend to have far lower status than the locals).

These results suggest that the restrictions on women working outside the house are not fixed and are a function of economic needs and opportunity. During my visit to the women's college in relatively wealthy Saudi Arabia in 2012, I was told by a college administrator that employable young women have become more attractive marriage candidates as family income needs have grown. The results shown in Figure 9.7 also support the work of Michael Ross, a professor at UCLA, who has suggested that women's political rights in the Middle East are connected more to the political economies of the Middle East than to religion or culture. Ross argues that women in the Middle East lag behind women in other regions in making political and economic gains principally because "oil production reduces the number of women in the labor force, which in turn reduces their political influence. As a result, oil-producing states are more strongly dominated by men than similar states without oil."[11]

When women have the chance to earn their own wages, they are more likely to delay childbirth and to have fewer children, and parents are more likely to invest in their daughters' health and education when they see them as future contributors to family income. Women's entrance into the workforce results in more political power.

In Ross's view, there are two reasons oil wealth keeps women in the home. First, the more oil a country produces, the more difficult it is for manufacturing companies to remain profitable, as a rise in the exchange rate makes imported goods cheaper. The types of factories that are most likely to hire women are export-oriented companies that rely on low-wage labor, and the increase in oil production will almost certainly make them unprofitable. Most of the jobs produced in an oil-based economy will be in construction, retail, and government. Unless women can find positions in these sectors, a booming oil industry will make it harder for them to enter the labor force.

---

11. See Michael Ross, "The Impact of Oil Wealth on Women in the Middle East," in *Oil, Globalization, and Political Reform*, ed. Shibley Telhami (Washington, DC: Brookings Institution, 2009), 17. Available online at: www.brookings.edu/~/media/research/files/papers/2009/2/oil%20 telhami/02_oil_telhami.pdf.

Second, oil production creates large government revenues that encourage women to stay at home. Governments transfer more money to households as oil revenues rise, through welfare programs, subsidies, and tax reductions. While increased household income may make life more comfortable, it reduces the need for a second income and may result in daily life being more male-dominated as fewer women work outside the home.[12]

> In general, the states that are richest in oil (Saudi Arabia, Qatar, Bahrain, United Arab Emirates, and Oman) have been the most reluctant to grant female suffrage, have the fewest women in their parliaments, have the fewest women in their nonagricultural workforce, and offer women the fewest rights. States with little or no oil (Morocco, Tunisia, Lebanon, Syria, Djibouti) were the first to grant female suffrage, tend to have more women in parliament and the workplace, and grant women more rights.[13]

Whether or not one completely accepts the argument about the specific effects of the oil economy on employment and politics, there can be little doubt that women's empowerment often follows economic empowerment through earning wages, which in turn leads to cultural and normative change. Unless opportunities and incentives are created to increase women's participation in the workforce, women's empowerment in politics and society will remain stagnant. That said, cultural and religious norms as well as man-made laws will continue to place limits on women's freedom in the Arab world, despite revolutions advocating freedom, and even with expanding educational opportunities for some women, particularly in the oil-producing states.

As with freedom and democracy in a rapidly changing Arab world, the future role of women is a balancing act in the short term that can fall in either direction. But the bet in the long term favors more women's rights, partly because of rising economic needs and partly because women, like the rest of society, are increasingly empowered by the information revolution.

---

12. Ross, "The Impact of Oil Wealth on Women in the Middle East," 18–19.
13. Ross, "The Impact of Oil Wealth on Women in the Middle East," 20–22.

CHAPTER 10

GLOBAL PERSPECTIVES

ONE MANIFEST ARAB PUBLIC ASPIRATION since the end of the cold war has been to counter American power, which is seen to have empowered Israel and limited the prospects of Arab influence in the Gulf and elsewhere. Two decades of continual U.S. military activity and political intervention in the region, especially after the horrific attacks on American soil on 9/11, cemented among Arabs the need for a global counterweight to the United States. But there is a second, related, political desire through which Arabs view the larger world: a craving for Arab advancement and empowerment. This overarching need has a much longer history than resistance to the United States. It is rooted in two centuries without an indigenous Arab power able to resist incursion and lead its people into the modern political era.

Two Centuries of Arab Aspirations

Beginning in the nineteenth century, Arabs felt that intrusive Western powers were preventing the emergence of a powerful Arab center on the world stage. Still under the domination of a decaying Ottoman Empire, Egyptians had a golden opportunity to expand their power at the Ottomans' expense. In 1839, for example, Egyptian forces advanced against the weakened Ottomans and might well have emerged as a dominant power in the region had it not been for Western intervention aimed at preventing the empire's collapse. Europe's later division of Arab lands after World War I—and the inevitable dissolution of the remnants of the Ottoman Empire—has had a lasting impact well into the twenty-first century.

Most Arab states had achieved independence by World War II. The exceptions were Algeria, controlled by the French until 1962, and the small states in the Gulf region, controlled by Britain until 1971. But for most Arabs, independence did not equate with true freedom. The second half of the twentieth century would see continued Western suppression of strong Arab states. The most promising flash of regional leadership began in the 1950s with the rise of Pan-Arabism under the leadership of the widely admired Egyptian leader, Gamal Abd al-Nasser. But Arab ambitions to control their destiny were confounded in 1956 when England, France, and Israel attacked Nasser's Egypt in a dispute over the Suez Canal. The United States also sought to limit Nasser's power by supporting his enemies in the region, most prominently through the 1955 "Baghdad Pact," a military alliance with the United Kingdom, Pakistan, Turkey, and Iran.

In the 1950s, the Eisenhower administration secretly went beyond even its stern public posture of calling Arab states out on the cold war confrontation with the Soviet Union. Ike's message had been basically "If you are not a friend, you are an enemy." But fearful that an anti-Western regime could control critical oil resources, the president privately broadened a Truman administration policy that sought to deny the Soviet Union control of Middle Eastern oil. If the USSR invaded the Arabian Peninsula, Truman's "oil-denial" strategy included blowing up the region's oil fields, and indeed, the CIA was ordered to place explosives in these fields, without the knowledge of host governments. As Nasser and his supporters gained more power in the late 1950s, the policy was broadened. If a hostile regional regime emerged, the United States would deny that regime control of its own natural resources by blowing up its oil fields. It has never been confirmed when or whether this policy was discontinued, but it was nonetheless indicative of the American fear of the emergence of local powers independent of or hostile to Western interests.

The biggest setbacks to hopes of Arab revival and power on the world stage came at the hands of Israel, in the disastrous 1967 war. Egypt's Nasser had given Arabs their greatest modern hope for achieving their aspirations. Yet, in six short days, Israel decisively defeated Syria, Jordan, and Egypt, seizing territory from each nation. Given Arabs' belief that Israel's devastating modern military was possible only as the result of Western support, it has since been hard for Arabs to separate Israel's humiliating victory from

Western domination. Not only did the Western powers, especially France before 1967, provide Israel with essential military hardware; the link between the West and Israel has been strong throughout Israel's relatively brief history—even though the Zionist movement that led to the creation of Israel had little to do with Western aims or interests. European countries like France, and then later the United States, have long provided critical political, economic, and military backing for Israel. This support has also allowed Israel to maintain policies that have often been opposed by most nations around the world. So when Arabs are angry at Israel or blame it for a particular policy or outcome, it is automatically associated in their minds with the West, principally the United States since 1967, for empowering Israel.

Arabs looking for a strong, vibrant Arab state have had few signs of hope since Nasser's death in 1970. Egypt, the most powerful and populous Arab state, made peace with Israel in 1979 and became a close ally of the West. Few other Arab states offered even the potential to become contending powers on their own. The one possible Arab power was Iraq, which had emerged as a leader of those opposing Egypt's peace with Israel and became a wealthy state following the oil boom of the 1970s. But hopes for a dominant Iraq faded after the nation launched a bloody and economically draining eight-year war with Iran during the 1980s.

As the twentieth century drew to an end, Arab frustration over Western and Israeli control and influence in the region manifested itself in conspiracy theories. Though the enormous waste of lives and resources during the Iran-Iraq war could not be laid at the feet of Western powers, popular conspiracy theorists nonetheless suggested that the West and Israel had somehow "lured" Iraq into attacking Iran to weaken two promising Muslim states; or that, at a minimum, the West did little to stop the grinding war because it benefited from the weakening of the two Muslim states. Later theories held that the United States gave Iraq's Saddam Hussein the "green light" to invade Kuwait in 1990 so that the United States would have an excuse to position its forces in the oil region. The 2003 U.S.-led invasion of Iraq, which was difficult for most in the region to understand, was seen as a more blatant attempt to dominate the region.

Whether the conspiracy theories regarding American motivations and involvement in Iraq were mere figments of Arab imagination or had a kernel of truth, they nonetheless illustrate the framework through which many

Arabs view global realities. These fears of Western designs in their region have roots in a century of very real conspiracies and unilateral action against Arab interests. And Arabs' angry perception that some of their rulers often acted as instruments of Western powers is more than just fantasy.

Arab Public Views of World Powers

Today, Arabs' perceptions of global power are inseparable from what they regard as dominant and threatening states: Israel at the regional level and the United States at the international level. Many also embrace ideas or models to be emulated in the pursuit of Arab progress. In my polls following the 2003 U.S.-led invasion of Iraq, I have sought to gain some insight into these two driving trends.

These dynamics played out in an interesting way during the American occupation of Iraq. When asked which two countries pose the biggest threat to them, Arabs consistently rank Israel number one (Figure 10.1). This is never a surprising result: Israel is the strongest military power in the Middle East; a non-Arab, non-Muslim state that has been engaged in almost continual armed conflict with its neighbors since 1948 and occupying Arab lands since 1967. What was noteworthy following the U.S. occupation of Iraq was

FIGURE 10.1 The Two Countries That Pose the Largest Threat, Six-Country Totals, 2005

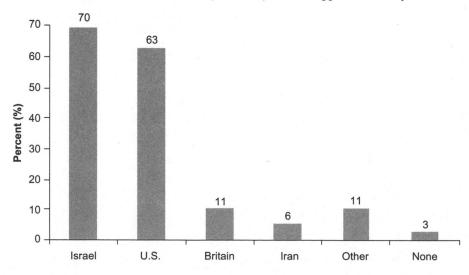

Name the TWO countries that you think pose the biggest threat to you:

that a large majority of Arabs perceived the United States—a country that implicitly or explicitly provides military protection for several of the polled nations—to be almost as threatening as Israel.

Another question asked annually has respondents express their preferences for a world power from a list of seven countries: the United States, the United Kingdom, France, Germany, China, Russia, and Pakistan. Respondents were asked, "In a world where there is only one power, which of the following countries would you prefer to be that superpower?" The most obvious change since the start of the uprisings came at the top, where long-standing number one France was dethroned by China, but making sense of Arabs' perceptions of seven very different countries provides a unique insight into how long-standing Arab desires are playing out today.

The biggest single factor in these answers is the long-standing concern about an unchecked U.S. role in the region. Unsurprisingly, the United States and its presumed ally Britain finished near the bottom. Anger with U.S. policies in the region led respondents to embrace the country they feared less. But the shifts in rankings were also driven by perceptions of which countries had the demonstrated capability to be a world power. For example, Pakistan, the only Muslim country on the list, has not ranked high, particularly in recent

FIGURE 10.2 Preferred World Power, 2005–2011

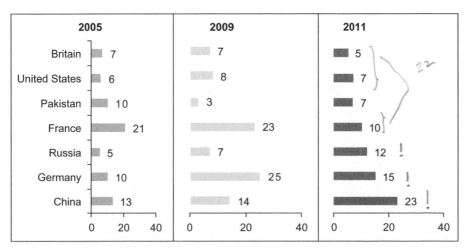

In a world where there is only one power, which of the following countries would you prefer to be that superpower?

years. This is probably because, despite the country's nuclear capacity, Arabs do not see Pakistan as having real capabilities to play the role of superpower.

The movement among the other four countries is more interesting. Russia's historically low rankings were in part due to the perception of a decline in power following the end of the cold war, especially a lag in technological progress in contrast to Western states or China. Few products are sold in the Middle East with a "made in Russia" label, and technology is a psychological indicator of capabilities. But there is another factor: the Chechnya war, which has been very unpopular in the Arab world as in other Muslim-majority countries, as it pitted Russia against a Muslim population. But although it has ranked low as a preferred superpower throughout the period, Russia has risen along with China in the post-Arab uprisings poll—most likely because Arabs were passionately divided on the desirability of international intervention, particularly in Syria, and Russia's opposition earned high marks with a segment of the Arab public, while alienating others.

Meanwhile, Germany, France, and China are the biggest movers on the list—each of them changed rankings and moved at least 10 percentage points in various directions between 2005 and 2011. Since the end of World War II, Germany has played a limited political role in the Middle East but has generally been admired for its technological and financial power. It has been somewhere in the middle of the preferred powers by Arabs, but it has gained at the expense of France since 2009. Germany has taken a cautious approach toward the Arab uprisings, but in recent years it has become more involved in the arms trade to both Arabs and Israelis, something that has at times made Israel uneasy. As Germany raises its profile in the Middle East, it will increasingly face the tension of trying to please both Arabs and Israelis.

France, a Western power with a Middle Eastern colonial history, has long been an Arab favorite on multiple dimensions, and it is striking that Arab admiration has declined since the Arab uprisings, although it is not clear whether this will be a lasting effect. France's relationship with the Arabs since the end of World War II is a tale of two chapters. France was Israel's central military backer before the 1967 war. Israel's successful offensive in 1967, particularly from the air, was carried out with French-supplied airplanes, and its nuclear reactor in Dimona was built with French help. In North Africa, France remained engaged in bloody battles in Algeria and did not withdraw from that country until 1962. So, though I didn't have public opinion polls at that time, it isn't hard to imagine what Arabs thought of France during this period.

But in 1967 France shifted its policy almost entirely. That shift began with a decision to stop supplying Israel with weapons, after which the United States moved to become Israel's key supplier. The public French explanation had to do with the 1967 war itself, when the French warned the Israelis to not initiate a full war in the face of Egypt's threatening moves. When Israel failed to heed French warnings, France stopped sending military supplies to Israel. But in reality, French interests were shifting in favor of trade with the Arab world.

Since then, France regularly took positions on Middle Eastern issues that were far more sympathetic to the Arabs than Washington's, and as noted earlier, its efforts seemed to pay off—climaxing in the years immediately after the 2003 Iraq war. Although prime minister Nicolas Sarkozy failed to achieve the personal popularity of his predecessor in the Arab world, France remained the prefered power until the start of the Arab uprisings. Remarkably, France's popularity continued despite tension within its Arab and Muslim immigrant communities, particularly over the ban on wearing the Muslim *hijab* to public school. As noted earlier, though, two Muslim countries, Turkey and Tunisia, had also banned the head scarf in public institutions, and in Egypt, public television announcers were not allowed to wear the *hijab* until 2012.

China's rise in Arab public opinion over the decade is the leading indicator of Arab perceptions of a shift in global power, as well as of the value the region places on finding a legitimate counterweight to the United States. At the end of the cold war, when Arab elites were looking to foreign powers to compensate for the loss of the balancing power of the Soviet Union, the focus was on European and Japanese capabilities—China was hardly on the radar screen. But by the time of the Iraq war, it was clear that Japan was stuck in the economic doldrums, whereas China had become a rising star.

As a member of the United Nations Security Council, China stood with France in refusing to support the Iraq war. Both France and China, although to a more limited extent, were rewarded for their stances in Arab public opinion. The trillions of dollars and thousands of American lives that the United States lost in that war not only stoked Arab anger but, taken with the subsequent financial crisis, projected a weakened American power. As my

2011 poll shows, the greatest beneficiary has been China, a seemingly vibrant nation flush with cash.

Saudi Arabia did not even have official relations with China until 1990, but along with many other Arab nations, it has since developed strong pragmatic economic ties. Today China buys about half of its oil from Arab states, a volume that will only increase as China's economy continues to grow.[1] On his first official trip outside the Arab world, Egyptian president Morsi traveled to China with a large delegation that included scores of businessmen to clinch deals on trade and economic development. Some of America's close allies in the Gulf now visit China more frequently than they visit the United States, now that trade and development projects are growing as substantially as China's thirst for Middle East oil.

Little wonder, then, that China should be soaring in Arab eyes. China received much favorable attention in the Arab media in the lead-up to the 2008 Olympics. In addition, "the China Model" of rapid technological development has captured the imagination of some, bolstered by governments who feel safer touting a model that doesn't stress rapid democratic reform. However, China's quick rise as a preferred superpower should be read less as a full embrace than as a sign of hunger for a real counterbalance to American power. In this regard, China's top ranking in the 2011 poll suggests that Arabs believe that China is the country most likely to supplant the United States as global superpower.

Turkey Through Arab Eyes

These choices about preferred global superpowers were expressed in polls of a limited set of countries. In the May 2012 Egypt-only poll, I asked the same question about the preference for a superpower in a world where there is only one—but outside their own country—without providing a list of countries to choose from. The number one answer (41 percent) was Turkey.

As a leading Sunni Muslim democratic state at a time when Arabs are seeking a similar democracy, Turkey has much to recommend it. Historically, though, Turkey provided the "other" against which Arab political identity

1. Emile Hokayem, "Looking East: A Gulf Vision or a Reality?" International Institute for Strategic Studies, September 29, 2011. Available online at: www.iiss.org./whats-new/iiss-experts-commentary/looking-east-a-gulf-vision-or-a-reality/.

emerged in the nineteenth century. Many of Arabs' earliest battles were wars of independence fought against the Ottoman Empire. Arab national identity, as it emerged in the nineteenth century, was less a secular movement and more a differentiating feature of Muslim Arabs versus Muslim Turks. And Arabs were later prepared to join forces with the West to help bring down the Ottoman Empire, a fact that has remained a source of tension in relations between Turks and Arabs into modern times.

During the cold war, Turkey's membership in NATO and its friendship with Israel even during the intense years of Arab-Israeli conflict were not received well by many in the Arab world. And although it seems "natural" that Arab aspiration for an Islamic democracy would bring Arab nations closer to Turkey, Turkey has been a democratic nation for some time. Even after the rise of Islamic-affiliated parties and the decline of the power of Turkey's military, Arabs did not take particular note of Turkey and its leaders until the country took a position against the Iraq war, despite its NATO membership. Even then Turkey's leaders did not top the list of most-admired world leaders until Turkey's prime minister was seen to stand up to Israel more boldly than Arab leaders over the 2008 Gaza war between Israel and Hamas, in which about 1,400 Palestinians were killed versus only 13 Israelis.

In the end, Arab preference for a Turkish superpower is less about the nation's democracy and more about its embrace of Arab and Muslim aspirations and its projected ability to go its own way, to stand up to Israel on Gaza and to the United States on Iraq, and, as a Muslim country, to persist in the face of its rejected membership in the European Union, despite its role in NATO.

The case of Turkey reinforces the idea that Arabs are generally passing judgment about the world through two separate prisms, one of which seeks a balance to those threatening them while the other searches for a model to admire and emulate if they want to acquire their own independent power. These two frequently don't lead to the same place—Turkey's appeal is a rare convergence of both.

Arabs First

In 2009 and 2011 I also asked a question with a different angle on Arab opinions toward global powers. For the same list of seven countries, respondents

179

FIGURE 10.3 Preferred World-Power Country to Live in, Six-Country Totals, 2009–2011

If you had to live in one of the following countries, which one would you prefer most?

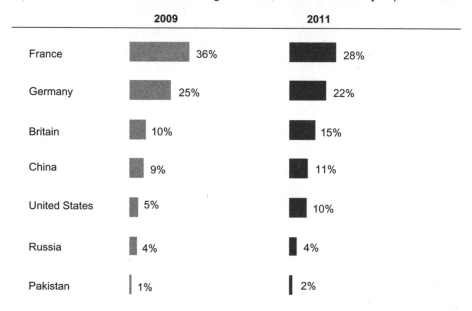

	2009	2011
France	36%	28%
Germany	25%	22%
Britain	10%	15%
China	9%	11%
United States	5%	10%
Russia	4%	4%
Pakistan	1%	2%

were asked, "If you had to live in one of the following countries, which one would you prefer most?" (Figure 10.3).

Of the top five nations, four of the selections are not surprising, given that they are generally considered to have a much higher standard of living than the bottom two. China's ranking above the United States reflects many of the considerations we have just been looking at: both an enthusiasm for China's booming economy as well as residual anger over U.S. policy, and perhaps a belief that Muslims and Arabs are routinely discriminated against in America. That Russia and Pakistan are the two lowest choices generally reflects the lower quality of life those nations offer, as documented in the United Nations Human Development Index—although it is worth mentioning that Russia (66) does finish significantly higher than China (101) in the UN index.[2]

It is, however, somewhat curious that Pakistan, a majority-Sunni Muslim country, was selected by almost no one. Though Pakistan is a very populous

---

2. The Human Development Index Rankings of 2011 is available online at: hdr.undp.org/en /statistics/.

country with a large middle class, it is also underdeveloped—a fact that would have been driven home to respondents in Saudi Arabia and the United Arab Emirates by their countries' large number of immigrant Pakistani workers. Nonetheless, most Arabs are Muslim and identify with other Muslims and care about crises and pain in other Muslim communities around the world. Arabs' Islamic focus was also increased by the confrontations that followed the tragedy of 9/11 and the Iraq war. But Pakistan's low ranking also reflects the fact that Arabs tend to focus more on Arab issues—even most of their Islamic movements are locally focused.

In fact, global jihadist groups like Al Qaeda have criticized just that Arab-first tendency among the dominant Islamist groups in the Arab world, from the mainstream Muslim Brotherhood to the Palestinian Hamas and the Lebanese Hezbollah, accusing them of being too provincial and internally focused. These jihadist groups cite, for example, Arab countries' failure to send fighters to help other Muslim communities in Bosnia, Chechnya, and Afghanistan.

FIGURE 10.4 Most Disappointing Policy of the Obama Administration, Six-Country Totals, 2010–2011

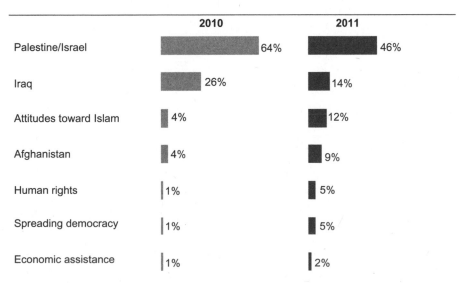

When you look back at the past year of the Obama administration, which one of the following policies are you most disappointed with?

	2010	2011
Palestine/Israel	64%	46%
Iraq	26%	14%
Attitudes toward Islam	4%	12%
Afghanistan	4%	9%
Human rights	1%	5%
Spreading democracy	1%	5%
Economic assistance	1%	2%

Arabs' concern for other Arab nations versus other non-Arab Muslim nations could also be measured by reactions to the Afghanistan war. Arabs did follow events in Afghanistan, which fueled their anger with the United States, but that war was not nearly as central as the one closer to home in Iraq or the Palestinian-Israeli issue. For example, when Arabs were asked which Obama administration policy disappointed them most in the prior year, policy toward Afghanistan lagged behind Arab issues even as late as October 2011 when American forces had almost been completely withdrawn from Iraq (Figure 10.4).

Above all, Arabs hunger for Arab power, Arab progress, Arab democracy, and an Arab state that would help take Arabs to what they perceive to be their rightful place among nations. This is why, of all the remarkable revolutions that have swept the region, from the courage of Tunisians and Libyans, the sacrifice of Yemenis, Bahrainis, and Syrians, the one place that captured the public's imagination more than any other was Tahrir Square. And it is the course of change in Egypt that will likely have the most impact on the future of the Arab uprisings and on how Arabs evaluate other world powers.

CHAPTER 11

FROM 9/11 TO TAHRIR SQUARE: THE ARABS THROUGH AMERICAN EYES

THE UNFORGETTABLE PICTURES FROM TAHRIR SQUARE of marginalized, ordinary Arabs risking their lives for freedom had an emotional impact on people everywhere, including Americans. Not only did the images cast the citizens of the long-undemocratic country in a new light; they inspired Americans to similar protests. In February 2011, immediately after the fall of the Mubarak regime in Egypt, demonstrators in Wisconsin took to the streets over labor issues. One demonstrator captured the mood: "Watching Egypt's story for a week or two very intently, I was inspired by the Egyptian people, you know, striving for their own self-determination and democracy in their country. I was very inspired by that. And when I got here, I sensed that everyone's in it together. The sense of solidarity is just amazing."[1]

Similarly, the "Occupy Wall Street" gatherings had their own causes, but inspiration from Tahrir Square was also readily evident. In October 2011 the *New York Times* reported that "Are you ready for a Tahrir moment?" had become a call to action among occupiers. Newcomers to Zuccotti Park—ground zero for the Occupy movement in Manhattan—were given leaflets explicitly connecting the movements: "We are using the revolutionary Arab

---

1. Andy Kroll, "Cairo in Wisconsin: Eating Egyptian Pizza in Downtown Madison," Tomdispatch .com, February 28, 2011. Available online at: http://truth-out.org/index.php?option=com_k2& view=item&id=98:cairo-in-wisconsin-eating-egyptian-pizza-in-downtown-madison.

Spring occupation tactics to achieve our ends and we encourage the use of nonviolence to maximize the safety of all participants."[2]

In the previous ten years, a decade that began with the horrible 9/11 attacks, war and fear of terrorism weighed heavily on the American public's mood and its perceptions of Arabs and Muslims. Did the Arab uprisings replace the painful and ugly prism through which Americans had come to see Arabs and Muslims? Are Americans now looking at and interpreting events in the Middle East through a more positive "Tahrir Square prism"? According to our polling evidence, the uprisings have affected American perceptions, but Americans' views on the Arab world are still heavily affected by other factors, including the previous two decades of interaction between the United States and the Arab world.

American and Arab perceptions of each other are somewhat interactive and can have policy consequences. In the decade after 9/11, a common American perception was that the problem with what seemed like a unified "Muslim world" was likely a result of a clash of values and that Islam, the religion, may be part of the problem. This perception not only was reflected in the American public discourse but also was heard and viewed by many Arabs and Muslims. It gave the impression that Arabs and Muslims were under assault for who they are and in turn played into the hands of those among them, especially Islamist militants, who were all too happy to use it in their confrontation with the United States. Thus the importance of the question: Have the Arab uprisings changed American public perceptions of the region?

Exceptionalism and Exhaustion

The 1990s saw unprecedented American power and influence. Over ten years, the United States basked in the glow of having won the cold war, successfully confronted the Iraqi invasion of Kuwait by building an extraordinary and unprecedented international coalition, and then enjoyed an enormous economic expansion. It is hard to find a decade when America reigned more supreme.

---

2. Anne Barnard, "Occupy Wall Street Meets Tahrir Square," City Room, *New York Times*, October 25, 2011. Available online at: http://cityroom.blogs.nytimes.com/2011/10/25/occupy-wall -street-meets-tahrir-square/.

But 9/11, as we all recall, shattered the country's confidence and imbued the American public with an instant sense of vulnerability and helplessness. Within days of that event, a congressional leader said to me during urgent consultations what many others quietly feared: "This can defeat us."

In less than a month, the United States invaded Afghanistan. The ensuing triumphalism over the relatively quick collapse of the Taliban, the leaders of a poor and war-torn nation, was not mere arrogance, because it helped rejuvenate public confidence and reassert American power. While people in the United States continued to feel vulnerable to terrorism, their initial sense of helplessness and, yes, weakness was overshadowed by B-52 bombers over Tora Bora, which appeared to accomplish in mere days what the Soviet Union had failed to do in years. And that exultant mood continued through the "shock and awe" bombings of Baghdad, climaxing in George W. Bush's "mission accomplished" speech.

But these quick victories were followed by grinding, bloody wars on two fronts. In Iraq, the anarchy, mounting U.S. casualties, bloody internecine terrorism, and extraordinary sectarian violence quickly revealed not only that the mission was far from accomplished but also the limits of the unequaled U.S. military power. The inability of American forces to stomp out the Taliban in Afghanistan only added to the feeling of impotence.

Even the celebration following the successful May 2011 killing of Osama bin Laden was haunted by the knowledge that it took the world's only superpower ten years to find the world's most wanted and recognizable terrorist. Worse, he was discovered hiding under the noses of the United States' presumptive ally, the Pakistani army. In my 2011 poll, I found that while most Americans feel that the killing of bin Laden was a setback for al Qaeda, they don't believe the organization is significantly weaker. A sense of exhaustion with the costly, seemingly endless wars abroad was also evident: A majority of Americans felt that the United States has overinvested in the Iraq and Afghanistan wars as well as in building alliances in the war on terrorism.

This mood was captured in two polls of Americans I conducted in March and August 2011. The American public had come to endorse full U.S. withdrawal from Iraq, and it wanted a reduction in the presence in Afghanistan. In my August 2011 poll, two-thirds of respondents expressed the view that

America's influence around the world had declined in the decade that followed the 9/11 tragedy. A large majority of Americans, 71 percent, expressed the view that the United States had "overinvested" in one or more aspects of its response to 9/11, and of those, 59 percent said that this overinvestment contributed to America's economic problems.

Those same 2011 polls also found American public opinions toward the people of the Middle East changing, sometimes dramatically, in the wake of the events in Tahrir Square and elsewhere. In my April 2011 poll, the American public had a somewhat positive view of the Arab uprisings. A plurality, 45 percent, expressed the view that the Arab uprisings "were more about ordinary people seeking freedom and democracy," while only 15 percent said they were "more about Islamist groups seeking political power" (Figure 11.1). At the same time, 37 percent said the uprisings were about both equally. This sense that the uprisings reflected both a universal drive for freedom, on the one hand, and an Islamist power grab, on the other, was even more evident in the poll I conducted a few months later, in August 2011. In that poll, 45 percent said the uprisings were equally about ordinary people seeking freedom and about Islamist groups seeking power.

FIGURE 11.1 Americans' Views of Arab Uprisings, April and August 2011

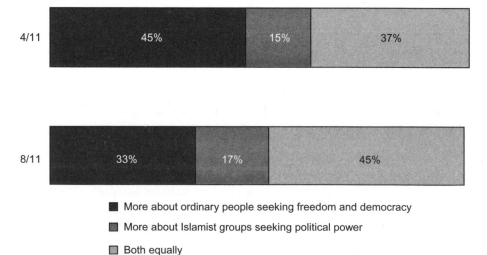

Do you think the popular uprisings in the Arab world are:

4/11   45%   15%   37%

8/11   33%   17%   45%

■ More about ordinary people seeking freedom and democracy
▣ More about Islamist groups seeking political power
□ Both equally

Unity and Division in Current American Opinion

While the horrific shock of the 9/11 attacks bound Americans together in the early months following the tragedy, this national unity eventually became a casualty of the subsequent wars and occupations. Today there are significant differences in the attitudes of Republicans, Democrats, and independents on issues relating to the Arab world, whether they are matters of opinion or fact. A plurality of Republicans (43 percent), for example, remains convinced that Saddam Hussein provided substantial support to al Qaeda, and 41 percent (compared with 15 percent of Democrats and 23 percent of independents) believe that Iraq possessed actual weapons of mass destruction before the Iraq war, even though both claims have been persuasively debunked. A majority of Republicans continues to feel that the Iraq war was justified, while Democrats and independents take the opposite position. Such differences are also reflected in a host of other issues, including attitudes toward terrorism, Islam, and the Arab-Israeli conflict.

If there is one thing Americans can agree on, it's that there is a shell-shocked public mood that adds up to increasing isolationism: a reluctance to intervene internationally or even, in some cases, take sides in foreign conflicts. So while the American public's attitudes toward the uprisings were decidedly in favor of the people against their governments—even governments that have been key American allies, such as Jordan and Saudi Arabia—the majority of Americans generally wanted their country to remain neutral in response to the uprisings (Figure 11.2). Consistently, two-thirds of those polled expressed the view that the United States should not take a position on the uprisings, perhaps reflecting fear of a slippery slope leading to military intervention or at least to more overinvestment, particularly at a time of economic crisis.

Arabs Versus Muslims

Despite an unwillingness to intervene in the conflicts, Americans notably embraced the people involved in the uprisings. I cannot be entirely certain that these attitudes are primarily a reflection of the Arab uprisings—because I don't have data from prior years on attitudes toward the Arab "people" specifically—but the clear indication is that the uprisings had caused a strong uptick in Americans' positive feelings toward Arabs: 39 percent said that their sympathy for the Arab people had increased.

FIGURE 11.2 Position United States Government Should Take Toward Arab Uprisings, 2011

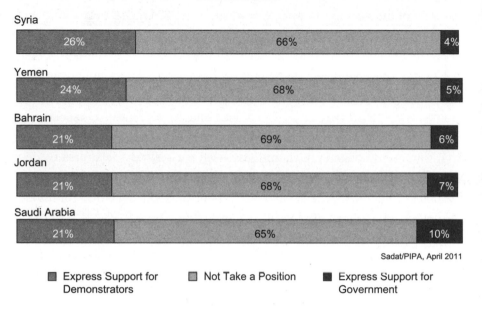

In responding to the popular uprisings in the following countries, do you think the U.S. should:

Syria

| 26% | 66% | 4% |

Yemen

| 24% | 68% | 5% |

Bahrain

| 21% | 69% | 6% |

Jordan

| 21% | 68% | 7% |

Saudi Arabia

| 21% | 65% | 10% |

Sadat/PIPA, April 2011

■ Express Support for Demonstrators　　□ Not Take a Position　　■ Express Support for Government

Regardless of the exact reasons for these attitudes, they were remarkably positive, particularly when contrasted with the mostly negative attitudes expressed about "Arab countries"—with the exception of Egypt. Overall, 56 percent had positive views of Arabs generally and 57 percent expressed positive views of the people of Saudi Arabia (Figure 11.3). A large majority, 70 percent, had positive views of Egyptians, which was comparable to American public attitudes toward the Israeli people.

Attitudes toward Islam and Muslims have also changed significantly over the past decade—but not as a result of the Arab uprisings. Instead, a majority of Americans reported negative views of Islam, reflecting a decade-long increase in antipathy toward the religion. Strikingly, right after 9/11 more Americans had a positive view of the Islamic religion than a negative view, but by the time of my August 2011 poll, a majority of Americans (61 percent) were on the negative side of the ledger (Figure 11.4), including many respondents who didn't have an opinion in the past.

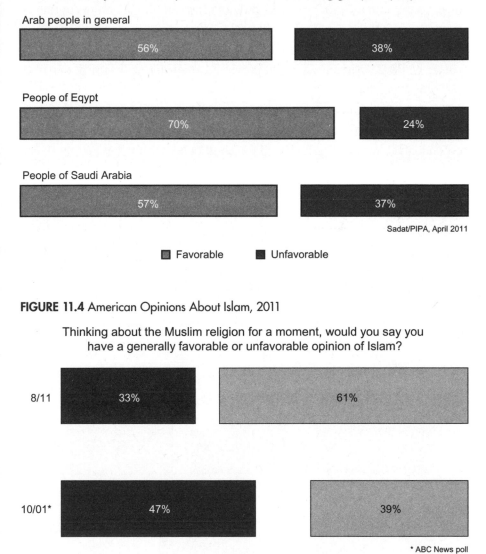

FIGURE 11.3 American Opinions About Arab People, 2011

What is your overall opinion of each of the following groups of people:

Arab people in general

| 56% | 38% |

People of Eqypt

| 70% | 24% |

People of Saudi Arabia

| 57% | 37% |

Sadat/PIPA, April 2011

■ Favorable   ■ Unfavorable

FIGURE 11.4 American Opinions About Islam, 2011

Thinking about the Muslim religion for a moment, would you say you have a generally favorable or unfavorable opinion of Islam?

8/11 | 33% | 61% |

10/01* | 47% | 39% |

* ABC News poll

■ Favorable   □ Unfavorable

This adverse view of Islam exists without a corresponding number of Americans blaming Islam for the 9/11 attacks. In fact, a stable majority continues to think that the 9/11 attacks did not represent the intentions of mainstream Islam. Of those polled in 2011, 73 percent (compared with 87 percent in October 2001) said that the attacks represented the views of a radical fringe, while 22 percent said it represented mainstream Islam (compared with only 7 percent in 2001).

Despite these negative views of Islam itself, most Americans don't think that conflict between Islam and the West is inevitable (Figure 11.5). Most respondents in my 2011 poll viewed the conflict between Islam and the West as driven more by political than cultural factors, and most continued to express confidence that it is possible to find common ground between Islam and the West, though this percentage is down somewhat from late 2001. Likewise, a negative view of Islam didn't directly translate into a dislike for its adherents: Nearly 50 percent of Americans expressed positive views of Muslims.

Not surprisingly, given their mixed sentiments toward previous U.S. military interventions, Arabs, Islam, and Muslims themselves, Americans remain divided when it comes to assessing the likely outcome of the Arab uprisings. In the April 2011 poll, 51 percent said they believed that the uprisings would lead to democracy in the Middle East, while 47 percent felt that

FIGURE 11.5 American Views on Conflict Between Islam and the West, 2011

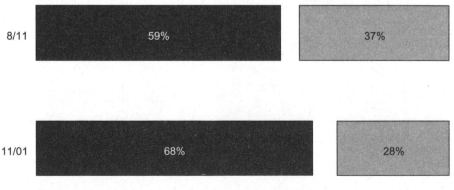

8/11   59%   37%

11/01   68%   28%

■ Though there are some fanatics in the Islamic world, most people there have needs and wants like those of people everywhere, so it is possible for us to find common ground.

▨ Because Islamic religious and social traditions are intolerant and fundamentally incompatible with Western culture, violent conflict is bound to keep happening.

they would not. Democrats and independents tended to be far more optimistic than Republicans, but there was agreement across the party divide that if the uprisings did, in fact, lead to democratic change in the Middle East, this would be positive for the United States in the short term (65 percent) and even more so in the long term (76 percent). More strikingly, a majority of Americans (57 percent) wanted the United States to support democratic change in the region even if the outcome was less positive for the United States (compared with only 48 percent in September 2005).

American Public Attitudes Toward the Palestinian-Israeli Conflict

Earlier I argued that the Palestinian-Israeli conflict is the prism of pain through which Arabs see the world, especially the United States. What is often not fully recognized is that, over the years, it has also become a central prism through which the United States evaluates events in the Middle East. This is certainly true at the level of government, especially Congress, where the events taking place in the region, from the growing power of Iran to the revolution in Egypt, have been evaluated to a great extent in terms of their ramifications for Israel. But where does the American public stand on this issue? Have the Arab uprisings changed American public attitudes?

For nearly two decades I have conducted polls to study American public attitudes toward the Arab-Israeli conflict, and there have been two clear and relatively consistent responses: When given a choice, most Americans preferred that the United States not lean toward either Israel or the Arabs/ Palestinians. What's more, those who ranked this issue high in their priorities were a relatively small portion of the population. But it has been equally clear that those who did attach great weight to the issue were more likely to act on it through voting or campaign contributions and tended to favor supporting Israel over the Palestinians, by ratios ranging from 2 to 1 to 6 to 1 over the years and in different polls. This tended to hold, to varying degrees, for both Republicans and Democrats.

Recent years, though, have brought some important, even startling shifts: More Americans rank the Palestinian-Israeli conflict high in their priorities; and the difference between the Republican desire to lean toward Israel and the reluctance of Democrats and independents to do the same has grown dramatically, a phenomenon that is largely related to shifts and alliances within American politics.

FIGURE 11.6 American Views on Position U.S. Government Should Take on Israeli-Palestinian Conflict, 2010 and 2011

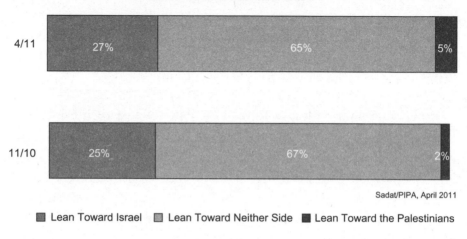

In its efforts to resolve the Israeli-Palestinian conflict, what position do you believe the U.S. should take?

4/11 — 27% / 65% / 5%

11/10 — 25% / 67% / 2%

Sadat/PIPA, April 2011

■ Lean Toward Israel   ▢ Lean Toward Neither Side   ■ Lean Toward the Palestinians

In the April 2011 poll, I asked respondents if they wanted the United States to "lean toward" Israel, the Palestinians, or neither side (Figure 11.6). Consistent with results in prior years, roughly two-thirds chose leaning toward neither side, which was nearly identical to the results of a poll I conducted in November 2010. Also consistent with prior trends, those who wanted the United States to lean toward one side chose Israel by a margin of 5 to 1.

But the breakdown of attitudes along demographic lines is telling: This issue has become far more important to Republicans than to Democrats. Among Democrats, 79 percent want the United States to lean toward neither side, compared with 73 percent of independents and 50 percent of Republicans. Meanwhile, 46 percent of Republicans want Washington to lean toward Israel compared with only 14 percent of Democrats and 11 percent of independents.

Similarly, older Americans, whites, and men tend to want the United States to support Israel more than younger Americans, minorities, and women. But the consequential political story may be in how Americans rank the issue, given that ranking is important for the way people tend to behave. In the April 2011 poll, one in four Americans ranked the Arab-Israeli issue "among the top three issues" for U.S. interests, and nearly two-thirds ranked it among the top five issues.

FIGURE 11.7 American Views on Position U.S. Government Should Take to Resolve Israeli-Palestinian Conflict, 2011

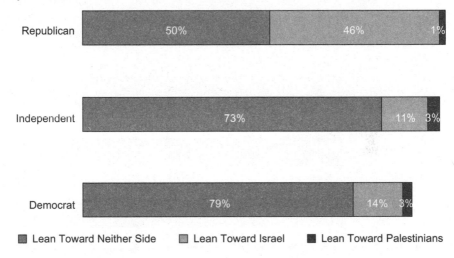

In its efforts to resolve the Israeli-Palestinian conflict, what position do you believe the U.S. should take?

Party Affiliation:

Republican: Lean Toward Neither Side 50%, Lean Toward Israel 46%, Lean Toward Palestinians 1%

Independent: Lean Toward Neither Side 73%, Lean Toward Israel 11%, Lean Toward Palestinians 3%

Democrat: Lean Toward Neither Side 79%, Lean Toward Israel 14%, Lean Toward Palestinians 3%

■ Lean Toward Neither Side   □ Lean Toward Israel   ■ Lean Toward Palestinians

But those who ranked the issue highest tended to most strongly want Washington to lean toward Israel; of those who ranked the issue as "the single most important" issue for U.S. interests, 50 percent wanted the United States to lean toward Israel. And those who didn't rank the issue among the top five at all tended to overwhelmingly favor neutrality. Those urging Washington to lean toward the Palestinians were few, across the demographic categories, although there were signs of an increase in the August 2011 poll.

These results indicate that the most passionate support for Israel in recent years has not been in the Democratic Party, which is the home of the overwhelming majority of Jewish Americans, but in the Republican Party, the home of an evangelical Christian right that has grown to rank Israel high in its priorities, for ideological as well as political reasons. Polls of American Jews specifically show that, while they care about Israel, many don't rank the Israel issue particularly high in their priorities, and they don't interpret their support for Israel to coincide with the articulated position of the Israeli right.

The largest segment of Americans overall remains those who want neutrality—an opinion in line with Americans' growing isolationism. Nonetheless, those Americans who do favor neutrality don't tend to be passionate

FIGURE 11.8 Position U.S. Government Should Take on Israeli-Palestinian Conflict, by Importance of the Issue, 2011

In its efforts to resolve the Israeli-Palestinian conflict, what position do you believe the U.S. should take?

Importance of Arab-Israeli Conflict:

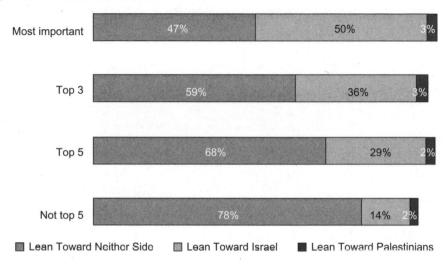

enough to make a difference in the political arena. And while demographic trends seem to suggest reduced support for Israel among the young and the growing minorities, these segments could in the long term be socialized into the prevailing American mood as they become more empowered.

Even following the Arab uprisings, Israel will likely remain the central prism through which Americans view events in the Middle East. As long as the Arab-Israeli conflict remains unresolved, this will continue to be a sore point in the way Arabs see America and evaluate American foreign policy— especially in times of crisis. This has clear implications for congressional attitudes: Even if Egypt does turn into a genuinely democratic state, any confrontational moves against Israel will inevitably sour relations between Washington and Cairo.

The Road Ahead

Whether the Arab uprisings will continue to project positive images of ordi-nary Arabs and Muslims seeking freedom and democracy—and continue to have a positive impact on American public attitudes—remains to be seen.

How much the 9/11 paradigm will be replaced by a "Tahrir Square prism" will depend on how events unfold in the streets and capitals of the Middle East in the months and years ahead.

One of the appeals of the early Arab uprisings was their relative peacefulness; another was the apparent absence of political ideology as a driving force and the fact that Islamists were only one of many groups, including a large number of liberal activists. But the violence that ensued, especially in Libya and Syria, may create a different impression—even if most of the violence has come from the regimes, not from the rebels. And the victories of Islamists in Tunisia and Egypt have created a level of discomfort that will ultimately be a function of how the new rulers behave, not only in relation to their own people but also in their foreign policies.

Already by October 2012 my American public opinion polls conducted after attacks on the American diplomatic missions in Libya and Egypt showed that more Americans were characterizing the Arab uprisings as being driven by Islamist groups than as being a reflection of ordinary people seeking freedom and democracy—although their views of the Arab people remained slightly more favorable than unfavorable.[3]

One certain thing is that it is less the 9/11 attacks themselves than the long, bloody, and complicated response to them over the past decade that has taken its toll on the American mood and perception of the region. Wars have a way of trumping all perceptions. If Americans find their country engaged in other wars in the Middle East, whether in Iran or through an intervention in the Arab world, that commitment will transcend peacetime perceptions. Rallying around the flag settles ideational battles in the short term, but they endure until the next crisis. And regional crises over the Arab-Israeli issue, even ones that don't involve the United States militarily, will continue to provide a prism through which the American public and the American elites view Arabs and Muslims. But for now, even as most Americans continue to view Islam negatively as a religion, the Arab uprisings have gone a long way to humanize the Arab people in American eyes and to generate a degree of empathy with their aspirations.

---

3. Anwar Sadat Chair, "Americans on the Middle East: A Study of American Public Opinion," October 8, 2012, University of Maryland and Program on International Policy Attitudes. Available online at: http://sadat.umd.edu/MiddleEast_Oct12_rpt.pdf.

CHAPTER 12

ARAB PUBLIC OPINION AND THE RESHAPING OF THE MIDDLE EAST

S INCE THE BEGINNING of the Arab public uprisings in 2010, scholars and analysts have debated their roots, alternately describing them as an "Arab awakening," an "Islamic awakening," or an "Arab Spring." But almost everyone agrees that the political environment in the Middle East has changed and that public opinion will count more than ever before in the internal politics of countries in the region, and in strategic calculations.

In a previous work published just before the 2003 Iraq war,[1] and well before the Arab uprisings, I argued that even in countries where rulers retained the capacity to ignore their public, and still maintain power, there were four strong countervailing factors that made public opinion important:

- Every government needs a degree of public legitimacy, to govern effectively. The more illegitimate a government feels, the more repressive resources it has to deploy, and there is a cost for deploying those resources. Legitimacy also provides a protective cushion in times of crisis by buying governments time when there is a temporary reduction in their coercive capabilities.
- The rise of transnational media and the information revolution has taken away much of the governments' monopoly

---

1. Shibley Telhami, *The Stakes: America and the Middle East* (Boulder, CO: Westview, 2002).

over an important instrument of control previously at their disposal. When they can no longer control the narrative, it is much harder to hide their flaws.

- The capacity of disaffected individuals and groups to inflict pain on states has dramatically increased in an era when states have decreased capacity to control weapons technology and information. Whether or not states can suppress opposition, which increases public anger even more, and contain terrorism at the same time is less certain than in the past.

- Despite the record of stability of authoritarian governments in the region, there have also been marked episodes of consequential public opposition. To cite one prominent and tragic example, former Israeli prime minister Menachem Begin convinced Egyptian president Sadat that he should ignore his public during the 1978 Camp David peace negotiations, and Sadat ended up paying with his life for his courage. Although revolutions are scarce in history, and certainly in the Middle East, they do occur, often unpredictably.

Narrative Control

Now that these factors have helped produce actual regime change in multiple Arab nations, a new debate, one regarding the nature of the uprisings, has opened. In these arguments, the battle for narrative control is even more important than the battle to occupy Tahrir Square. My Arab public opinion polls indicate that a majority of Arabs see the uprisings simply as a revolt of ordinary people seeking dignity, freedom, and democracy—the same aspirations expressed in the chants of Arab revolutionaries in the streets and public squares. But doubters existed from the outset; and they were bound to use the bloody path revolution took in Syria—massacres, refugees, sectarianism, and the involvement of many foreign hands—to author a narrative that helped their case. In a culture that has a rich history of real and imagined conspiracies, narratives are *never* in short supply.

Some narratives that emerged from the Arab awakening were predictable, others had aspects of reality, still more were fanciful. One of the first issues of debate was whether the uprisings constituted an "Arab" or an "Islamic" awakening. Iran potentially stood to lose more than it could gain by the rise of assertive and proud Arab governments, not only strategically but also in the potential revival of an Iranian public revolt against the regime. So it is not surprising for Tehran to posit to its own people that Arabs were actually witnessing an "Islamic" revolution akin to the one it had already experienced in 1979.

And yet Iran's hand was present but also exaggerated in the Bahraini uprisings by the Shiite majority against the Sunni-dominated monarchy. Supporters of the Bahraini regime in the Gulf, including governments of the Gulf Cooperation Council, sought to explain the Bahraini revolts in Shiite-Sunni sectarian terms or, more frequently, with direct reference to Iran, partly because they had real fears of Shiite revolts in their own countries and of Iran. But the sectarian explanation also helped them deflect real challenges they face from their own Sunni populations, especially the young and restless.

Still others, especially those with political interests in supporting the Syrian regime, told a narrative about foreign intervention, especially American and Israeli. For example, Hezbollah leader Hassan Nasrallah framed the events that threatened his patrons in Syria in terms of a foreign plot. But during Libya's uprising, which was openly supported militarily by the United States, Nasrallah had taken the opposite position: that accusations of a foreign plot were demeaning to the sacrifices and aspirations of ordinary Arabs. Clearly these were narratives of convenience, at least to some extent.

Many groups on the losing end of change, including liberals and secularists in Tunisia and Egypt, voiced fears that the revolutions had been "hijacked" by Islamists. The electoral victories of Islamist parties and the seeming concentration of power in Egypt in the hands of Islamists generated the sort of fears that some had warned of years earlier: that Islamists would use democracy to rise to power and then find every way, including undemocratic methods, to maintain that power. Soon after Morsi's election in Egypt, some critics compared his rule with that of the ayatollahs in Iran.

There were also surprising categorical interpretations of events by people who were initially inspired by the uprisings. Muhammad Hassanein Heikal has been one of the most influential columnists and political writers in the Arab world for over a half century, dating back to his time as a close advisor to Egyptian president Gamal Abd al-Nasser. Despite Heikal's long-standing support for Arab self-determination, in August 2011 he argued that the Arab revolutions were "not an Arab Spring but a new Sykes-Picot deal to divide the Arab world and share its resources." The reference, well known to Arabs, is to the post–World War I treaty in which European powers sliced up and occupied much of the Arab world. Heikal suggested that the change is merely "turning over the keys" to new drivers, suggesting that Washington had a hand in these events and that its dealings with the Muslim Brotherhood are sinister.[2]

These interpretations were partly reflective of the positions of winners and losers in the ongoing battles to define the future of each country in the inevitable competition for power. But they were also an expression of at least three major battles exposed in the events unfolding in the ongoing Arab uprisings—even aside from power struggles and the secular-religious divide that remain central in every case:

- The battle that captured the imagination regionally and globally: a genuine public awakening that challenged repressive regimes and sought freedom and dignity
- The sectarian battle fought in countries where sectarianism has deep roots, especially Syria and Bahrain, but also Yemen
- The battle for power of many regional and global powers seeking influence in a region where suspicion and fear of foreign intervention is almost always on the people's minds

How people ranked these issues in their immediate priorities largely determined the narratives they adopted about the uprisings.

Despite competing story lines, the rising role of the Arab people in determining the shape of their future has been a starting point for most narratives. What's next? I close with eight conclusions that can be drawn about how Arab public opinion will help reshape the unfolding political course in the Arab world.

---

2. "Muhammad Hassanein Heikal on the New Sykes Picot," Arabist.net. Available online at: www.arabist.net/blog/2011/11/13/in-translation-muhammad-hassanein-heikal-on-the-new -sykes-pi.html.

First, the processes unleashed by the Tunisian and Egyptian revolutions are not episodic and are likely to endure: They represented an unprecedented public empowerment that transcends national boundaries, an awakening on a greater scale than ever before. Although the Arab public uprisings were not "caused" by the information revolution—we've long known about pervasive anger in the Arab world—the tools of information revolution constituted new mechanisms for effective organization, raised expectations, and empowered individuals in the region in hitherto unavailable ways. Given that this information revolution continues to expand, public empowerment, restlessness, and assertiveness are not likely to go away. *New York Times* columnist Thomas Friedman put it this way, long before the Arab uprisings:

> The third balance that you have to pay attention to in the globalization system—the one that is really the newest of all—is the balance between individuals and nation-states. Because globalization has brought down many of the walls that limited the movement and reach of people, and because it has simultaneously wired the world into networks, it gives more power to individuals to influence both markets and nation-states than at any time in history. So you have today not only a superpower.... You have Super-empowered individuals. Some of these Super-empowered individuals are quite angry, some of them quite wonderful—but all of them are now able to act directly on the world stage without the traditional mediation of governments, corporations or any other public or private institutions.[3]

Second, the uprisings and their consequences will play themselves out differently in each country, and the key factors in most instances will be the relative ethnic and religious homogeneity of the populace, relative wealth of the state, and the government's flexibility in providing credible steps for reform.

Public empowerment does not entail public unanimity; in fact, divisions contained in the past are likely to rise. These divisions include, but are not

---

3. Thomas L. Friedman, *The Lexus and the Olive Tree* (New York: Farrar, Straus and Giroux, 1999), 12.

limited to, sectarianism. The more heterogeneous a country is, the more likely it is to experience extended conflict. Certainly this has been true in Yemen, Syria, and Bahrain, where there is sectarian diversity, but it is likely to be true also in countries like Egypt and Tunisia, where there are sharp ideological divisions between secularists and liberals, on the one side, and those who are more determined to see stronger intrusions of religion into politics. Each can mobilize an empowered constituency, which is a normal part of mature democratic politics, but in environments of unstable transitions, it is also a potential recipe for confrontation—and exploitation.

Public empowerment can be a subversive tool. In recent times the Middle East witnessed more than its share of this type of exploitative motivation, particularly in Egypt and Yemen, and in Libya where four American diplomats, including the ambassador, paid with their lives.[4] Even an elected Egyptian government with strong Islamic credentials had difficulty containing an anti-American revolt, spurred by a film that most Muslims found deeply insulting. Yes, the U.S. government had nothing to do with the film, but the ability of determined groups to generate a confrontation clearly demonstrates the destabilizing potential of public empowerment.

Third, no government in the Arab world is fully immune to revolt, including the oil-rich countries. Yes, secure, well-paying jobs and generous public services certainly remove one source of public discontent. And governments of oil-rich states, particularly Saudi Arabia, have the capacity to buy time by improving in these areas. Indeed, one of the first moves made by the king of Saudi Arabia as the Arab uprisings spread in 2011 was to announce the most extraordinary, expensive, and sweeping welfare measures ever introduced in any Arab country.

As anyone who has ever been out of work knows, the absence of a job is more than just the absence of income—it's an assault on one's dignity. And even when economic desperation is not a factor, the prevailing sense of utter dependence on forces ordinary people cannot control for their own advancement and welfare, and on the arbitrary decisions of their own rulers, instills a deep sense of resentment—one regularly reinforced by media images of

---

4. In the Libyan case, there was early evidence that militants may have planned the attack on the American consulate in Benghazi and exploited the demonstrations as a cover.

increasing freedom in other lands. As was the case in most of the initial revolts in Tunisia and Egypt, those who led the revolts were neither the most
desperate nor unemployed—although jobs and food became factors as the
revolts expanded.

Of course, rich states also have the resources to spend on more effective
security, and it is evident that many of the economic packages offered by the
king of Saudi Arabia targeted improvements for the security and policing
personnel in the kingdom. These steps help buy time, but the expanding
public empowerment in the region aspires for much more than economic
improvements. Hosni Mubarak's problem was *not* the absence of effective
security forces. Unless these economic steps are accompanied by serious
political reforms, voices of dissent will likely find their way into the public
square.

One possible place for an uprising to occur is among Saudi Arabia's
Shiite community, which has already confronted government forces multiple
times since the beginning of the Arab uprisings. But Shiites remain a minority in Saudi Arabia (about 10 percent of the population), and most live in isolated communities in the oil-rich eastern part of the country, and so have a
below-average rate of unemployment. The Saudi government has deployed a
large security force in the region to confront any revolt. More centrally, given
their limited size, a Shiite uprising is unlikely to threaten the royal family and
could even play into its hands by mobilizing the Sunni majority behind it.

More challenging to the Saudi government is a generation of young Saudis who are globally connected through the Internet and social media and
are tweeting criticism of the royal family. These young men and women feel
empowered by discovering that others share their views, and their expectations are being informed by the possibilities of liberty and opportunity that
they can glean from the outside world.

Fourth, while the importance of public opinion is increasing, public sentiment is never the only factor in determining political outcomes or directions
of policy. This is, of course, true even in mature democracies: Witness the
relatively low turnout of the American public in elections and the increasing
role of campaign contributions in shaping the outcome of American elections. In practice, individuals and groups don't count equally even if they do
in theory.

The power of people to demonstrate and to revolt does not translate into parallel power in democratic politics. This was visible early on following the Egyptian revolution, as Egypt embarked on a democratic electoral course. If the Arab uprisings were particularly remarkable in the seeming lack of need to rely on strong political institutions and organizations to mobilize large numbers of people, the electoral politics that followed showed how important organizations remained for effective politics.

In particular the Egyptian presidential elections in May 2012 showed the critical centrality of political organizations. Despite an early lead in the polls for two independent candidates for president, Amr Mousa and Abdel Moneim Aboul Fotouh, both were defeated in the first round of elections in favor of candidates backed by the two best-organized groups in the country: the Muslim Brotherhood and the National Democratic Party that had governed the country before the revolution. Only 46 percent of Egyptians voted, giving those who were able to get out the vote a decided advantage. Here is another striking aspect of that round of the election, which took place in the middle of a revolution and public empowerment: The two candidates who survived the first round, combined, drew less than 50 percent support from the 46 percent who voted in the elections.

Organizations are partly dependent on resources, and resources will continue to be unevenly divided across society. Commercial interests will find a way to organize and to have their voices heard disproportionately. The media are increasingly diverse, but given their modest ability to generate income, most media outlets remain dependent on those who have resources—and a political agenda. The fight for narrative is in part influenced by media and resources: Witness how quickly opponents of the Muslim Brotherhood in Egypt, particularly those from among the elites behind the Mubarak regime, were able to turn the table and accuse the Muslim Brotherhood of being an American ally.

The militaries in every Arab country will continue to matter. In Tunisia, one reason for the rapid fall of the Bin Ali regime was that the military in essence decided not to risk a confrontation with the public. To a lesser extent the same could be said about Egypt. In Syria the military became the instrument of the regime against the opposition, even if the price was some defections. But even in cases where the military appeared to be increasingly subordinated to elected governments, these institutions remain well organized and sometimes have vast economic interests that they will need to protect. And rulers will continue to need their backing in unstable transitions.

Fifth, the short- to medium-term course of the uprisings is bound to lead to some reevaluation of the initial assumptions about their nature and their causes. There has already been much of that witnessed in the battle of narratives fought by competing regional and global forces. But there is one arena that may be central: the means and consequences of the uprisings.

One of the early aspects of the Arab uprisings that captured the Arab as well as international imagination was the relatively peaceful nature of the revolts in Tunisia and Egypt, and even in Yemen (despite the widespread presence of arms across the population). This is one reason why there was such considerable regional and global rallying against the government of Muammar al-Qaddafi as soon as it mounted ruthless military means to suppress its own peaceful uprisings. But much has changed since then.

The Arab public immediately recognized the power of peaceful demonstrations, as demonstrators in Yemen, Egypt, and Syria deliberately chanted in the face of government forces, "silmiyya, silmiyya" (peaceful, peaceful). Even the leader of the Palestinian militant group Hamas, Khalid Mashal, who had long argued that only armed struggle can help Palestinians achieve their goals, was so taken by what he witnessed that he spoke of moving to rely on peaceful resistance, which he likened to a tsunami.

On the day Mubarak fell, I suggested in an article that the sight of the Egyptian president falling under the pressure of a peaceful revolt constituted "Osama bin Laden's nightmare":

> In seeking to overthrow Arab governments, long before the 9/11 horror, Al Qaeda leaders, including the second-in-command Ayman Zawahiri, an Egyptian doctor, told the Arab people to take on the seemingly overwhelming power of the state—with bloody attacks against its symbols. The Al Qaeda leadership insisted that militant Islam was the way. No one else seemed to have an answer. Enter the Tunisian people and now the Egyptian people—in some of the most extraordinary peaceful non-ideological revolts in history. If they succeed, Al Qaeda may

remain a force, but its public appeal will ring hollow. If they fail, the energy, the mobilization, the taste of pride and empowerment, will not go away—but could be channeled somewhere else. These forces could turn into Egypt's and the world's nightmare.[5]

But the paths of the uprising and of governments' responses have changed. Peaceful uprisings have failed in several places and turned violent in others. In Bahrain the government has acted with an iron fist. In Syria what started as a peaceful rebellion was met with a ruthless response by the rulers in Damascus—as the rebellion itself became an armed struggle.

There is another possible outcome of the prolonged and bloody conflict in Syria: It may spread fear of the possible outcome of the uprisings or at least may exhaust the energies of Arabs in the short to medium terms. Just as happened in the early days of the Iraq war, when massacres, death, destruction, and threats to family and community helped Arab rulers promote the value of relative stability in their countries, there is some chance that the Syrian bloodshed will have an impact on potential revolutionaries in other Arab countries—but not in the long term.

Still, sustained instability and accompanying economic deprivation can provide opportunities for new dictatorial rule. The public empowerment sweeping the region may provide a buffer against this possibility, but as we have witnessed even in what seemed enlightened places in history, extremes of hunger, fear, and insecurity can trump almost all other human aspirations.

Sixth, the outcome of the uprisings is at least in part a function of regional forces, and the uprisings themselves have had an impact on the configuration of those forces. The immediate impact has been on a shift of influence in Arab politics toward the oil-producing states, especially Saudi Arabia. This was in part a function of a vacuum of power: Iraq had not returned to its position of influence since the war, Syria was undergoing a devastating revolt that marginalized its government's influence regionally, and Egypt was going through a revolutionary transition that limited its ability to lead, even after the election of its first postrevolution president. The states of the Gulf

---

5. Shibley Telhami, "Bin Laden's Nightmare in Egypt," Politico.com, February 11, 2011. Available online at: www.politico.com/news/stories/0211/49333.html#ixzz26NPm1Yzq.

Cooperation Council were united by the common interests of regime survival in the face of popular revolutions and concern for the unfavorable outcomes in other Arab countries. Saudi Arabia and Qatar, which have sometimes pursued competitive policies, were brought together more than at any point in the previous twenty years. Using their economic power to provide aid, especially to other Arab monarchies in Jordan and Morocco, they expanded their influence and hoped that the latter two could assist them in the security arena.

While the Arab public watched, hopes were pinned on the assertive power of a democratic Egypt. But as Egypt emerged economically weakened while at the same time pursuing a policy that could potentially reduce aid from the West, particularly the United States, its short-term economic options were limited. The Saudi government was known to have favored Mubarak and wanted to see him survive the forces of revolution, but realism prevailed, and their confidence in the influence they can acquire through economic assistance moved them to accept and work with President Morsi. For his part, Morsi made Saudi Arabia the first country he visited after his election. Qatar, too, was there to offer financial assistance. This use of aid by rulers of the rich Arab states toward democratizing countries, whose populations see these rulers as being part of the problem, is one of the anomalies of the Arab uprisings. Whether these relationships can be sustained in the long term remains an open question—particularly if the uprisings expand more forcefully to the rich states.

The economic clout of the GCC is also visible in the dominance of their media in the Arab world. Besides the Qatari Al Jazeera, which singlehandedly commands nearly half of Arab news viewers as a first choice, and many more as second choice, Saudi-owned Al Arabiya and MBC are among the most watched. Resources matter in putting out fresh content that Arab audiences want to watch, and that remains a serious limitation for those trying to compete. Egyptian media may rise again regionally, but this will take time and will be hampered by a media that remains mostly government-owned, even if there is a proliferation of private but less well-funded media.

Seventh, more than any other factor, what happens in Egypt and Saudi Arabia in the next decade will affect not only Arab aspirations and the pursuit of democracy in the region but also the shape of regional alliances and the relations between Arabs and the rest of the world. Arabs want a model to embrace and leadership to admire. And the two most powerful states in the Arab world remain Egypt, as the most populous and historically influential, and Saudi Arabia, both as the wealthiest and as the birthplace of Islam.

Egypt's experiment is well under way, and most Arabs are watching carefully. They hope that sometime soon, when they are asked what political system they most want their own to look like, they will have reason to answer Egypt's instead of Turkey's, and they dream of admiring an Arab leader more than anyone else. Egypt's attempt to fulfill these aspirations will be closely watched.

The Saudi case is far more complicated—and challenges to the regime could pose an even greater dilemma to American foreign policy than the Egyptian revolution did. Newly elected leaders in the Arab world in Egypt, Tunisia, and Yemen, who will continue to rely on Saudi and other GCC support, could be challenged even more because their publics will inevitably sympathize with the Saudi and other Gulf peoples. Part of this tension is sometimes addressed by rulers and elites, including religious leaders, by highlighting the Sunni-Shiite divide and implicating Iran's hand. This can help up to point, as we have seen in the case of Bahrain, but the Arab public's hearts will mostly remain with other Arabs aspiring for freedom from authoritarianism.

For all the talk of energy independence in the United States, America and the rest of the industrialized world remain—and are likely to remain—dependent on Middle Eastern oil in the foreseeable future. And Saudi Arabia's oil reserves remain the largest in the world. It isn't about where the United States imports its oil from; the real issue is that oil prices globally are affected by supply and demand, and how much oil comes out of the Middle East will have inevitable and potentially grave implications for the global economy. This sense of importance, coupled with the fear that any hostile power controlling so much oil could pose greater challenges to the United States, has defined the American approach to Saudi Arabia. In a sense America's historical approach to Saudi Arabia cannot be separated from its bargain with the Saudi monarchy. If a genuine threat against the monarchy emerges in the birthplace of Islam, the United States will face its most difficult challenge of the Arab uprisings.

Eighth, Arab identity and sense of threat will continue to be defined in relation to Israel and the United States. The most consequential measures of this sense of threat remain the Palestinian-Israeli conflict and the presence of American forces in the region. When Al Qaeda sought to achieve its ideological agenda of a Taliban-like Islamic order, and tried to rally Arabs and Muslims behind its militant means, it appealed first and foremost to the Arab discomfort with the large presence of American forces in the Arabian Peninsula and to their anger with American policy on the Palestinian issue. And it appealed to public anger with regimes that limited their freedoms and frustrated their aspirations. The same anger and aspirations remain, even if Al Qaeda's methods have been delegitimized and its core ideological aspiration for a theocratic state never embraced. As I argued earlier, these two issues, Palestine and the American presence, have more than any other defined the prisms through which most Arabs see the world and how they define their enemies and friends.

Yet these issues are often misunderstood. When there is anger with the United States over an issue like the horrible film denigrating Islam that surfaced in September 2012, it is hard to understand how Libyans, whom the United States helped to topple a repressive regime, and Egyptians, the recipients of billions of dollars in American aid, could direct their anger at Washington—especially over a film in which Washington had no role. Of course, those who take the lead in demonstrations or, even more so, in violent confrontations are almost always minorities, often opposed by majorities, and this was probably the case in Libya when the American consulate in Benghazi was attacked and the U.S. ambassador, Christopher Stevens, and three other Americans were killed. But what those who take the lead count on is the deep sense of mistrust of American intentions pervasive among Arabs. As the adage goes, if you don't trust the messenger, you can't trust the message, even when it is seemingly appealing.

That sense of mistrust of America has deep roots that are at their core linked to a long history connected closely to these two trumping issues. They are not always the cause of what happens in episodes of anger with America, and they are not always articulated, but their impact is ever-present.

It is improbable that Washington can transcend the core issues through American aid and public diplomacy. Every good U.S. act, even when well intentioned, will be attributed to sinister aims.

In contrast, decades of French policy to cultivate positive perceptions in the Arab world, especially on the Palestine issue—and following decades of hated colonialism—paid off handsomely. When French prohibition of the *hijab* in public schools was widely debated in France and the Arab media, what could have turned into anti-French anger in the Arab world was mitigated by French policies on the Iraq war and the Israel-Palestine issue—to the point that even Islamic authorities like Sheikh Yousef Qaradawi refused to criticize France directly, praising it instead for its foreign policy.

This is not to say that the United States should forgo aid and public diplomacy. Even aside from humanitarian and moral aims, these do matter for governments and segments of the public, whose cooperation will remain indispensable for American foreign policy. But nothing short of transformative change in policy that includes withdrawal of American forces from the region and a breakthrough in the Palestinian-Israeli conflict is likely to reverse the deep mistrust of American aims among the Arab public.

The issue of Israel and America is important in other ways to the aspirations of most Arabs and many Muslims. America is seen as empowering Israel, which feels insecure. A nation of 8 million people with limited resources imagines itself potentially facing 350 million Arabs and many more millions of Muslims. Its strategy for survival, especially if it continues to occupy Arab territories, is to be in a position to defeat all Arab forces combined if the need arises. Above all, Israel makes a goal of maintaining "qualitative" technological and military superiority over the Arabs and also over Iran. In that goal, it has the stated and practical support of the United States. Seen from the Israeli perspective, this is simple survival arithmetic.

Seen from the Arab public's side, this is a direct assault on their aspirations for prominence, technological advancement, and military and political power on the world stage. It goes beyond the immediate impact on Palestinians and directly into who Arabs aspire to be and who they identify as the central barriers to their aspirations. This is a zero-sum game so long as the Palestinian-Israeli conflict remains unresolved and even more so when there is intense fighting and bloodshed. As Israel's principal backer, the United States will remain the target of anger and suspicion. For this reason American policy must never waiver in its efforts to resolve the Palestinian-Israeli conflict in particular and the Arab-Israeli conflict more broadly.

In the end, it is important to keep a sense of modesty about predicting the shape of things to come as the Arab uprisings continue to unfold. There are too many moving parts within each country and across countries. The paths taken have their own impact on aspirations and motivations. There is much learning that occurs, not only by publics but also by rulers, businesses, organizations, and foreign powers. The distribution of resources, especially economic and military resources, will continue to be a central factor in shaping events within each Arab state and across the region, and that, too, can shift as events slide this way and that.

But with all the unpredictability of the Arab uprisings, one can be confident about the forces at play, particularly about the rising Arab public empowerment and its importance as a factor in local, regional, and international politics. Even as many Tunisians, Egyptians, Yemenis, Syrians, and other Arabs strive for a better life and more freedom for themselves at home, their aspirations remain connected to the aspirations of other Arabs and Muslims, and to a vision of their collective place in the world. Above all, they want to hold their heads high.

ACKNOWLEDGMENTS

The research on which this book is based has been undertaken with the support of many institutions and individuals. I am particularly grateful to the Carnegie Corporation of New York, which has supported my public opinion research in the Middle East and the impact of the information revolution on identity and opinion. Vartan Gregorian, Stephen Del Rosso, David Speedie, Deanna Arsenian, Hilary Wiesner, and Patricia Rosenfield have been particularly supportive and helpful over the years. My students and staff at the University of Maryland have inspired me in ways that went beyond my actual research. I am particularly grateful to my research assistants and staff for the polling project, including Shana Marshall, Mike Lebson, Guy Ziv, Jonathan Pearl, Hyo Joon Chang, and Bilal Saab. My office staff, Awet Sellers, Gulnur Valiullina, Grace Boyle, and Lori Shin. The Program for International Policy Attitudes partnered with me for research on American public opinion, and in some cases, Israeli public opinion. Steven Kull, both as director of PIPA and a close colleague, has been particularly supportive. PIPA staff, including Clay Ramsay and Abe Medoff, provided indispensable help. Evan Lewis, both as a research assistant and as a member of the PIPA staff, has provided excellent analysis of the data. My colleague and friend, Joshua Goldstein, has not only given excellent advice but participated in designing some of the research and helped create our data archive. My colleagues at the Brookings Institution and the Saban Center, Martin Indyk, Kenneth Pollack, Tamara Wittes, Marshall Lilly, and Gail Chalef, have been supportive, particularly in hosting my poll unveilings over the years. I'm grateful to Basic Books and its staff, to the former publisher who solicited this manuscript, John Sherer, to my editor, helpful Tim Bartlett, and to two external editors, Howard Means and Nathan Means. Debbie Masi of Westchester Publishing Services and Wendy Nelson helped with the production and editing. Michael Hopps also provided constructive editorial advice.

Most of the polls in the Arab world were conducted through the services of Zogby International and JZ Analytics. I'm particularly grateful to John Zogby, Chad Bohnert, and Joe Mazloom. Polls among Israelis were mostly conducted by the Dahaf Institute and I am especially appreciative of the services provided by its director, Mina Zemach. Public opinion polls in the United States were conducted through Knowledge Networks, which always carried out the work in a timely and professional manner.

Above all, I am especially grateful to my wife and partner, Kathryn Hopps, who has been my first critic and a constant source of inspiration; and to our two children, Ramsey and Ruya, who have displayed immense patience during periods of busy research and travel, with Ruya providing occasional help with research and typing.

PUBLIC OPINION POLLS

Six-Country Arab Polls (Egypt, Saudi Arabia, Morocco, Jordan, Lebanon, and the United Arab Emirates)

- The *2011 Annual Arab Public Opinion Survey* was conducted in Egypt, Saudi Arabia (KSA), Jordan, Lebanon, Morocco, and the United Arab Emirates (UAE) with 3,750 participants from October 20, 2011 to November 4, 2011; the margin of error was +/–1.6 percent. The poll was fielded for the Anwar Sadat Chair by JZ Analytics.

- The *2010 Annual Arab Public Opinion Survey* was conducted in Egypt, Jordan, Lebanon, Morocco, Saudi Arabia (KSA), and UAE with 3,976 participants from June 29, 2010 to July 20, 2010; the margin of error was +/–1.6 percent. The poll was fielded for the Anwar Sadat Chair by Zogby International.

- The *2009 Annual Arab Public Opinion Survey* was conducted in Egypt, Jordan, Lebanon, Morocco, Saudi Arabia (KSA), and UAE with 4,087 participants from April 21, 2009 to May 11, 2009; the margin of error was +/–1.6 percent. The poll was fielded for the Anwar Sadat Chair by Zogby International.

- The *2008 Annual Arab Public Opinion Survey* was conducted in Egypt, Jordan, Lebanon, Morocco, Saudi Arabia (KSA), and UAE with 4,046 participants from March 10, 2008 to March 26, 2008. The margin of error was +/–1.6 percent. The poll was fielded for the Anwar Sadat Chair by Zogby International.

- The *2006 Annual Arab Public Opinion Survey* was conducted in Egypt, Jordan, Lebanon, Morocco, Saudi Arabia (KSA), and UAE with 3,850 participants from November 11, 2006 to November 21, 2006. The margin of error was +/–1.58 percent. The poll was fielded for the Anwar Sadat Chair by Zogby International.

- The *2005 Annual Arab Public Opinion Survey* was conducted in Egypt, Jordan, Lebanon, Morocco, Saudi Arabia (KSA), and UAE with 3,617 participants from October 15, 2005 to October 24, 2005. The margin of error was +/–1.7 percent. The poll was fielded for the Anwar Sadat Chair by Zogby International.

- The *2004 Annual Arab Public Opinion Survey* was conducted in Egypt, Jordan, Lebanon, Morocco, Saudi Arabia (KSA), and UAE with 3,300 participants in May 2004; the margin of error was +/–1.7 percent. The poll was fielded for the Anwar Sadat Chair by Zogby International.

- The *2003 Annual Arab Public Opinion Survey* was conducted in Egypt, Jordan, Lebanon, Morocco, Saudi Arabia (KSA), and UAE with 3,300 participants from February 19, 2003 to March 11, 2003. The margin of error was +/–1.7 percent. The poll was fielded for the Anwar Sadat Chair by Zogby International.

2012 Egypt Poll

- The *2012 Public Opinion Survey* was conducted in Egypt with 773 participants polled from May 4, 2012 to May 10, 2012; the margin of error was +/–3.6 percent. The poll was fielded for the Anwar Sadat Chair by JZ Analytics.

Polls of American Public Opinion

- The *Americans on the Middle East: A Study of American Public Opinion* was conducted in the United States with 737 participants polled from September 27, 2012 to October 2, 2012; the margin of error was +/–4.6 percent. The poll was fielded for the Anwar Sadat

Chair by the Program on International Policy Attitudes (PIPA), and the Knowledge Network.

- The *Americans on Israel and Iranian Nuclear Program* survey was conducted in the United States with 727 participants polled from March 3, 2012 to March 7, 2012; the margin of error was +/–4.5 percent. The poll was conducted by the Anwar Sadat Chair and the Program on International Policy Attitudes (PIPA), and fielded by Knowledge Network.

- The *American Public on the 9/11 Decade: A Study of American Public Opinion* was conducted in the United States with 957 participants polled from August 19, 2011 to August 25, 2011; the margin of error was +/–3.2 percent. The poll was conducted by the Anwar Sadat Chair and the Program on International Policy Attitudes (PIPA), and fielded by Knowledge Network.

- The *American Public and the Arab Awakening* survey was conducted in the United States with 802 participants polled from April 1, 2011 to April 5, 2011; the margin of error was +/–3.5 percent. The poll was conducted by the Anwar Sadat Chair and the Program on International Policy Attitudes (PIPA), and fielded by Knowledge Network.

- The *2010 U.S. Public Opinion Survey* was conducted in the United States with 1,486 participants polled from October 8, 2010 to October 22, 2010 and from November 6, 2010 to November 15, 2010; the margin of error is +/–2.5 percent. The poll was conducted for the Anwar Sadat Chair and fielded by Knowledge Network.

Israeli (Arab and Jewish) Polls

- The *Israeli Public Opinion Survey* was conducted in Israel with 500 participants polled February 22, 2012 to February 26, 2012; the margin of error was +/–4 percent. The poll was conducted for the

Anwar Sadat Chair by the Dahaf Public Opinion Research Institute.

- The 2011 *Public Opinion Poll of Arab Citizens of Israel* was conducted in Israel with 500 Arab/Palestinian participants polled from November 13, 2011 to November 20, 2011; the margin of error was +/–4.5 percent. The poll was conducted for the Anwar Sadat Chair by JZ Analytics.

- The *2011 Public Opinion Poll of Jewish Citizens of Israel* was conducted in Israel with 510 participants polled from November 10, 2011 to November 16, 2011; the margin of error was +/–4.4 percent. The poll was conducted for the Anwar Sadat Chair by the Dahaf Public Opinion Research Institute.

- The *2010 Israeli Jewish Public Opinion Survey* was conducted in Israel with 500 participants polled from November 17, 2010 to November 24, 2010; the margin of error was +/–4.5 percent. The poll was conducted for the Anwar Sadat Chair by the Dahaf Public Opinion Research Institute.

- The *2010 Israeli Arab/Palestinian Public Opinion Survey* was conducted in Israel with 600 participants polled from October 20, 2010 to November 3, 2010; the margin of error was +/–4.0 percent. The poll was conducted for the Anwar Sadat Chair by the Zogby International.

- The *2009 Israeli Arab/Palestinian Public Opinion Survey* was conducted in Israel with 600 participants polled in August 2009; the margin of error was +/–4.1 percent. The poll was conducted for the Anwar Sadat Chair by Zogby International.

INDEX